MW00679946

CBF at 25

Stories of the
Cooperative Baptist Fellowship

Aaron D. Weaver, Editor

© 2016

Published in the United States by Nurturing Faith Inc., Macon GA,

www.nurturingfaith.net.

Library of Congress Cataloging-in-Publication Data is available.

ISBN 978-1-938514-97-5

All rights reserved. Printed in the United States of America.

For Free and Faithful Baptists on the
25th Anniversary of CBF

CONTENTS

AFTERWORD

APPENDIX

ACKNOWLEDGMENTS

PREFACE

Story of a Name

By Aaron D. Weaver

When Page Fulgham stepped up to the microphone during the last session of the Consultation of Concerned Baptists in Atlanta on August 25, 1990, he knew the group of some 3,000 moderate Baptists needed a name. The theme of the three-day gathering was "For Such A Time As This," and Fulgham, like so many others, felt the gravity of the moment—"a feeling of euphoria in the sense that we had finally come home," as he would describe it to me 25 years later.

For such a time as this, the pastor of nearby First Baptist Church of Lawrenceville, Georgia, leaned in to the microphone and made a last-minute motion to name the new group the "Cooperative Baptist Fellowship."

Jimmy Allen, presiding convener of the Consultation, quickly responded and urged Fulgham and the attendees to refer to the new group as simply "the fellowship" for the time being. "If you name it, you might lose it," Allen warned, alluding to the *other home* that the room of concerned Baptists had helped build and sustain, only to later lose to fundamentalism.

Persuaded by Allen, a past president of that *other home*, Fulgham returned to the microphone and rescinded his motion. A formal name would have to wait for another time.

"We were Baptists who were cooperating together for a mission, a cause, a purpose and, unlike our former associations, we felt a great sense of togetherness," Fulgham explained to me, noting that the name carried with it the tradition of the Cooperative Program of the Southern Baptist Convention, the single giving plan that had united Southern Baptists for decades.

"The name, I think, was good, so I made the motion. It just kind of came to me in the moment, sort of a moment of inspiration."

Over the next year, the journey to adopt the name Cooperative Baptist Fellowship took a tortuous path. Five months later, the Interim Steering Committee of "the fellowship" agreed to recommend the name "The Baptist Fellowship" to the upcoming Convocation scheduled for May 9-11, 1991, at the Omni Coliseum in Atlanta.

That proposal was short-lived, as the committee soon discovered that another group of Baptists had already registered the name with the Georgia Secretary of State—ironically, an independent Baptist group with past ties to the fiery fundamentalist preacher (and former Southern Baptist) J. Frank Norris.

Discussion of what to formally call "the fellowship" came up again a few months later at the Interim Steering Committee's May 8-9 meeting immediately preceding the founding Convocation. At the meeting, committee members learned that lawyers for "the fellowship" had reserved several potential names, including "Fellowship of Baptists Inc." and "Baptist Congress."

During the meeting, one member recommended the name "Fellowship of Cooperating Baptists" to be listed on the group's proposed constitution. Another member asked if "cooperating" could be changed to "cooperative"—and one high-profile member said "cooperative" had become "a chain at my church."

"If we're going to break free, I'd like us to try some new language," the member said.

Another well-known voice spoke up and expressed his unease with both "cooperating" and "fellowship": "I no longer like the term 'fellowship,' and we are not at this point 'cooperating'."

More names were suggested, such as "The Association of Baptists," "Baptist Assembly," "Baptist Cooperative Missions Association" and "Free Baptists." With no agreed-upon name looming on the horizon, a five-member subcommittee was appointed to take a few hours and return with a list of three names for the committee to choose from.

Later in the evening, three names were recommended: "United Baptist Fellowship," "Fellowship of Baptists United" and "Baptists United." With all five members in agreement, the subcommittee moved that the group adopt the name "United Baptist Fellowship."

They did and did so unanimously. But the story doesn't end there.

Less than 48 hours later, Daniel Vestal stood behind the podium as Moderator of the founding Convocation, alongside lay leader (and fellow Texan) Patricia Ayres, and introduced to attendees the proposed Constitution and Bylaws bearing the name "United Baptist Fellowship."

As Vestal prepared the group to discuss Article 1 of the Constitution, attendees lined up at microphones spread out across the room to weigh in on the proposed new name. John Dunaway, pastor of First Baptist Church in Corbin, Kentucky, was first up.

"What United Baptist means in our area of the country," Dunaway told the crowd, "is an extreme Calvinistic view, a view of Baptists there who are considerably different . . . whose concept of education is different from ours, whose concept of the ministry is different from ours, whose concept of mission is different from ours, whose concept of evangelism is different from ours.

"To identify, in my mind, with a group called 'United Baptists', whether it's simply with the term 'fellowship' added to it, would be in contradiction to what we ourselves have said we are, who we are and what our purpose is," Dunaway continued. "It would appear to me something to the term of 'Cooperative Baptists' would include far more than this and would make possible an easier relationship for all Baptists who choose to cooperate on the basis of missions, evangelism, education and ministry.

"I move that the words 'United Baptist' be amended to 'Cooperative Baptist' throughout the document," Dunaway said.

After an explanation from a member of the Interim Steering Committee on how they came up with the name "United Baptist Fellowship," Ed Vick, a layman from Raleigh, North Carolina, was recognized to address the assembly.

"In our group, we have discussed the name and feel that the word 'united' breeds two problems. One, the first image that comes to your mind is our good friends the Methodists. And second, I don't believe Baptists in the truest sense of the word are united. We are cooperative, but we're not united," said Vick, receiving applause and chuckles from the crowd.

Next up was Mike Queen, pastor of First Baptist Church in Wilmington, North Carolina, who joined Dunaway, pointing to the potential confusion the name "United Baptists" would bring in certain parts of the country.

"When I left my home in West Virginia to go to Southeastern Seminary, the United Baptists that are part of the Queen family all prayed for me . . . but what they prayed for was that I wouldn't learn anything when I went to seminary," Queen said to loud laughter. "I have disappointed them, I think. What the brother from Kentucky said is true—in that part of the country, United Baptists mean something so radically different from who and what we are."

The debate over the name would continue as two more individuals weighed in, one speaking in favor of Dunaway's motion and another suggesting the need to move away from the term "cooperative" and its connection to the past.

Then Dunaway returned to the microphone to speak to his motion.

"The word cooperative . . . is not a bad term. But it is the idea that we are a cooperating body . . . and this places the emphasis on freedom, of voluntarily committing ourselves to work together."

After Dunaway was done, Vestal exclaimed: "Isn't it great to be in a meeting where you can talk?"

The crowd began clapping, and a moment later the assembly adopted the name "Cooperative Baptist Fellowship."

"And the motion does carry. You have voted yourself a name," Vestal announced as the clapping continued.

This *story of a name* is just one of the stories of the Cooperative Baptist Fellowship over the past 25 years. The stories in this anniversary volume reflect our shared heritage and hope through the stories of individuals, congregations, pastors and professors, lay leaders, young Baptists, field personnel and short-term missionaries, chaplains and pastoral counselors, partners and friends. They are the stories of being the presence of Christ and forming together in Christ.

When newly elected CBF Moderator John Hewett stood behind the podium at the Omni Coliseum in 1991 to offer parting words to the three-day gathering, he gave voice to the Convocation's theme— "Behold, I am doing a new thing!" He spoke of the pilgrimage that they as Baptists were on together: a journey to their new spiritual *home*.

"I am no longer worried about the future," Hewett said. "I'm convinced we are heading someplace free and faithful."

As we look forward to the next 25 years as Cooperative Baptists, may we remember the journey while also continuing to do bold new things together as a Fellowship. Happy 25th Anniversary!

Aaron D. Weaver is Communications Manager for the Cooperative Baptist Fellowship, where he serves as editor of fellowship! *magazine.*

Heritage and Hope

By Daniel Vestal

Since the birth of the Cooperative Baptist Fellowship 25 years ago, the world has changed. I often tell friends that we have lived through a period of societal, cultural and denominational deconstruction and reconstruction in the past quarter century. For thoughtful Christians who want to be true to scripture and authentic in ministry, it has not been easy. It still is not easy. Personal discipleship, congregational formation and public witness remain daunting challenges for Baptists.

The Church in North America finds itself in a secular and sometimes hostile environment. Partisan rhetoric fuels division among us. "The color line" still divides large portions of our society, and 11 o'clock on Sunday morning is still the most segregated hour of the week. These also are daunting challenges for Baptists.

Yet the gospel is as true today as ever. God is on a mission of reconciliation. The Spirit is at work within the Church as well as outside it. The Kingdom has come, is coming and will come. Jesus Christ is Lord. We need not be afraid. There are hopeful signs in the midst of the challenges. Millions of people are coming to Christ in the Global South, and the Global Church is growing. Even in our country, there is an awakening to spirituality which provides all kinds of opportunities for witness. Younger people do care about issues of justice, and they offer visionary and passionate leadership.

The past 25 years, though a significant amount of time in the life of one person, is but a "blip" on the timeline of history. While it is difficult to evaluate what is of lasting importance and what should be forgotten, let me offer a few personal reflections on my experience in CBF.

First, *the joy is in the journey.* In our beginning, there was a sense of wonder at what was happening among us and through us. Many of us realized early that we were participating in the creation of something much bigger than ourselves and that we were not the primary architects. Nobody recognized this more than Cecil Sherman, the first Executive Coordinator of CBF. He was a discerning and perceptive leader.

Along with Walter B. Shurden, Cecil prepared a document, "An Address to the Public," that was approved by the Interim Steering

Committee of the new movement and then presented to the CBF founding Convocation in 1991. The strong sentiment in the room when the committee received and read this profound statement was great joy. In spite of uncertainty and anguish, there was joy. We adopted it unanimously without changing a word.

Our joy in CBF has not usually been one of giddiness. Rather, it's been expressed in a more subdued manner. But our joy has been real and, at times, euphoric. Some of the greatest worship experiences I have known were at CBF General Assemblies where I wept and laughed simultaneously from sheer joy. Some of my richest spiritual experiences were in CBF prayer retreats and leadership conferences. Even when participating in disaster relief in Southeast Asia (2004), New Orleans (2005) and Haiti (2010), those who were involved exhibited a joyful gratitude in the midst of very difficult work.

A second reflection is that *we are laborers together with God.* I would be remiss if I did not bear witness to what I have seen of providence in the sacrificial service of CBF field personnel. JoAnn and John David Hopper, one of the first missionary couples to be commissioned, had a ministry in Eastern Europe that was legendary even before they retired. More than 325 CBF field personnel appointments have followed in the past 25 years. These missionaries have served in some of the most difficult and dangerous places in the world, and they continue to inspire us to greater sacrifice.

The word "partnership" has defined CBF's mission initiatives from the very beginning. The idea behind such a strategy is the presupposition that we can do more together than we can alone. Hence we have had influence in the world mission enterprise far beyond our size and dollars. The list of mission partners is long and illustrious: World Vision, Baptist World Alliance, Buckner International, Habitat for Humanity, Bread for the World, Volunteers of America, American Baptists, Passport, Wycliffe, American Bible Society and thousands of churches and hundreds of nonprofit organizations that encircle the globe.

Partnerships have also defined our "labors together" in spiritual and congregational formation as well as in leadership development. But it has been in theological education where the Fellowship's partnering with new seminaries has been transformative. These schools, which function independently of one another but form a consortium with one another, have changed the face of Baptist life. Their influence and impact are truly remarkable.

Conversations—serious conversations—have also defined our "labors together." These Fellowship-wide conversations have been intentional, giving us clarity and conviction about our identity and mission. The topics have included strategic visioning (1998), the missional church (2000), rural poverty (2001), HIV/AIDS (2006), the United Nations Millennium Development Goals and global poverty (2009), human sexuality (2012), organizational structure (2010-2012) and advocacy for social justice (2013-2016). They have required us to listen to one another and to the Spirit in ways that have formed and transformed our understandings of ourselves, the world and the gospel. This, too, has been the work of the Lord.

A final reflection is that *there's a sweet, sweet spirit in this place* called CBF. If asked to define my most rewarding memory of the past 25 years, I must say that it has been the personal relationships that have been birthed and nurtured during these years. My life has been changed because of the friendships that would not have happened if it were not for the Cooperative Baptist Fellowship. Clergy and laity, male and female, young and old make for a rich tapestry that is then made even richer by geographical, cultural and theological differences.

We are a work of God's grace and a renewal movement within the Baptist family. One reason I believe this so strongly is because we have stayed focused on our oneness in Christ even though we have great diversity. Our commitment as Baptists to soul freedom, Bible freedom, church freedom and religious freedom has allowed us to disagree with one another, sometimes strongly, and yet to share ministry and life together in mutual affection.

I have seen and experienced this affection from our very beginning, and I see and experience it still. We are surely not perfect and will no doubt face more "growing pains" in the next 25 years. But the Christian witness in America needs the Cooperative Baptist Fellowship. The Global Church needs the Cooperative Baptist Fellowship. Local churches need the Cooperative Baptist Fellowship.

So with deep gratitude for the past and great hope for the future, I join my voice with the voices of friends and colleagues who offer the following reflections and stories in a chorus of doxology. Praise be to God for the Cooperative Baptist Fellowship.

Daniel Vestal served as Executive Coordinator of the Cooperative Baptist Fellowship from 1996 until 2012.

*For Such
A Time As
This . . .*

**Consultation
of Concerned Baptists**

INFORUM

Atlanta, Georgia
August 23 - 25, 1990

Convened by
BAPTISTS COMMITTED

THE • BAPTIST
FELLOWSHIP

*"Behold, I Do
A New Thing"*

CONVOCATION

May 9-11, 1991

Omni Coliseum

Atlanta, Georgia

Following the 1990 annual meeting of the Southern Baptist Convention in New Orleans, Daniel Vestal, pastor of Dunwoody Baptist Church in suburban Atlanta, called for Baptists concerned about the fundamentalist takeover of their denomination to gather at Atlanta's Inforum Convention Center. Several hundred were expected to attend but several thousand showed up for the August 23-25 meeting. The next May, the group gathered again in Atlanta and voted to form the Cooperative Baptist Fellowship. The following are stories from the Fellowship's early years. They are the stories of Fellowship founders, pastors, staff, lay leaders and mission advocates. —**Editor**

1

And So It Begins . . .

By Clarissa Strickland

With apologies to Charles Dickens, it was the *best* of times and it was the *worst* of times—*worst* in that moderate Baptists who had long fought the fundamentalist takeover of the Southern Baptist Convention had pretty much given up the ghost at the 1990 SBC meeting in New Orleans with the loss of the presidential election yet again; *best* in that there was something new afoot, and a fresh wind of freedom was about to blow through this disheartened group and change things in a huge way.

When I began working for the Cooperative Baptist Fellowship, it was really *not* the Cooperative Baptist Fellowship but the Baptist Cooperative Missions Program, Inc. (BCMP). It was June of 1991. The new organization had just been named CBF a month earlier at the 1991 Convocation of The Baptist Fellowship at the Omni Coliseum in Atlanta. But it had not yet merged with the original BCMP, which was formed after the initial Consultation of Concerned Baptists—an August 1990 meeting in Atlanta called by Daniel Vestal. It was at that meeting that the winds of freedom grew to hurricane strength.

BCMP was established as a way to bypass funding through the SBC Cooperative Program because it was felt that Southern Baptist leaders had violated historic Baptist principles in the fundamentalist takeover of the convention.

This funding arm, famously called a "bucket" by David Sapp at the 1990 Consultation, was set up with a board of directors. Many moderate Baptists began channeling their gifts to the Cooperative Program with the noted exceptions—or bypassing the Cooperative Program altogether. An office was established at Oakhurst Baptist Church in Decatur, Georgia, and Hettie Johnson, a former employee of the old SBC Home Mission Board, volunteered to set up the necessary mechanisms.

Some months later, in April of 1991, Sandra Davey, a member of Heritage Baptist Church in Cartersville, Georgia, who was a former banker, was hired as the first full-time employee of the BCMP. Space was found for a one-room office in the Fairview Office Building in downtown Decatur. In June of that year, Sandra hired me on a temporary basis to work one or two days a week. My "temporary job" was to become a 23-year career with CBF!

Before I could agree to take this temporary position, I sought the approval of Daniel Vestal, who was chair of the Interim Steering Committee. At the Convocation in 1991, I had been elected as a representative of Georgia to the first CBF Coordinating Council—the governing entity of the new organization. I was concerned that my employment would be a conflict of interest.

Daniel told me not to worry about it; it was, after all, just a temporary, one-day-a-week kind of thing. However, as CBF became more structured, it was decided that my employment was indeed a conflict of interest, and I was asked to choose whether to remain in the job or on the Coordinating Council. I chose the one that was paying me a little bit of money and resigned from the council.

The early days of CBF (BCMP soon merged into CBF) were heady ones, filled with enthusiasm and excitement. The oft-used analogy was that we were "building this airplane while we flew it." In the midst of all the excitement and newness, the two of us who were working in the one-room office in Decatur conducted the mundane affairs of the business.

Our office was sparsely furnished—one computer and one phone line with call waiting. I worked at a folding table with such rudimentary equipment as a roll of stamps. There was no such thing as email. I remember our excitement the day we purchased our first fax machine!

My main duty in those early days was to sit at the computer and weed out the many duplicates in our database, or mailing list, which had been compiled from many different sources. I also did some correspondence. Sandra handled the financial aspects, receiving contributions and distributing checks. Eventually, three separate giving plans were established from which contributors could choose to designate their funds. One funneled most of the money through to the old Cooperative Program, with the exceptions noted above; one divided funds pretty much half-and-half between the new CBF and the old Cooperative Program; the third directed that all funds remain with CBF. This financial arrangement was greatly simplified in 1994 when the SBC voted at its Orlando meeting to refuse any contributions that came through CBF, specifying such gifts as "tainted." Henceforth, all contributions remained with CBF.

In those early days, Sandra and I had no daily oversight—no executive coordinator, no "boss." We commuted together the 40 miles from Cartersville, where we both lived. On one memorable day, when I was in the office alone, I made lunch plans with my sister, who also worked in Decatur. I was to pick her up in front of her building, and we would go to lunch from there. As I left, I locked the office with a key on the keyring with all my other keys—car, house, etc. Our office building had restrooms on the halls, and I stopped by there on my way out. Without going into too much detail, suffice it to say that I flushed *all* my keys down the toilet. I could not get back into the office or into my car! My sister was standing out on the street waiting for me, and this was long before the advent of cell phones. The final solution was an expensive call to a locksmith, who had to break into my car and create a key for it.

I had been employed for 10 months when the most exciting thing of all happened. In April 1992, CBF's first executive coordinator was to begin work at CBF. This was, of course, Cecil Sherman, the one who, for a number of years, had so courageously tried to warn Baptists of what was happening in regard to the takeover of the SBC. In many ways, I saw him as a voice crying in the wilderness. For me, he already had hero status, and that perception would only increase in the years ahead.

The first day Cecil was to visit the office in Decatur (when he was still living in Fort Worth), Sandra and I, with a great deal of anticipatory excitement, watched out our office window, where we had a clear view of the sidewalk by which he would arrive, walking from the nearby MARTA station. Pretty soon, his lanky, Ichabod Crane-like frame appeared, carrying only a briefcase. Cecil was to spend the night in Cartersville with my then-husband and me. When I asked him where his luggage was, he promptly opened the briefcase. On top was a neatly folded dress shirt. (I did not inquire as to what else might be under the dress shirt.) I thought of Jesus' command to the disciples to "travel light," taking neither two coats nor shoes nor scrip. Cecil was one who traveled light but seemed to carry a hefty stick.

In preparation for the coming of our first Executive Coordinator, we had moved to a three-room suite of offices in the same building. I did not know it then, but this was the first of seven moves and/or expansions I was to experience in my 23 years of employment with CBF. Three of those locations were on the Atlanta campus of Mercer University, with each in a different building.

Cecil Sherman was a dedicated and disciplined coordinator. In his four-year tenure, he was tireless, traveling to churches everywhere to build the case for the Fellowship. He also expanded the staff, including the call of Keith Parks as CBF's first Coordinator of Global Missions. But at that time, almost everything was a "first."

Cecil took very seriously his stewardship of the financial resources of the growing Fellowship—what he referred to as "minding the store." He was always apprised of where we were financially, and money was never spent carelessly or without thought. An example of this is the first move we made to the Mercer campus, to the Davis Administration Building. Rather than hiring professional movers to make the transition, Sandra Davey, Cecil and his secretary, Janice Brake, and I—along with a couple of guys from Sandra's husband's company in Cartersville—made the move. The Davis Building had no elevator, and our new space was on the second floor. Everything had to be carried up a flight of steps. It was an exhausting experience—but no one could say it was not an economical one!

Cecil and I shared a love of Diet Dr Pepper. More than once, I would find one of my Dr Peppers missing from the office refrigerator—but with 50 cents left in my chair. Or he would ask me to pick up a six pack for him at the grocery store.

For a number of months, a young man named Mark Brazil—whose family Cecil had known while pastoring in Asheville—joined our little staff. One of his duties was to be Cecil's driver. When Mark was in the office, we shared a workspace. Mark told me that one day, as he and Cecil were on the road, trying to decide on a place to eat, they passed a sign for Hooters. Cecil suggested that they try it. Mark diplomatically told him that he did not think Cecil would care for Hooters!

Cecil was a master with words. Without any superfluous rhetoric, he had a rare ability to cut immediately to the meat of what he wanted to say. This also came through in his writing (always done on his faithful IBM Selectric typewriter), especially in the commentary he penned for the Formations Sunday school literature produced by Smyth & Helwys Publishing, Inc.

Cecil was just the right person and uniquely gifted to act as midwife (midhusband?) in the birth of the Fellowship. I heard him say more than once that "this baby will survive." And it did!

Cecil led CBF as Executive Coordinator for four years, followed by Daniel Vestal and then Suzii Paynter. It was my high privilege to work with all three—each with very different gifts, but each with great capabilities. And I have been blessed to call each friend.

During my 23 years as an employee of CBF, I watched the organization grow and morph, shaped by time and events. My own duties were constantly changing as well, as I worked with different supervisors in different areas of the organization. In the early years, I was what David Wilkinson, then Coordinator of Communications, called a "generalist," with many different responsibilities. The last 10 years or so, I was the Reference and Referral Specialist—working with churches who were seeking ministers and with ministers looking for places of service. But no matter what my duties were, it was pure joy to feel that I was in the right place and doing what I should be doing.

Cecil Sherman pretty much voiced my feelings during those early years when he stopped by my desk one afternoon. He said, "You know, Clarissa, this is just the perfect job for you!"

And it was just that way for 23 years! Thanks be to God!

Below is a brief excerpt of a tongue-in-cheek tribute that I gave to Cecil at his retirement dinner in Richmond, Virginia, in 1996.

Third Clarissa 4:7-11; 16-20

4:7 And it came to pass in 1979 that insanity began to reign in the land of the SBC. [8] And many were they who witnessed it; but behold they were blind, for they would not see. [9] And lo, there came the voice of one crying in the wilderness, saying, "Make straight this mess before it is too late!" And this prophet came clothed with the guts of wild animals, eating nails, and drinking Dr Pepper. [10] And all they that heard him wondered at his saying, and cast in their minds what kind of wild-eyed liberal this should be. [11] And so it was that this Sherman on the Mount was scourged, and reviled and persecuted in the press.

4:16 But out of the darkness cometh those with a vision of a new place; for the first place was passed away and there was no more freedom. [17] And behold, all things were made new. [18] And they who saw it said, "Let us now go even unto Fort Worth and find this Sherman on the Mount; for he shall lead us." [19] And they came with haste and found Cecil and Dot and brought them unto Atlanta. [20] And thus it was said, "Behold! Sherman hath come to Atlanta again!"

Clarissa Strickland worked for the Cooperative Baptist Fellowship for 23 years before her retirement in June 2014. She declares that she is "Baptist born and Baptist bred"—and when she dies, will likely be "Baptist dead."

Standing Room Only

By Helen Moore-Montgomery

There was standing room only on the train!

Bruised and battered, I moved cautiously, looking for a home. I heard the invitation as it rang out—"Get on board the train." The words powerfully beckoned me as I let my barriers down, opened my heart and accepted John Hewett's opening message in 1991 to the Convocation of The Baptist Fellowship, where the Cooperative Baptist Fellowship was birthed. I still hear that invitation today as I serve with my Cooperative Baptist family, who have formed together to be the presence of Christ in a changing world.

My search for my Baptist roots is akin to that of many of you. I had faithfully attended the annual meetings of the Southern Baptist Convention, though I had never been recognized as a voice of laity. I had served alongside staff in my church as a lay minister to students. My call to serve with students came early in my life and, even today, my heart remains focused as God opens doors late in my journey. As I listened to the young future leaders of the church, I sensed their frustrations within our Baptist family. I grieved as they walked away in large numbers, searching, struggling, and many leaving to seek a more perfect relationship with their God, weary of the fighting within their beloved faith family.

My pastor invited me to represent my congregation at the 1991 Convocation in Atlanta. With fear and trembling, I agreed to go along with Charles, my husband (now deceased) and encourager. We began our journey having no idea what to expect. Those who know me know the rest of the story.

Little did I expect to find that there was standing room only on the train. Many had come to learn the truth about the takeover and to look for free and faithful Baptists. I am careful as I mention names, but I will forever give thanks to Steve and Jennifer Graham and the Oklahoma delegation, who would not hear "*No*" and named me to serve on the charter CBF Coordinating Council.

Clergy, laity, preachers, educators, university and seminary professors, church staff, community leaders, businessmen, retired military, disillusioned missionaries, chaplains—all of them faithful, historic Baptists—came together, and heaven came down. Wounded and weary, we joined in a reunion of the Christ community and, with God's blessing, we walked through an open door and began to sing "The Servant Song": "We are here to help each other walk the mile and bear the load."

There were so many voices, free at last to speak, to vote, to express what was in their hearts. It was a bit like Babel as we all contributed to the chorus, touting our own interests. As CBF was organized, I chaired the Equipping the Laity Committee. With no budget, we found creative ways to educate the people in the pews. All the committee chairs stood strong together for the work assigned and, with time, we formed that beautiful cooperative spirit that permeates our Fellowship today.

As I share these thoughts of yesteryear, I wonder again at the myriad ways we reached out and drew crowds to our meetings. Fax machines ran late at night with news of the day in an effort to answer every inquiry that came our way; no question was ignored and no phone call unanswered. Laity rose from the pew and joined the effort to provide open dialogue, become inclusive, share the story of historic Baptists and accept committee assignments—each of us paying his or her own way.

The need was great, and we dug deep to give of our resources. Small and large gifts were received, and we sang "hallelujahs" as we commissioned our first field personnel. Our best days were yet to come!

Now, as I walk the halls at our General Assembly each year and share hugs with the "charter family," welcome new young families with babies in tow, listen to the students who share 24-hour Facebook fellowship with me, hear young pastors call out for my wisdom of the ages, and feel the presence of Christ among our Fellowship family, I bow and give thanks for a place to call *my home*.

I can hear the invitation today: Get on board the train, standing room only; but we have made room for you! Young, well-equipped, called leaders are on board today, and we bow in gratitude for their servant hearts. May they let their little lights shine and send God's light into our needy world. May God go before them and smooth the way.

The Fellowship: brothers and sisters forming together in celebration of free and faithful Baptists.

Cooperative—what a beautiful word!

Helen Moore-Montgomery served on the CBF Coordinating Council from 1991-1998 and 1999-2001. She serves as a lay leader at Community North Baptist Church in McKinney, Texas, and has devoted her life to encouraging young people.

Forming Something New

By Pat Anderson

My wife, Carolyn, and I have been involved in the Cooperative Baptist Fellowship since its nameless beginning after our exit from the Southern Baptist Convention. It was in 1987 that we joined the effort to "save" the SBC, then our denominational home, from the fundamentalist takeover that climaxed at the 1990 SBC meeting in New Orleans. During the 1980s, I was involved in Southern Baptist life as a consultant in the fight against legalized gambling and, in our home state of Florida, Carolyn and I had each served as vice president of the Florida Baptist Convention.

We were well aware of the wave of political shenanigans coming from fundamentalists and worked hard to stem the tide. Our efforts were defeated, and victorious fundamentalists turned to purging the SBC of anyone in leadership who did not hold firm to "biblical inerrancy" and a host of narrow beliefs that lent themselves to literalism, including a seven-day, 24-hour-day creation and the subjugation of women. We realized in New Orleans that we could no longer be Southern Baptists, although we were not sure what we would become regarding our larger church identity.

Those of us who participated in the struggle were invited to attend a meeting in Atlanta called the Consultation of Concerned Baptists in August 1990. Carolyn was unable to attend, but I was there. The 3,000 or so persons who attended became the core group out of which the new organization, later to be known as CBF, emerged. I remember it was like a family reunion—joyful, hopeful and exciting. I returned home on cloud nine and quickly organized a gathering of like-minded Baptists at the annual meeting of the Florida Baptist Convention in Tampa that November. I was voted off the board of the Florida Baptist Theological College located in Graceville, Florida (now known as the Baptist College of Florida). That week, we saw the beginning of what became the Cooperative Baptist Fellowship of Florida.

By May 1991, CBF emerged as an organization both in Florida and nationally. I served on the first CBF Coordinating Council, and the next several years were marked by a gumbo of feelings of uncertainty, grief, anger, freedom, joy and optimism. Some of the early leaders, including members of the Coordinating Council, were former

Southern Baptists who had "left" the SBC earlier to form the Southern Baptist Alliance (now known as the Alliance of Baptists). Others were still SBC loyalists and dreamed of a day when their beloved denomination would be won over again and the glory days of yesteryear would return.

Meanwhile, some of us were interested in creating a new thing, a more modern organization of individuals and churches committed to historic Baptist principles and not tied to traditional denominational models. Those three groups did not always see things the same way, were often at odds with one another, and did not all share the same view of the future.

This made for lively and energetic council meetings in the early- and mid-1990s. Some folks felt that rather than creating a new organization, we should just join the Alliance. Others thought we should scheme to retake the SBC. The rest tried to develop a new way of being Baptist. Our shared support for women in leadership resulted in a significant number of women in positions of responsibility. Consternation about a perceived lack of pastoral leadership in the struggles against fundamentalism, and the over-representation of pastors in SBC leadership, resulted in a significant number of laity in leadership positions.

We shared a deep distrust of strong leadership because of the way that a few strong people had taken the SBC away from us. We also had regional differences. Few of us knew many people in Baptist life outside our own circle of friends, and we were just learning to know and appreciate our larger family. We chose not to use titles like "Doctor" or "Reverend," preferring a "level field" for clergy and laity, male and female. We named our executive leader the executive coordinator, reacting against an executive "director" terminology.

Instead of an executive committee, we had a Coordinating Council. Some worried about a possible future takeover of this movement and sought mightily to avoid any semblance of bureaucratic leadership or executive rule. The result was the development of an unwieldy organization that was difficult to manage. We were distrustful, wounded and unsure of ourselves.

CBF meetings became rich with humor, strong opinions and skewed loyalties. Coordinating Council meetings usually lasted for three days. Nothing seemed to get accomplished easily. Everyone seemed to want to be heard on every issue. Perhaps it was because we had all been shut out of discussions or involvement in the decision-making of the SBC, or perhaps some of us just enjoyed talking and arguing. Regardless, I remember many occasions when the simplest matters took an inordinately long time to finalize.

We were also awash with money in the early years. For one thing, we did not have much of anything to spend money on, and the churches were trying to figure out how to defund the SBC while at the same time funding this new venture called CBF. The largest portion of money came from Southern Baptists redirecting missions gifts to CBF. By the time Keith Parks became our Global Missions Coordinator, we had a large sum of money available for missions.

Some Cooperative Baptists believed that the money would continue to flow, adopting a belief that since we had lost the SBC with votes like 45 percent to 55 percent, we would somehow accumulate 45 percent of the budget of the SBC. The error of that thinking quickly became evident.

Deep friendships developed during the early years. Many of us would have never known each other had it not been for CBF. Today, after 25 unbroken years of work in the Fellowship, Carolyn and I still feel the annual CBF General Assembly is like a family reunion. And what a rich family fellowship it is! We are amazed at the growth of the Fellowship movement toward a young generation that is attracted to CBF not as a reaction against fundamentalism (although one would be hard-pressed to find a fundamentalist in our ranks), but as a network of Baptists that is forward-thinking, global, inclusive, happy and committed to following Jesus.

I look back on the 1990s with a smile. I can close my eyes and see the faces and hear the voices of so many interesting personalities. I miss those who have passed on—Cecil Sherman, Steve Tondera, Jack Snell, Carolyn Weatherford Crumpler, to name just a few. When we who remain are together, no matter how long the separation, it is as though we have never been apart. What a fellowship!

Pat Anderson served as Interim Executive Coordinator of the Cooperative Baptist Fellowship from July 2012 through February 2013. He also was Moderator of CBF in 1995-1996. The Cooperative Baptist Fellowship of Florida was organized in his home in 1990. He served as its Coordinator until 2002, when he joined CBF as a missions advocate, speaking on behalf of CBF Global Missions and taking groups of pastors to difficult places where CBF field personnel work.

Free and Faithful

By John Hewett

During the summer of 1990, following the final loss in a decade-long series of dispiriting defeats, moderate Southern Baptist leaders called a meeting in Atlanta named the Consultation of Concerned Baptists—a "last waltz" for those of us who had been laboring first to stop, then at least to slow the fundamentalist movement seizing control of the Southern Baptist Convention. The annual meeting of the SBC in New Orleans signaled the end to organized opposition to SBC fundamentalism.

They'd won. We'd lost. It was time to fold our tents and consider other lands of promise.

Two hundred people were expected at Atlanta's Inforum Convention Center that August; 3,000 showed up. The next few days were dramatic, to say the least. Some mourned over what they'd lost. Others raged against the dying of the light. The Old Guard longed for "the way things used to be," when the fish were jumpin' and the cotton was high. Young Turks caucused in the hallways, impatient with the "Back to Egypt" crowd. It was not at all clear at first what was happening.

But it became clear soon enough. By the time we left, we had blessed the conception of a new Baptist organism, called simply "The Fellowship," and had elected an Interim Steering Committee to spend the next nine months guiding its gestation and birth.

I served on that Interim Steering Committee. A few months into it, our leader, Daniel Vestal, asked Oeita Bottorff and me to plan the initial gathering the following spring in Atlanta. There was so much to do—with no staff, no budget and no infrastructure. I reserved the Omni Coliseum on my credit card. Oeita and I learned to master the "new technology" of the fax machine, sending program proofs back and forth between Texas and North Carolina.

Some of those early meetings of the Interim Steering Committee were painful therapy sessions for the disaffected and exiled among us. We talked and talked and talked, but couldn't find our way toward much action. Nostalgia for the SBC wonder years was often palpable. As one of those mournful episodes was peaking, I remember turning to a similarly frustrated friend and saying, "If Morris Chapman [the newly elected SBC president who had defeated Daniel Vestal in New

Orleans] were to call right now and say, 'We're sorry, please come back home,' half this crowd would be on a plane to Nashville within the hour."

Somehow, we muddled through. One of the biggest reasons was a gentle soul named Daniel Vestal, who was the right person at the right time. Daniel knew Baptists had forgotten how to do two important things: disagree and laugh. So he regularly asked us to look around the room, find someone with whom we might disagree on an issue, then go out for 20 minutes to talk together, heart-to-heart. When we reconvened, we always seemed to approve the next motion unanimously. After learning "holy war" in the SBC, we built this new organism from consensus to consensus.

And Lord, how we laughed! We rediscovered the joy of our particular outcropping of the Kingdom and the joy of our salvation. I experienced more authentic "church" in those meetings than in any other religious gatherings before or since. Blest were the ties that bound our hearts in Christian love.

So we sent out an invitation and, at the May meeting in Atlanta— called the Convocation of The Baptist Fellowship—5,000 noble souls arrived to claim their future. I was elected as the first Moderator of what was eventually named, after lengthy debate, the Cooperative Baptist Fellowship. As we were leaving, I called us "free and faithful Baptists." The label stuck.

Six months later, I had the great privilege of traveling with a group of those free and faithful Baptists to the International Baptist Theological Seminary in Rüschlikon, Switzerland, where we delivered to President John David Hopper a check for $250,000—funds lovingly contributed by CBF supporters to replace those rescinded by the SBC. That's what the first year was like. Every ground we broke was new ground. We were composing anthems on Saturday night and singing them Sunday morning.

It was the best and noblest work of my life.

Twenty-five years on, I've had occasion to reflect on those heady days of denominational fermentation and ponder the power of new wine in new wineskins. The people who birthed and shaped CBF brought a variety of hopes and dreams to the task. Some envisioned it as little more than the SBC-in-Exile, a shadow convention offering churches a pre-1979 structure of cooperation and mission support. But there also lived among others of us the vibrant hope that we could fashion in the Baptist tradition a home for brave, progressive Christianity.

One of my vivid memories from the early days was the constant pressure to "go slow" from those resistant to the new winds of changes. After the Consultation in 1990, I heard from a lot of brand-new Cooperative Baptists who were mightily chagrined that we had too many women on the platform and sang too few gospel songs. The pressure to crawl was intense. *Go slow on women in ministry,* many urged. *Go slow on liturgical renewal. Go slow on anything friendly to the sensibilities of the Southern Baptist Alliance* (later renamed the Alliance of Baptists). *Go slow on leaving the SBC.*

Twenty-five years on, all that hesitancy seems almost comical. Other denominations had embraced the giftedness of their prophesying daughters decades ago. CBF churches were slow to follow. We waited so long to leave that the SBC finally expelled us, depriving us of the joyful responsibility to shake their pharisaic dust off our feet and seek more fertile fields of ministry. Our fears deprived us of a chance to offer a welcoming voice of love and justice to our LGBT brothers and sisters, sons and daughters. And while we were clinging to denominational identity, the post-denominational world arrived and moved right on past us.

Lately I've become convinced that church was always supposed to be about life, not life about church. I was raised a wall-to-wall Southern Baptist: Sunbeam, Royal Ambassador, youth group member, Baptist Student Union leader, Southern Baptist seminary student, Southern Baptist pastor, state convention leader. My entire world had church as its axis. And church was about *Baptists,* "free and faithful" ones to be sure, but congregational life was lived out within the narrow constraints of our tradition.

How I wish now I had sent us forth from the Omni in May 1991 with the call to be free and faithful *Christians.* And how I repent over being held captive by an insular theology which assumed that life at church was the only life we could know.

But today I am greatly encouraged by the leaders emerging among the CBF family—young women and men offering us all an opportunity to catch a fresh vision of what God is actually doing in God's world and encouraging us to go and do the same things. CBF appears to be in glad, good hands. Free and faithful Christians, indeed.

So I cheer us on, albeit from the sidelines, praying that the original dream of a brave and progressive Christianity in the Baptist tradition might yet come to pass, to the praise of God's glory for Christ's sake and our sakes.

John Hewett served as the first Moderator of the Cooperative Baptist Fellowship from 1991-1992. He is founder and President of Hewett Consulting LLC, a Charlotte, North Carolina firm serving churches and other nonprofit organizations nationwide. A native of Florida, he graduated from Stetson University (Bachelor of Arts, 1974) and Southern Baptist Theological Seminary (Master of Divinity, 1977; Doctor of Philosophy, 1981). His pastoral ministry included Kirkwood Baptist in St. Louis, Missouri, and First Baptist Church of Asheville, N.C. His family includes two grown sons and one perfect granddaughter.

All About Missions

By Catherine Allen

Between 1984 and 1990, the Southern Baptist Convention showed that it would sacrifice its own missions in order to hobble women. In defense of Baptist missions, I participated in the neonatal days of the Cooperative Baptist Fellowship. I had no time to unpack after the 1990 Baptist World Congress of the Baptist World Alliance in Korea before immediately traveling to Atlanta to join caring, concerned Baptist friends on August 23. I was happy to vote for a new way of Baptist cooperation.

It was Christ's love for all the world—women included—that compelled me. On August 24 and 25, we dug the foundations of what would become the Cooperative Baptist Fellowship. I led one of 20 discussion groups to build consensus and, at a plenary session, I hoisted my open umbrella over the pulpit as a symbol that we must shelter the people of missions from the storms pounding them. Then I turned the umbrella upside down, like a basket—a symbol that we had to collect piles of money to fund missions. Without money, the new movement could not lead far enough into places where Christ was calling.

A committee met until midnight, dialing pay telephones and asking friends to serve on an Interim Steering Committee. I had to decline a place on the committee, as I was to spend much of the next five-plus years in other countries. I saw clearly the urgent necessity for an organization like CBF. I believed with all my heart that CBF would do the global mission of Christ more effectively and more zealously than any organization since the Apostle Paul and his supporters.

To me, CBF was and is all about missions. Everything else is secondary to that high calling. This movement cannot succeed unless and until strategic missions reign. This is what so many of us early adopters expected. The cream of Baptist missions leadership in the 1990s aggregated with CBF.

We must continue to build a more excellent homeplace from which the love of Christ can compel us into all the world.

Catherine Allen served as Associate Executive Director of Woman's Missionary Union. She has written or contributed to several books on missions and Baptist history. While serving on the staff of Samford University in Birmingham, Alabama, she was also President of the Women's Department of the Baptist World Alliance. She remains an advocate for women in missions and ministries.

West of the Mississippi

By Bill Bruster

Following the 1979 meeting of the Southern Baptist Convention in Houston, Cecil Sherman organized a group of Baptist leaders called the "Gatlinburg Gang." Cecil saw the future more clearly than the rest of us and knew the direction the denomination was headed. The first meeting was held in Gatlinburg, Tennessee, thus the name. I was out of the country and missed that first gathering. This was a political group designed to "save" the SBC. The mission failed, and after 10 years of utter disappointment, we knew something else had to be done.

When Daniel Vestal gathered a group of us in his hotel room after the 1990 meeting of the SBC in New Orleans, we began to look to the future. The Cooperative Baptist Fellowship was soon born. The highlight of the 1990 Consultation of Concerned Baptists in Atlanta, which would later birth CBF, came when a pastor of a small church in Kentucky stood with a small bag of money and proclaimed, "This is the VBS offering by our church collected for missions. We are not giving it to the SBC. Tell me where to send it."

That first meeting was electric. We divided into small groups and brainstormed about what we would do about missions, theological education, literature, media and public relations. We were determined to find a way for that Kentucky pastor to spend his church's contribution.

Months later, I spent three days in a San Antonio motel, rooming with Cecil Sherman as he was wrestling with the decision to become CBF's first Executive Coordinator. He drew a line down the middle of a yellow notebook page. On one side, he wrote the words, "Why I should take the job," and on the other side, "Why I should not take the job."

As the left side of the page filled, he said, "If I take the job, I want you to help me."

Cecil later asked me to become the Western Coordinator for the Fellowship, developing the work west of the Mississippi, while he worked east of the river. He and I called on pastors, asking them if we could visit their churches and speak to them about CBF. Many pastors were reluctant to "bring the controversy into their church."

CBF was a reactionary movement in the beginning. We were much more focused on "what was wrong with the SBC" than "what is right with CBF." Thus, we often faced hostility from laity who were not aware of the changes in the SBC.

Cecil was a dear friend and had as much integrity as anyone I have ever known. He was very careful with money sent to CBF. When the staff traveled with him and he really wanted to splurge on a meal, we stopped at Shoney's. He would often say, "We are spending Baptist money. The churches send this to us to do the Lord's work."

When Cecil retired and Daniel Vestal was elected to succeed him, I offered Daniel my resignation. I wanted him to be free to bring in someone of his choosing. He asked me to stay but wanted me to move from Texas to Atlanta and work to develop the state organizations. I gladly did so.

Daniel brought the gift of organization to CBF, and I found in him the same integrity that guided Cecil's life. I served with CBF for 12 years before retiring. I cherish and will forever be grateful for my colleagues in the organization. I thank God for calling CBF into being and especially for the privilege of working with Cecil and Daniel. I now pray regularly for CBF Executive Coordinator Suzii Paynter and those who work with her.

Bill Bruster served the Cooperative Baptist Fellowship as Western Coordinator from 1994-1996 and as Networking Coordinator for CBF from 1997-2006. A pastor for 35 years and author of three books, he received his Doctor of Theology degree from Southwestern Baptist Theological Seminary in Fort Worth, Texas, and completed postdoctoral studies at Regents Park College in Oxford, England. He and his wife, Charlotte, have two children and three grandchildren.

Living Out an Incarnational Theology

By Charles R. Wade

Frustration and discouragement filled the hearts of the 3,000 Baptist pilgrims who found themselves in Atlanta in August 1990 at the Consultation of Concerned Baptists. Responding to a call from Daniel Vestal and Jimmy Allen for all Baptists who longed for a new future, these men and women had traveled from across the country to meet together. We prayed. We sang. We preached. We listened. We found encouragement in one another and dared to hope that a new future for these Southern Baptists was possible.

For several years, we saw ourselves as a loyal opposition to the new leadership among Southern Baptists. We still believed in the Cooperative Program and the mission endeavors and had some hope—though it was rapidly diminishing—for the seminaries. But the attempt to remain Southern Baptist was thwarted by the determination of the denomination's leaders to brand the Cooperative Baptist Fellowship as a disloyal and separate group. CBF declined to identify as a new and separate denomination and intentionally continued to relate to churches who wanted to be involved with both CBF and the SBC.

These were years of trying to find our way organizationally as we struggled to be inclusive and respect the voices of all our Baptist family. We were focused on missions, hoping to channel the funds of our Baptist people into what we saw as holistic mission efforts that listened more carefully to the people we felt called to serve. We also wanted to support theological education that we felt would better prepare our young ministers—including women—for effective ministry in a changing culture.

A powerful vision for our movement is to encourage our churches to be the presence of Christ in their communities. This incarnational theology is lived out across the Fellowship in work with churches, ministers and the communities we serve. Some of the greatest achievements and future possibilities are found in our continuing emphasis on creative mission efforts, thoughtful theological education and the embodiment of a kind of Baptist life that honors religious freedom and encourages missional congregations.

One of the pivotal moments in CBF history was applying to be full members of the Baptist World Alliance. As CBF went through the process of identifying with the global Baptist family, CBF leaders had to admit that the SBC did not consider CBF a part of the SBC family. Therefore, the Fellowship finally declared itself a new union of Baptist people and churches, committed to historic Baptist theology and practice and determined to be both free and faithful in the pursuit of glorifying and serving God.

We have had the blessing of three of the finest human beings in Baptist life serving as our Executive Coordinators: Cecil Sherman, Daniel Vestal and Suzii Paynter. They have each brought specific and courageous gifts of leadership and service. The future of our movement pulses with hope and excitement as CBF models a vision of what Baptist life can and should be.

Charles R. Wade served for eight years as Executive Director of the Baptist General Convention of Texas (1999-2008). He was also pastor of First Baptist Church of Arlington, Texas, from 1976 to 1999. While he was pastor, FBC Arlington became nationally known for its outreach and community ministry through Mission Arlington.

Keeping the Promises at Rüschlikon

By Earl and Jane Martin

We felt betrayed! It was a blatant breach of promise. The Southern Baptist Convention had pulled the rug out from under Baptist Theological Seminary in Rüschlikon, Switzerland. In December 1991, the SBC's Foreign Mission Board suddenly withdrew its financial support by unilaterally rescinding its 15-year funding commitment to the seminary.

When this happened, we had been serving as Southern Baptist missionaries for more than 30 years. The first 25 years in Eastern Africa were followed by five years in Europe, where we served in a dual capacity. On the Rüschlikon Seminary faculty, Earl taught courses in missiology and world religions. At the same time, we directed the Institute of Mission and Evangelism for European Baptists, which involved conducting short courses in missions and world religions among European Baptist churches. Many courses were in the Communist bloc prior to its downfall. The direction and policies of the control-minded Foreign Mission Board had changed intolerably to something beyond authentic mission endeavor. We registered our protest by an immediate request for retirement.

Despite our sense of betrayal, neither we nor our Rüschlikon colleagues yielded to panic. Assurance came from faithful Baptists who promised to fill the gap for us. The fledgling Cooperative Baptist Fellowship was already in place.

Retirement from the Foreign Mission Board did not mean our service in Europe was finished. We sensed that our mission was yet to be fulfilled. European Baptists agreed, requesting that we remain both on the faculty and with the Institute. However, we needed a support base. We immediately requested to join CBF's new venture in missions, and in due course our request was approved. We were officially commissioned at the 1993 CBF General Assembly in Birmingham, Alabama.

The Rüschlikon Seminary also was not left in the lurch. On March 1, 1992, 50 sympathetic Baptists from the United States arrived on campus to offer earnest encouragement. There was a rousing chorus of support in the chapel service when CBF Moderator John Hewett delivered a resounding affirmation of reinforcement. The presentation of a batch of checks from churches and individuals totaling nearly $250,000 was a tangible sign of support.

Next, Hewett invited the mission personnel serving at the seminary to come front and center. The 50 CBF representatives encircled the missionaries, laying hands on them while Hewett offered a commissioning prayer.

It was an epiphany. The seminary would not be abandoned!

Since retiring from Europe in 1995, we have continued to be wholehearted advocates on behalf of CBF missions and ministries. From our European experience, we gained a deep compassion for the greatly marginalized Roma people. We gave strong encouragement to the Fellowship-supported ministry of the Ruth School in Bucharest, Romania, in its early years. Three years after retiring, in 1998, we volunteered to serve as the national prayer coordinators for CBF's Roma ministries. For the next eight years, we were associated with the cluster of field personnel serving among the Roma.

CBF's efforts to be the presence of Christ around the world through global missions and other manifold ministries continue to inspire our enthusiastic support at the local church level.

Earl and Jane Martin were part of the first class of Cooperative Baptist Fellowship missionaries (later called field personnel) commissioned in May 1993. The Martins served as missionaries in East Africa from 1955-1977, in Rwanda from 1977-1982, and to the European Baptist Federation in Rüschlikon, Switzerland, from 1987-1994.

Giving Hope

By E. Glenn Hinson

On a visit to the Baptist Theological Seminary in Rüschlikon, Switzerland (now International Baptist Theological Seminary*), where I was teaching in 1994, Cecil Sherman, the first Executive Coordinator of the Cooperative Baptist Fellowship, chidingly attributed to me a significant role in the launching of CBF in 1991. I can't recall his exact words, but I think he intended to say something like this: "Had you not managed to get the Foreign Mission Board of the Southern Baptist Convention to defund Rüschlikon, this new venture wouldn't have had the *cause celébre* it needed to help people see why it should come into existence and what it should do."

As a church historian, I would hesitate to give myself much credit in the conceiving and birthing of the Fellowship. I had taken part in some preliminary meetings but, for obvious reasons, I wasn't in Atlanta when it began and wasn't in a position to do much more than offer a prayer for those who met there. To the contrary, I was on sabbatical leave from Southern Baptist Theological Seminary, teaching church history and spirituality in Rüschlikon, when the trustees of the Foreign Mission Board dropped their bomb defunding the school on October 9 —ostensibly because I was teaching there, although conservatives on the board had tried to defund it for several years.

When President John David Hopper gave me the news, the bottom dropped out of my stomach. The seminary depended on the Foreign Mission Board for more than half of its budget. The question "What can I do to make up for the loss?" obsessed me. It kept me awake at night. I wrote letters to every person I knew who might offer some help, and quite a few did. Lots of individual contributions poured in, but nothing mattered as much as the forming of an organization (CBF) that would rally to the seminary's aid. One could hardly think of it as anything other than providential.

Providence reached a hand out to me, too. As I wallowed in despair over what had happened, Tom Graves invited me to join the faculty of the Baptist Theological Seminary at Richmond, also founded in 1991. Thanks to Cecil Sherman, CBF supplied a significant part of the budget for the seminary. Organizers of the Fellowship invited me to speak at the General Assembly in Fort Worth at the end of May 1992.

I'm almost embarrassed to admit that my family's financial situation had gotten so bleak by this time that I had to ask them to pay my way. They did, and I spoke twice to enthusiastic audiences about what happened in Rüschlikon. I would have to write a long essay to explain what the invitation to speak at that second meeting meant at a time when my future looked murky, but I will sum it up in these words: CBF gave me hope then, and it gives me hope now.

International Baptist Theological Seminary is a CBF partner theological school now located in Amsterdam, the capital of the Netherlands.

E. Glenn Hinson is Emeritus Professor of Spirituality and John Loftis Professor of Church History at Baptist Theological Seminary at Richmond in Richmond, Virginia.

Flying This Plane
While We're Still Building It

By Hardy Clemons

When the Nominating Committee of the Cooperative Baptist Fellowship Coordinating Council approached me to see if I would take the job as the third moderator of this fledgling organization, to say that I was surprised is a major understatement! The churches I had served since 1961 through the 1990s were clearly "moderate" churches. So with the approval of the leaders of First Baptist Church of Greenville, South Carolina, where I served as pastor, I told the committee I was honored to be invited and overwhelmed at the enormity of the task.

I had experienced some heavy encounters with people who were much more fundamentalist than moderate. These included Paul Pressler, who was at the University of Texas Law School while I was the Baptist Student Union Director at the University of Texas, and Paige Patterson, who was still in school but who wrote often about his criticisms of the direction of the Southern Baptist Convention. Both these men and their followers had little tolerance for the ideas of "unity in diversity" or "soul freedom."

So I knew it would not be a smooth ride.

My assignment would be to serve as Moderator-Elect for a year, then Moderator. And in those days, it became clear that to begin building an institutional memory, we needed another two years from our leaders. So, each Moderator served an additional two years as Past Moderator and "Past, Past Moderator," making a total of four years of service.

The early moderators were, in order, John Hewett, Patsy Ayres, myself, Carolyn Crumpler and Pat Anderson, who would become "past, past moderator," as did I. Cecil Sherman was our worthy coordinator.

At some point, it was decided to discontinue the Past, Past Moderator's job, which in hindsight works very well.

So, why did I agree to take the job?

1. The committee assured me that this was not a political job—that CBF was about missions, ministry and education, and not about political action.

2. We are about all three words in our title:
   a. We live and work in *Cooperation* with each other.
   b. We are *Baptist* Christians.
   c. We are a *Fellowship* and not a denomination.
3. We cooperate with all who are willing to engage with us in moving to serve those who live and work in a world without borders.
4. We respect and utilize both laity and clergy, women and men, older and younger.
5. We are "free and faithful" Baptists who take both sides of that polarity with faith and fun.
6. Since we did not want to become a denomination and had no models by which to go, we often admitted that, to quote one of our philosophical members: "We seem to be flying this plane while we're still building it."

Holding this concept made for a firm trust in God, cooperation with each other, and fidelity to scripture and to our ancient heritage, when Baptist Christians were indeed both free and faithful.

Hardy Clemons served as CBF Moderator from 1993-1994 and served on the CBF Coordinating Council from 1992-1996. He is a CBF-endorsed chaplain and served as the pastor of multiple churches from 1961 until 2008, when he retired from Trinity Baptist Church in San Antonio, Texas.

Editor's Note: The following is an edited excerpt from a previously unreleased video interview with Dr. James M. Dunn, then Executive Director of the Baptist Joint Committee on Public Affairs, at the 1990 Consultation of Concerned Baptists in Atlanta, which was instrumental in birthing the Cooperative Baptist Fellowship.

Real Baptists

By James M. Dunn

Religious liberty is important to Baptists and always has been because it is the social—or the corporate—expression of our most central belief, which is soul freedom. That's the Baptist spin we put on priesthood of all believers—the competence of the individual before God. And since we insist upon that for ourselves, we believe that we either follow Jesus Christ really or not really.

Ethics and common sense and history demand that we want that same freedom for everybody else. We want that freedom because we believe with all our heart that when anyone's religious liberty is denied, everybody's religious liberty is endangered. And it's important today especially, because in our pluralistic society, in our secular world, in our complicated urban life, it is so easy to run roughshod over the minority, to ignore the spiritual dimension of life, to let other concerns that relate to our life together overshadow and completely obscure the freedom of the individual before God. And so it's terribly important that we maintain it.

I'm with this group of like-minded Baptists in Atlanta because I, as well as the majority of people here, am deeply committed and convinced that real Baptists still believe in religious liberty and church-state separation as they always have. The creedalism that says, "Since the majority of us believes *this*, *you* have to believe it," is the absolute antithesis of what it means to be a Baptist. Baptists have been, at their heart and soul, dissenters from the very beginning, and are still to this day dissenters. This crowd who is meeting here are still as committed to real religious liberty and church-state separation as Baptists have always been, and that's the essence of what it means to be a Baptist.

There are other people who do a better job of evangelism than we do. There are other people who do a better job of stewardship than we do. There are a lot of other people who use as much water as we do to baptize people as we do. But there's no group on the face of the earth by their very identity and history and theological centrism that focus on the freedom of the individual before God in the way that Baptists have. To be a real Baptist is what it's all about as far as I'm concerned and as far as these people are concerned. I wouldn't be anywhere else than here with my friends.

A positive, upbeat affirmation of missions, evangelism and outreach of the gospel, unhindered and untainted to the world, is why these folks are together. They really believe in cooperation. These people affirmed in a vote a few moments ago that they no longer want to be coerced, but they want to cooperate. Cooperative—the word itself implies voluntariness and freedom and spiritual dependence upon the guidance of the Lord. It's not merely a question of human democracy; it's a commitment to be free to do that which we believe God is leading us to do. Baptists have always valued freedom more than uniformity.

Conformity and uniformity are dirty words to a real Baptist.

James M. Dunn served as Executive Director of the Baptist Joint Committee on Public Affairs from 1981-1999. After retiring from the BJC, he became Professor of Christianity and Public Policy at Wake Forest University School of Divinity in Winston-Salem, North Carolina. He continued teaching courses there until 2014. Dunn passed away at the age of 83 on July 4, 2015.

Field Personnel

CBF field personnel Sam Bandela presents a Bible and sewing machine to each graduate of a sewing class in India in January 2007. Following the tsunami in December 2004 that killed more than 178,000 people in Southern Asia, Bandela established ministries with the support of Cooperative Baptists to provide sewing classes to survivors as a means to support their families through microenterprise.

Since 1991, more than 325 persons have served as CBF field personnel among the most marginalized and least evangelized people in the world. Formed in September 1991 in a hotel conference room near the Atlanta airport, the Global Missions Ministry Group led by Jimmy Allen and Jeanne Bond began the process of putting the fledgling Fellowship on a path toward coordinated mission engagement in a "world without borders." A new missions entity was created from scratch, disaffected missionaries were hired and new career missionaries were appointed. Within two years, the CBF Coordinating Council would select Keith Parks as its first coordinator of Global Missions, bringing with him a deep passion for reaching the unreached with the gospel.

Twenty-five years later, CBF field personnel continue their work in a world without borders in the contexts of the global church, global poverty and global migration while living out the Fellowship's mission commitments to cultivate beloved community, bear witness to Jesus Christ and seek transformational development. These are their stories. —**Editor**

9/11—"All Are Welcome"

By Ronnie Adams

Since 1995, as one of Cooperative Baptist Fellowship's field personnel, I have been partnering with Metro Baptist Church, located in the Hell's Kitchen district of Manhattan, as well as with Metro's affiliated social service agency, Rauschenbusch Metro Ministries. A few blocks from popular attractions (Times Square, Broadway, the Hudson River) and just steps away from the Port Authority Bus Terminal and the Lincoln Tunnel, Metro sits in the midst of a high pedestrian and vehicular traffic area.

When called to missions, I had no idea that the call would lead me to New York City, where I—a Texan—had never been. I certainly had no idea that I would be in New York City on one of the most memorable days in that city's and our nation's history.

On that day, as I walked to Metro after voting in the mayoral primary, I thought, "What a beautiful September day." There was a deep blue sky and a north wind making it cool and comfortable. On my "to do" list was preparation for the arrival of our new CBF Global Missions personnel, Shonnie Ball. These are the first things I remember about September 11, 2001.

The morning continued as I arrived at my Metro office and delved into the day's tasks. Shortly afterwards, Marti Williams, Metro's associate pastor, came to tell me that a plane had hit the World Trade Center. I joined most of the world in thinking this was a horrible accident. Then, as the second plane hit, we knew instantly that we were under attack.

A few moments later, the Port Authority Bus Terminal began to close its huge metal doors. The roadway tunnels connecting the island of Manhattan to the other boroughs and mainland were closed, too. Thousands of people wandered the sidewalks and streets aimlessly, trying to figure out where to go and what to do.

David Waugh, then pastor of Metro, attempted to reach the World Trade Center site but was turned away at 14th Street, where police and military personnel had set up a perimeter. When he returned to the church, we had a quick meeting and prayed that God would use us.

Marti quickly made a sign that read, "All are welcome for prayer and refuge." Almost immediately, the small fellowship room filled with people watching television and using the church phones. Metro's sanctuary became a resting place and a place of prayer. We began to pass out water, trying to help in any way possible.

As noon approached, we decided to feed as many as possible. I went to the local stores, but their shelves had been nearly depleted by others frantically seeking to stock up on necessary provisions. Thankfully, there was another option. Metro's weekly food pantry ministry meant that canned and dry foods were available on site. Menus were created from those items, food was prepared, and people were served.

By early afternoon, people covered in white dust began to arrive. They had made their way on foot uptown, walking the three-and-a-half miles from the World Trade Center. I vividly recall two women dressed in professional business attire. In a state of shock, they told of their past few hours—how they had leapt over the bodies of those who had either jumped from the towers or been propelled out by the force of the explosions. I gave them wet towels to wipe their faces, served them food, said a prayer, and assured them that they were welcome to stay as long as they wanted or needed.

They soon decided to continue their journey, and I escorted them outside. I watched as these two women merged into the throng of hundreds walking silently down 40th Street past Metro's front doors. They were headed toward the Hudson River, where ferries across the water offered the only remaining transportation off the island.

Then came my tears as I watched this mass of moving people in the eerie quiet, broken by the sound of fighter jets as they flew low over the city. A young boy who attended the after-school homework center at Rauschenbusch Metro Ministries and who lived just around the corner walked up. He leaned against me and said, "I'm scared."

I could only reply, "I am too. But I know God is with us, no matter what happens."

While we were offering food, water and bathrooms, it became apparent that people would be stranded on the island and would need shelter. Mattresses were carried down from the fourth floor dorm space. Placing them on the sanctuary floor, we transformed the room into a temporary home for many as they waited for the bus, train and/ or vehicle transportation to resume.

A large crowd appeared at our door—young adults and families of all nationalities and faith traditions. Among them was a Kurdish Muslim family, newly arrived in the country. They had traveled by bus from the JFK Airport to the Port Authority to meet their sponsors.

31

They were stranded. One of our members saw them on the street and invited them to come to Metro for shelter. One of the most fearful was a French-speaking Muslim student from Morocco. Tony, a CBF Global Service Corp appointee turned volunteer, together with Jean, a French-speaking Metro member, assured the young man he would be both safe and welcome. Pastor David thoughtfully established a space for Muslim visitors to pray. Other foreign travelers included a group of Conservative Jewish students who had just arrived from a kibbutz in Israel. All were made to feel welcome.

Metro Baptist members represented the presence of Christ in so many ways during the hours and days after the attack—taking shifts to keep the temporary shelter open, manning the doors, cooking meals, researching available transportation options for those needing to continue their interrupted travels.

Members gave willingly and tirelessly for days, weeks and months following 9/11. However, Metro is a small congregation. The support CBF immediately offered was vital to continuing to meet the many needs precipitated by the attacks. CBF sent emergency funds to assist in meeting the immediate needs of the displaced and sought input on how the Fellowship might best provide further assistance. Through another partnering church, Greater Restoration in Brooklyn, and its connection with the Black Firemen's Union, funds were sent to assist with emergency needs in that area of the city.

Former Metro member Bob Freeman arrived from Atlanta, sent by CBF to help assess needs and determine how Cooperative Baptist volunteers might be most useful. I will be forever grateful for his presence and assistance during those tumultuous days. Within days of Bob's arrival, CBF sent crisis counselors to support New Yorkers in coping with the overwhelming loss, confusion and grief.

A few weeks later, David and Shirley Hall of Elon, North Carolina, made their way to New York City to coordinate the work of CBF volunteers. A partnership with Safe Horizon, a victim services agency, was established from which volunteers signed up for shifts at the massive Family Assistance Center established by the city on Pier 94, about a mile from Metro. Assistance was provided for the constant stream of people trying to navigate the process of obtaining emergency funds for housing, food and medical expenses.

Volunteers also worked at the center set up by the Tepeyac Association, an agency focused on assisting undocumented and underserved individuals who worked in the food courts, food trucks and souvenir stands in the World Trade Center (Ground Zero). Partnering with the Lower Eastside Coalition, volunteers cleaned apartments near Ground Zero, helping families who were impacted by the blast but not eligible for federal cleanup funds.

The stream of volunteers from CBF churches continued for months. Metro members also continued to volunteer and to offer the church's dorm space to house multitudes of volunteers. CBF emergency funds continued to support efforts to aid New York residents as they sought to function and recover—financially, emotionally and spiritually.

Then, as it does today, CBF sought to provide an active presence of Christ for a world in need. This was never demonstrated more beautifully than in the days following 9/11—a day that was meant to bring down and destroy, but instead brought people from all parts of the nation together, building relationships of love and support. Through the darkness of smoke and ashes, the love of God's people shone.

I will always be thankful for the hundreds of CBF volunteers who helped restore and lift up through their prayers, financial support and volunteer efforts.

Ronnie Adams has served since 1995 as one of Cooperative Baptist Fellowship's field personnel in New York City. He works with Metro Baptist Church in Manhattan and Greater Restoration Baptist Church in Brooklyn, serving the HIV/AIDS community as well as leading Bible studies and providing pastoral care.

The Matthew House Movement in Canada

By Marc Wyatt

For my wife, Kim, and me, missional journeys began in rather traditional ways. We were both raised at home and at church with the belief that everyone should live according to the Great Commission and the Great Commandment. That sense of being Christian became focused over the years into the deeply held belief that, because we had been given so much—grace, opportunity, material wealth, forgiveness—we had a responsibility to share with those who had not heard the Good News of God's love through Jesus Christ. For us, sharing would also mean going somewhere.

We first heard about the Cooperative Baptist Fellowship in the early 1990s. Dr. Keith Parks had just left the Foreign Mission Board of the Southern Baptist Convention, and his departure rocked our church and our personal plans to become missionaries. Our home church, Monument Heights Baptist Church, and the Foreign Mission Board (now the International Mission Board) are only a few stop lights apart in Richmond, Virginia. If Parks wasn't welcome in the SBC anymore, then maybe we weren't either.

We contacted Harlan Spurgeon, who had also recently left the Foreign Mission Board to join Parks and give form to the new CBF mission enterprise, and met with him in Richmond.

"You are our kind of people," Dr. Spurgeon told us. "But at this moment there are many moving parts. Be patient. You'll hear from us soon."

And so we waited.

We were commissioned as CBF field personnel during the 1996 CBF General Assembly in Richmond. Our families, friends and church community were all present as we shed tears of joy while holding our children in our arms. Rebecca was about to turn four, and Jon Marc had not yet celebrated his first birthday.

And then we said goodbye—goodbye to our families; goodbye to our home and cars; goodbye to the swing set Kim's dad and brother had built for Rebecca and Jon Marc. It was also goodbye to Christmas ornaments and all the other "stuff" of abundance and familiarity. We let go, left behind the privileged life we were given at birth, and flew halfway around the world to serve among a hill tribe of refugees living stateless, invisible, marginalized lives, unaware of Jesus.

The flight from familiar to foreign was long. We used every sticker and coloring book we had to help the children manage the journey east. With each new leg of the flight (and there were many), the sights, sounds and smells of our adventure changed. As the plane approached its landing at International Suvarnabhumi Airport in Bangkok, Thailand, I reached across the children's seats and took Kim's hand.

"Honey, we are here. Our mission dream has come true," I said.

Jet-lagged and exhausted from keeping the children in their seats for a full day, Kim gave me as loving a smile as she could manage. Then I promptly reached into the seatback and took out the little white paper bag and threw up! That was Day One.

The Thai language is tonal. It has a unique script. It doesn't use punctuation. Needless to say, language school was hard. Life in Bangkok was stressful. We were reminded daily that we weren't from there. Our little blonde and blue-eyed children stood out like lighthouses. Everywhere we went, locals wanted to touch their hair and pinch their plump white cheeks. It was annoying. Nothing resembled life as we knew it back home. The daily activities of life and the unrelenting heat made us weary. We were excited and committed, but we were also feeling a bit homesick.

I remember speaking with a veteran missionary one day about how difficult the language was and how hard life was for me and my family. He put his arm around my shoulder, gave me a hug and smiled.

"When you are reduced to zero, you will be ready to begin your work here," he said.

Being reduced to zero—starting completely over—wasn't what I wanted to hear. But that was the price of the call to be a missionary. Saying goodbye to family and friends and giving away possessions and privilege also means losing a part of yourself, your identity. It means becoming someone from here and there; a new person, an immigrant.

Our missionary journey took us next to Toronto, Canada's largest and most multicultural city, during the summer of 1998. The years spent in Canada greatly shaped our lives and influenced how we view God's work in the world.

We arrived in Canada from Northern Thailand; from tropical heat to sub-zero temperatures, from elephants walking in the street to moose crossing signs along the highways. There cannot be two more different places on earth. In Thailand, we were helping refugees from Burma.

There, they lived in thatch-covered bamboo houses and cooked over charcoal open fires. They lived with a fear that, at any given time, their enemies might attack.

In Canada, we found people—thousands upon thousands from every corner of the world—who had fled their homelands with the hope of finding a safe place to call home. The unfortunate reality is that in the world today there are approximately 16 million refugees who have left their homes and countries under fear of war, persecution and loss of life.

These displaced persons are moving along the refugee highway. It stretches from the war-torn corners of the earth that you see on the nightly news into the towns and cities of the Western world and into North America, to places of hope and safety and refuge. In 1998, we were unaware of this superhighway of homeless-yet-hopeful people.

CBF's response to this terrible reality was to send us to Canada to work alongside Canadian Baptists as they developed a ministry plan to serve refugee claimants seeking asylum there. Through partnership, we joined hands to help create what would become the first Matthew House in August 1998.

The name comes from the words of Jesus in Matthew 25:35: *"I was a stranger and you received me in your homes."* Matthew House is just that, a rather small and unassuming house. It is a place where a dozen refugees from a dozen global disaster zones share a home with Christians. It is a shelter for mothers and fathers, parents with small children, seniors and young adults who have lost everything but their lives.

Matthew House is a safe place for people who have been reduced to zero. It is a place for them to have the time they need to catch their breaths and to regain their given names—Tariq, Sara, Hiwot, Mohamed, David, Margret.

Not long into our work with Anne Woolger, the founder and Executive Director of Matthew House Toronto, Kim and I both found our places to serve. As in any home, the residents of Matthew House shared responsibilities, chores and meals together. It was always funny to me when men who believed that housework was a woman's work met Kim. She took it quite seriously to help them with their cultural orientation: This is a broom. This is a mop. This is how you wash dishes and this is how you wash your clothes. Your mother doesn't live here. Welcome to Canada. Welcome to the Matthew House family, she would say. And the men would scatter from in front of the television set, suddenly remembering appointments they needed to make, hoping to postpone their chores for a while.

Slowly and beautifully, Christian community would always come to have its transforming effect, shaping and giving life to everyone. The horror of a person's past or their religious or political positions did not seem to matter. The experience of life at Matthew House made us family.

It felt good to be useful at Matthew House. But little did Kim or I know that our traditional view of missions was about to be dramatically changed forever. I remember the day quite well. I was having lunch at Matthew House with those who were home. Jon Marc, my three-year-old son, was with me. He had become friends with Tariq, the four-year-old son of Juma, from Afghanistan. Juma spoke no English and was one of the men who received Kim's "Welcome to Matthew House" orientation.

Juma fled his homeland with his youngest child in hopes of one day bringing the rest of his family to safety in Canada. Juma looked every bit the part of a rough, war-torn Afghan. But he was also a father to a young son—just like me. Juma wanted the same things for his family that I wanted for mine.

Equally created in the image of God, our differences seemed to melt into our becoming a part of a sacred community. As I was passing the bread basket to Juma, I heard God speak clearly to my heart.

"I brought this man here by my own hand. You would have never met him except I brought you to this place at this time too. Love him. He is your neighbor. I am the Lord your God." At that moment, my heart and mind were changed.

I thought our time in Thailand had been for naught. What a waste of time and expense I believed it was to have lived overseas, but to have not completed the work. Suddenly, I saw that time differently. Those few years of stress, difficulty and disappointment had actually been a gift from God. Our time in Thailand—away from family, speaking the language like a child, unable to work until we could manage a new way of life—had been our training for the work God had prepared for us to do in Canada. We had been given the gift of being a foreigner. With that awareness, we began to understand mission in a new light.

I had never gone to Afghanistan. But here, during this ordinary meal time, God had opened my eyes to his amazing work. God brought an Afghan father to me, and somehow I missed an important point. Jesus commanded us to go to the people of Jerusalem, Judea, Samaria and the ends of the earth. But the places were not the point. It was always about the people. I felt a release from geography to humanity.

What started as just one small ministry in the corner of one city has since spread into five Canadian cities. There are now eight Matthew House refugee ministries in Canada. Each ministry home is dedicated to helping refugees from around the world reclaim their shattered lives in the name of Jesus. Joey Clifton, a member of First Baptist Church in Oklahoma City, Oklahoma, captures the growth of this ministry in his book, *The Above Ground Railroad: The Story of the Matthew House Movement in Canada.*

Because of faithful prayer and generous support from CBF churches and individuals, we were able to live our lives among people whose homelands are far away and whose hearts are very often spiritually far from a personal relationship with Jesus. Many have absolutely no knowledge of God. They may never have read or even heard any words from the Bible in their own language. They may have no church among their people, but when they move into Matthew House, it doesn't take long for someone to say, "Where's Matthew? I'd like to meet this man whose house I'm living in."

And so we get to tell the story.

Kim and Marc Wyatt have been Cooperative Baptist Fellowship field personnel since 1996, serving in Thailand, Canada and the United States. In October 2014, the Wyatts began a new assignment in the Research Triangle of North Carolina, an eight-county region with a population of approximately two million people surrounding the capital city of Raleigh. The Wyatts resource and mobilize churches as they discover their international neighbors and share the gospel in culturally appropriate ways.

A New Spiritual Family

By Allen and Verr Dean Williams

Our history with the Cooperative Baptist Fellowship began before there even was a Cooperative Baptist Fellowship! We had no idea what might come out of the 1990 Consultation of Concerned Baptists and 1991 Convocation of The Baptist Fellowship in Atlanta. We certainly did not go with the intention of helping to create an organization. Our sense was that Daniel Vestal was inviting us all to something more than an organizational meeting. We needed fellowship and community with like-minded Baptists.

Our experiences of Baptist life outside our local church in the 1980s were painful. We found ourselves in need of much more than a denominational identity; we needed a spiritual home. The fellowship and community we experienced in those early meetings in Atlanta met that need. As we all shared our stories, a renewed sense of community began to form. What we especially appreciated was the space that was created in which we all could make new commitments to maintaining fellowship with one another. We found a new spiritual family that encouraged our spiritual formation and honored the place where we were in our experience of God.

Within two years, we discovered another dimension to this group known as CBF. The Fellowship was ready to help us live into our mission calling. While we were asked many questions and given much advice, CBF also demonstrated trust in us. In 1993, CBF Global Missions appointed us to mission service, along with two other couples who had no previous service with a mission agency. CBF exhibited a commitment to God's mission in our world by providing a safety net for mission personnel who had been disenfranchised and by creating a mechanism for sending out new personnel into the field. Commitments old were renewed and new ones were formed, and we went out with a wonderful sense of affirmation and anticipation.

Our first ministry assignment was in the Czech Republic, where we began interacting with a group of people who became family. People like Jim and Becky Smith and "T" and Kathy Thomas shared their lives and their ministry experiences with us. They helped in our orientation to this new missionary life and saved us from many of the potential pitfalls that new missionary personnel are prone to experience.

There were others who can be described as CBF colleagues, but when we say their names and remember their presence, we would rather call them cherished friends. Alongside the Smiths and Thomases, people such as Rachel Stephen, Jay and Anita Lynn, and Don and Carolyn Berry were instrumental in the development of the partnership between the Czech Baptists and CBF. They became a nurturing community in which we could all grow. For our three daughters, these folks became aunts and uncles.

CBF Global Missions has never attempted to create cloisters or mission compounds, but rather to be in genuine, mutual relationships with partners around the world. When we say that we discovered fellowship and community in CBF, we must quickly add that the sense of community extended to relationships with other Baptists around the world.

Commitments to the larger Baptist family and its God-inspired visions and worthy aspirations helped to shape and guide us. Mission is a community enterprise that both positively impacts the world and transforms us individually. It was the Czech Baptists who invited us into their community for our initial ministry assignment. Iva and Milan Kernovi gave us time and space in the church community they led in Brno, Czech Republic. They were patient with us as we learned the Czech language and culture, offering explanations of situations that we simply could not have understood without their guidance.

But even as we struggled to express ourselves with an elementary level of Czech, the Kernovis invited us to share our thoughts and experiences. The more we tried, the deeper our conversations went, and the deeper our love for the Czech Baptist community grew. This was more than language acquisition. Hearing what the Spirit of God was saying to this community and through this community in the Czech language broadened our perspective of the Kingdom of God and the Mission of God.

The community of CBF Global Missions personnel and local partners came together to share the Good News in place after place, using a variety of methods. In the early 1990s, a local Czech Baptist congregation was reaching out to university students by offering opportunities for the students to improve their English language skills. The church invited us to teach in their English language camps, through which the students would both improve their English and be exposed to Christians who were interested in their lives.

For a week we lived together, packed into a 600-year-old cabin in the Czech highlands for in-depth English conversations. The majority of the university students who attended were not Christians; in fact, many were professed atheists. In the advanced class, the students became increasingly mesmerized with the unfolding story of Esther as we read and discussed each chapter.

One of the female students was visibly drawn into the story as copies of each chapter were passed out to the group. The narrative itself invited her into a world of intrigue, politics and ethics. After several days of discussions and anticipation of what would come next in this drama, we shared with her that the story came from the Bible.

She was shocked. She had never read the Bible, so she didn't realize the depth of interest God has in this world. During those days in the highlands, she opened her mind to the possibility that God was engaged in this world, and that engagement had meaning for her life as well.

Our time in the Czech Republic with our CBF Global Missions colleagues allowed for our understanding of calling to develop, and that calling took us to places and new ministries we had never imagined. Within the Czech Baptist community was a Roma group that held worship services in the basement of the Brno church. One of the early CBF mission efforts among the Roma was the printing of the New Testament in Romani.

Soon after that, we began to have conversations with our CBF colleagues and Czech Baptist ministers regarding a ministry among the Dom people in the Middle East and North Africa. The impetus for this new ministry was not ours; instead, it came from our CBF colleagues. Our decision to move into this new ministry was the result of deliberations within the larger fellowship that we experienced with both CBF and Czech Baptists. Missions for us was, and is, a community enterprise.

Our history with CBF Global Missions has included several other moves into new and different areas of ministry. Each change in ministry focus was made within community. In 2015, CBF Global Missions adopted a statement describing our mission commitments, one of which is "Cultivating Beloved Community." These are good words to describe our personal experience with our spiritual family, the Cooperative Baptist Fellowship.

Allen and Verr Dean Williams were commissioned as Cooperative Baptist Fellowship field personnel in September 1993. They have worked in the Czech Republic and the Middle East, and most recently they served as Area Coordinators for Mission Teams in Asia and with the Internationals of North America Team.

A Wonderful Journey

By Anita Snell Daniels

Wow! What a wonderful 25-year journey!

My reflection centers on the one I knew best—Jack Snell. Can't we all remember that wonderful laugh, the ready smile and the look of compassion as he helped commission field personnel for the Cooperative Baptist Fellowship?

Jack represented fully the spirit of CBF. His enthusiasm was contagious as he gave himself readily to any task required, and he led with dedicated humility. His understanding and care helped chart the course and direction during the early stages of CBF Global Missions.

Even when it took countless hours of late-night work, he never seemed to tire as the excitement of God's work unfolded in our midst. He helped form the Fellowship's identity through building strong relationships of trust. His love and care for others helped form many deep relationships that remain in place around the world today.

Our journey took us from the local church to work as CBF field personnel. What unbelievable joy! Although we served as Associate Coordinators for Mission Teams, we were also full-time workers in the field. Living in Singapore, Jack taught full-time with the Asia Baptist Graduate Theological Seminary. Through our friend and mentor, Dr. Lilian Lim, we came to know and understand the need for training Asian leaders within the Asian context.

Jack and I also led the English-speaking congregation of the oldest Baptist church in Singapore. As we helped them work through past difficulties, they won our hearts and patiently taught us the Asian culture. They even taught me to love durian—the foul-smelling fruit that is an acquired taste.

Living, traveling and working throughout Asia as representatives of CBF gave Jack and me the opportunity to build relationships with Baptist groups, educational institutions, national organizations and other sending agencies from around the world. An example is the collaborative Thailand Baptist Missionary Fellowship. When the horrific tsunami struck Indonesia in 2004, a skeletal framework built on trust was already in place for partnership in disaster relief.

Building relationships continues to be the hallmark of the Fellowship.

Another great example of partnership was CBF's work with the China Bible Exhibit in 2006. The story of China's Christian community was finally shared with a magnificent display of its history. CBF connections resulted in President Jimmy Carter helping to open the event. The hard work of field personnel and office staff, as well as the generosity of Second Ponce de Leon Baptist Church in Atlanta and countless volunteers, made this exhibit a huge success. More importantly, as we worked side-by-side, deep personal relationships developed. The connections built during this event have continued with individuals, churches and the China Christian Council through the years.

I continually experience meaningful relationships with our CBF field personnel. These individuals are uniquely gifted, highly qualified, passionate, called and committed. Their differing perspectives, from traditional to "out-of-the-box" missiology, means consensus building can be difficult—but not impossible.

Because of our strategic location, we were able to have the majority of field personnel and their families in our home in Singapore for extended visits. Getting to know each other more fully allowed us to lead with personal insight. I had fun finding western foods to serve a southern dinner from time to time. These times together built lifelong friendships that I still carry in my heart.

Countless church congregations, partner seminaries and divinity schools, CBF state and regional organizations, the Baptist World Alliance, Texas Baptists and Virginia Baptists have been vital partners. It takes all of us to make it work.

Our journey that began 25 years ago continues to change. Yet God sustains us through difficult and joyful times. We continue to be challenged to change, learn and grow. I get excited as I observe the emerging young leaders of CBF today filled with the enthusiasm and dedication that ensures CBF will continue its mission.

And Jack? Jack continues to cheer us on. Can you hear his joyful laugh?

Anita Snell Daniels served as Cooperative Baptist Fellowship field personnel from 2000-2012. She and her late husband, Jack, joined CBF Global Missions to minister in Asia after years of work in the local church and education. Jack passed away from pancreatic cancer in 2007. After retiring to Jacksonville, Florida, Anita met and married Lad Daniels, and they joyfully continue serving as advocates for the Fellowship.

Grace and Freedom Through Love

By Tina Bailey

As a female artist, dancer and cross-cultural minister, over the years I have been able to pursue and develop my passion and ministry organically as opportunities have emerged. I thank the Cooperative Baptist Fellowship for making this possible. Finding CBF meant finding a place where I could minister with all that I am.

My husband, Jonathan, and I were appointed as CBF field personnel in December 1995 and left the United States in 1996 for Bali, Indonesia, sight unseen. Since that time, Bali has been our home.

When we first arrived, creative arts were not specifically part of our job description. But as is the nature of CBF Global Missions, we gravitated to where our best skill sets lay, and that was in the arts and art community. I have a background in theatre, dance and visual arts, and Jonathan has a background in music and writing.

Over time in Bali, we found our people—fellow artists. As we began to work in this area, we were given the freedom to develop and explore new avenues of work in the arts.

Barbara Baldridge, CBF's Global Missions Coordinator at the time, and Jack and Anita Snell, our Associate Coordinators for Mission Teams, were instrumental in providing the encouragement and trust in our abilities to chart this new course. This was not something that we took for granted. It was a risk. Once you let artists out of the box, it is hard to get them back inside again!

By giving us this freedom, CBF was doing something that few organizations at the time would do. This freedom allowed us to explore many aspects of the arts and spiritual life within the community in Bali, moving away from the common perception in the church of the arts as a tool or a means to an end.

Over the years, I have personally experienced the importance of art and spirituality co-existing in my life and in the lives of those with whom we minister. From the work of the imagination to giving a voice to issues of social justice and managing the CBF Art Auction at General Assembly, artists have been encouraged, and awareness for their lives and cultures has been heightened.

Narwastu Art Community is the name given to the hub of our activities. We chose *narwastu* because this is the name in Indonesian of the oil that Mary poured on Jesus' feet and then, in passionate humility, washed with her hair. The disciples thought her action was extravagant, unnecessary and a waste of money, but Jesus affirmed that it was one of significance. We believe in the inherent value of the arts and imagination and are thankful to work for an organization that believes that what we do matters, even though it may not look like other ministries.

This work takes many forms with many partnerships about which I could speak, but at this point in my journey, my work in Kerobokan Prison in Bali is the story on which I would like to focus.

This work is an example of the journey that can happen when you allow yourself to dare to do something different and to be available and present. It was my life as a practicing artist that opened the door for me to go into the prison, and that is the person whom the inmates and staff know. They also know me as a minister and understand that I am both. But most importantly, they know I am who I say am. I am available to them in whatever way they need me to be, without an agenda. That is the power of being the presence of Christ. CBF gave us a gift to be this presence.

In February of 2012, I received a phone call from a friend telling me that inmates in the prison had started an art program and that they needed a teacher. I was asked if I would be open to meeting them and seeing the program. I said "yes."

Little did I know how much that single "yes" would change my life.

When I arrived at the prison, I was met at the gate by the man who started the program. His name was Myuran Sukumaran, and he would become a very good friend. He was one of the group known as the "Bali Nine" and was a death-row inmate. I immediately liked him and was at ease in his presence. Myu, as he is known by his friends, became one of the best artists I have ever had the privilege of working with. He cared deeply for those in the prison and ran a tight program with high expectations. I learned much from Myu and became close to his family.

That day I walked into Kerobokan Prison, I knew Myu had a death sentence and, in the back of my mind, I always knew the possibility existed that his life would end, although it seemed unlikely. He was a changed man and had already demonstrated his reformation in many ways through his own life and the number of lives he had impacted in the prison. But his execution day did come. On April 29, 2015, Myu was executed along with seven others.

The day before the execution, I found myself serving Myu and his family their last communion together. And then, on the day he was killed, I was caring for his last 15 paintings, still wet to the touch. At the moment when shots were fired, I was with his family singing his favorite songs. Unknown to us, he and the others were singing at the same time.

It was a path I wish with all of my heart I did not have to walk, but I did walk it and would do it again if called on. That is what we do. We find ourselves sometimes in places we did not choose, but we know we are right where we need to be.

During the past 20-plus years of ministry with CBF, I have grown in my understanding of grace and freedom. These things are possible only through love, and the work is not always easy. Sometimes it can break your heart, but it is this love that enables me to get through the hard times. And a lot of grace is needed when things don't work out as we hope.

Standing with Myu's family, stunned that he had been executed, we were left with the question, "Why, God?" There is no answer to the why—at least not a good one. Being part of a faith community like CBF that does not try to explain away the struggles and injustices of life empowers me to keep going when I feel powerless. I may have stood, feeling broken, with his family and a few friends, but I knew we were being held in prayer by many people on the other side of the world. That *knowing* is powerful and mystical.

So I will continue to love—even when it is hard—because I know that grace and freedom abound through love. By allowing me to minister in freedom and grace, CBF has taken me to amazing places and led me to face some of the most difficult situations in my life. The journey is long and hard—and worth every step.

My work in the prison, where I teach and care for other inmates who have also become dear to my heart, continues. Some inmates are there for only a short time, while others do not know if they will ever go free. But I am there, and I continue to learn from them and hope they learn something from me.

My hope is that CBF will continue to take the risk to be a community of grace and freedom, enabled by the power of love and knowing that we all can learn from each other along our shared journey.

Tina Bailey and her husband, Jonathan, have served as Cooperative Baptist Fellowship field personnel since 1995 and have lived in Indonesia since 1996. As an artist and minister, Tina's inspiration to create emerges from the desire to communicate beauty and truth. She uses her expertise to build relationships in the community as well as through prison arts ministries.

Zero to Ten

By Shane McNary

In April 2015, at a multi-team meeting in Katowice, Poland, my wife, Dianne, and I enjoyed having lunch with one of our favorite people, Becky Buice Hall. We have come to know and depend on Becky to help make life as Cooperative Baptist Fellowship field personnel bearable.

Going to be away from home overnight? Email Becky. Have a question about the sporadic finance report you were supposed to have received? Email Becky. New budget to submit? Spending receipts? Requesting a new project? Email Becky. And our favorite, though we try really hard never to do this: Need an additional amount of funds wired to you before the regular funds distribution day? That's right, email Becky.

However, this conversation around the lunch table that day was not focused on CBF Global Missions. It was just a friendly chat about life. Becky recalled the first time we had met. It was at the invitation to missionary service at the 2002 CBF General Assembly in Fort Worth, Texas. Becky met us at the front and gave us the response card to express our interest in serving with CBF Global Missions.

We all laughed when she recalled our responses to a particular question during the exploratory conference for potential appointees. We were asked to rate our marriage on a scale of zero to 10. We celebrated our 10th anniversary in 2002. Surely 10 years was enough time to work out any kinks in our relationship so that we could boast to these potential employers about how we had mastered marriage. Hence, our answer: "Some days it is a 10, and other days it is a zero." Candor of this sort is as memorable as it is rare.

It has been noted that the CBF Global Missions way of sending out field personnel in the early years was that they were "sent around the globe with little structure after arriving at their assignment." Having field personnel parachute in and then be left to figure things out for themselves continued longer, perhaps, than the subsequent structural changes intended.

I remember standing backstage during our commissioning service and hearing my own voice confess on video that about the only word I knew in Slovak before our arrival was *zmrzlina*, or ice cream. This comment was followed by the laughter of thousands of supportive voices that filled the convention center hall in Birmingham, Alabama. The memories of that evening seemed a lifetime away by the time we arrived in Slovakia. There have been times in the intervening years when we could no longer remember those voices. It was lonely.

Much of this experience was simply the natural process of cultural adaptation. Culture shock quickly replaced the honeymoon phase of our adaptation after we moved from rural Arkansas to Košice, Slovakia. The difficult early days of complete separation from all things familiar and total immersion into a different world are common to everyone who moves into a different culture. We took turns having "I hate Slovakia" days. When it was your day, it was a definite zero. But then you got to have a complete conversation at the bus stop. "What time is it?" the elderly man asked. Dianne's response: "Ten."

"Thank you," he said as he walked off. Break out the peanut butter! It was time to celebrate!

As we sought to focus on our task of language and cultural acquisition, we still longed for a connection back home. The occasional care package and calls home reminded us that we were not forgotten. We stumbled through the first several weeks, numbed by the overwhelming differences we experienced. The house we were moved into was not actually for rent, though we were asked for six months payment up front. It was for sale. Our relocation budget was spent, and we had to move after just a couple of months. We never recovered the full amount of prepaid rent. This was a big fat zero. But we moved into a modest home with a yard, garden space and the best landlords in all of Slovakia. That was a 10!

The day that Allie, our daughter, had to have an emergency appendectomy—and the doctor's utter failure in trying to get me to pay a bribe for a prompt surgery, since his negotiating skills in English were as inept as mine in Slovak—was a big fat zero for us and for him. The day Taylor, our son, was tutored in Slovak by our landlord's father, the man we affectionately called "Grandpa," as they worked together in the garden—a 10.

We remained constantly open to opportunities to interact and learn, to use what language we could, and to meet new people. We attended an event at InfoUSA, where Dianne would later become their longest-serving volunteer. The United States ambassador was to speak. At the back of the room were several students from a private Roma school we had discovered online. Google is, after all—with the exception of Google Translate—every missionary's best friend.

I spoke with the teacher. She invited us to meet the director of the school. Our decision to reach out and form a relationship with the school not only opened doors for us, it also became the location for a job for future field personnel. The day we decided to serve at the school was a 10.

I was asked to help the local Baptist church by preaching during the time it was without a pastor. I did not have to preach every week, and the opportunity to work closely with an incredible translator aided my language acquisition more than I could have imagined. The Sunday I told one parishioner in Slovak that I had "urinated" on a sermon (instead of "written" on the printed version of the sermon) was definitely a zero day for language proficiency, but a 10 for gracious friends. Friendships we have with so many of the members of the Košice Baptist Church still sustain us on those zero days.

Dianne attended a Czech and Slovak Baptist Union women's conference in the Czech Republic. While learning the significant difference between types of goulash, she also gained a deeper appreciation for the faith of our Czech and Slovak Baptist sisters. One of the ladies taught her to make *halušky*, the Slovak national dish. She was excited to be able to replicate it at home. Later, a Roma friend taught her another way to make it. "We make it cheaper," she insisted. Both cooking lessons and times of fellowship were 10s.

The impact of short-term mission teams and the ways we have utilized them has changed significantly over the past decade. Though technically our first team was a group of German students who came with Lindsey McClintock, our Global Service Corps colleague who served in Berlin, the Cooperative Baptist Fellowship of Arkansas was our first team from the United States. It was for one of the members of that team that I unknowingly agreed to commit larceny.

I had no idea that the waiter's agreement to sell me a wooden charger plate was done without his employer's knowledge until he placed it on the table and told me to cover it with my jacket! Breaking the eighth commandment notwithstanding, it was a 10 to be invited into that team member's home years later and reminisce about the charger plate she had proudly displayed in her northeast Arkansas kitchen. Now, a decade later, we see the fruits of investing in long-term relationships with local partners and utilizing the amazing skills of short-term mission teams to help them achieve their goals.

I recall the time I encountered the fabled thievery of the Roma people. Whether it was the flurry of four-letter words in four languages (all with impeccably placed accents) that filled my tirade, or the fact that I was storming through the train's sleeper car in only my underclothes, the shock on the faces of the half-dozen Roma men is a sight I doubt none of us will ever forget. They insisted that they did not steal my camera while they were pilfering things from adjacent compartments. After one of them returned and proved to me that they had moved, but did not take, my camera, I found new appreciation for the term "honor among thieves." Still, dealing with stereotypes about the Roma always makes for a zero day—stereotypes of the Roma as liars, thieves, dirty, dishonest.

"Don't you have lice from working with them?" I am asked by the tenor who stands next to me in the Baptist church's choir. We do not even recognize the Romani caricatures many of our Slovak and Czech friends seem to know so well. We simply have friends: Bartholomew, who may not be the best carpenter around, but who will drop everything he is doing to help us move; Jarmila, rarely on time with anything she has promised to give me so that I can get her new website completed, but who will pay for my coffee if I am not quick enough on the draw when the waitress comes by; Kristina, who always greets me with a kiss on both cheeks and then holds my hand as we sit and talk about how she had to reschedule her MRI because she was scared.

There is Rene, who speaks to everyone in town and is remembered by many as the hoodlum-turned-evangelist. There is Ladislav, who spent too much of his precious income to buy a gift of chocolate and alcohol to say thank you to the missionaries who led a team from the United States to come and make a difference in the lives of the children in a small settlement on the outskirts of town. And then there are Thomas and Peter and Olivia and Eva, whose commitment to completing their educations is worthy of everyone's respect and support. Every memory of them is a 10.

As CBF celebrates 25 years and looks toward the next 25, we look back with profound gratitude for the opportunity to serve. It is without platitude that we offer our thanks for continued prayers and generous support of the CBF Offering for Global Missions. We hope that a commitment to cooperative missions remains a part of the Fellowship's core identity. The individuals and churches that make up the beloved community called Cooperative Baptist Fellowship are certainly 10s.

We have spent more than half of our married lives together as CBF field personnel. The 11 years we have spent with CBF have presented their own opportunities and challenges. Like our marriage and our experience as field personnel among the Roma in Slovakia and the Czech Republic, our relationship with CBF is a big fat zero on some days. On other days—many, many more days—it is a big 10!

Dianne and Shane McNary have served as Cooperative Baptist Fellowship field personnel among the Roma people in Slovakia and the Czech Republic since 2004. They are both native Arkansans.

Whenever, Wherever, Whatever

By Butch and Nell Green

We were crushed. Leaving Africa was one of the most heartbreaking decisions we had ever had to make. Africa was all our children knew, and we all felt at home there. What would we do? Where would we go? Where did we *belong*?

We knew from the beginning of our call to missions that we were supposed to work as partners, sharing equally in responsibilities, decisions and relationships. Unfortunately that was no longer possible, as changes began taking place within our sponsoring mission organization. Not knowing what else to do, we went back to Texas.

We knew we were not "uncalled." So we wiped the slate clean and said, "OK. So we start from scratch, just like we did when we first went out."

We made a list of all the things we would like to do. We loved inner city work. We wanted to be in partnership with a local church. We had enjoyed prison ministry and ministry to the homeless. We wanted to have relationships with internationals and, for the previous eight years, we had loved working through a multidisciplinary social center.

This was our wish list to God. Our motto over the years was, "Whenever, wherever, whatever." With that motto in mind, we began making phone calls. We contacted numerous organizations. Either they did not have what we were looking for, or they were not appointing personnel at that time, or they were not enamored with a woman in ministry. One day, a friend called and asked if we had considered the Cooperative Baptist Fellowship.

We had heard of CBF, of course. Dr. Keith Parks, for whom we had great admiration and respect, had recently been hired by the Fellowship to lead its missions endeavors. While overseas, we had deliberately not followed CBF's beginnings. We wanted to stay focused on the work God had given us rather than the controversy that had birthed this new organization.

With our friend's encouragement, we called. We braced ourselves, not wanting to get too excited or hopeful. We visited on the phone with Parks' associate, Harlan Spurgeon, and then we waited. A couple of hours later, the phone rang.

"We would like to send you some job descriptions," Harlan said.

While our hearts were still overseas, we nevertheless told him, "Whenever, wherever, whatever." Finally, the packet arrived in the mail. We anxiously tore it open. The very first job description was for Miami, Florida. It asked for personnel to begin an inner city ministry in partnership with a downtown church. A federal detention center was located across the street. There was an ongoing ministry to the homeless. A college with a high percentage of international students was a block away. The city was home to many people from Cuba and Haiti. There was a need for a center that would address these needs. It was our wish list realized!

In May 1994, at the CBF General Assembly in Greensboro, North Carolina, we were commissioned as field personnel. A few months later, the new inner city ministry, Touching Miami with Love, was born. Since then, we have served as CBF field personnel for 22 years in Florida, Belgium, South Carolina and Texas. We have been honored and privileged to witness the growth and changes that have taken place. Yet, when we reflect on the memories of our service, it is the relationships that rise to the forefront.

We think of Angela*, the director of a childcare facility in Miami for children living with HIV (and most of them eventually dying of AIDS). Angela could not understand how we could gladly provide music and speech therapy at no cost. At the beginning of the partnership, she openly admitted that she was not a Christian. She watched and observed love given freely, asking for nothing in return. She cried as a young child lay dying and asked if his music teachers could visit him. Angela called Nell one day and said, "I want what you have."

We think of Peter*, a refugee forced to flee from his country because he disagreed with the regime's politics. During a movie night at the Centre Oasis in Belgium, he told Butch he didn't really believe anything but thought everyone should be free to believe as they chose. Peter began attending the Arab Evangelical Church with us. Each time, he mentioned the peace he felt while there. Later, incarcerated in a holding cell where he was being detained before being sent back to his country, Peter prayed. "God help me. Please get me out of here. I promise I will follow you." A few moments later, an officer came, called Peter's name and inexplicably released him.

We think of Harriet*, an international student in North Carolina. After coming to Christ through a student ministry in Florida, she found herself virtually ignored by the church. After hearing Nell speak, she wrote her an email and poured out her heart. She spent Christmas with us that year in South Carolina. Though she had been in the United States for seven years, she had never spent this amazing holiday in an American home. Everything delighted her—the fire, the singing, cinnamon rolls for breakfast, passing the plate, the gifts. As she put it, "My first Christmas stocking could not hold it all!"

We think of Mary*, an international student in Texas. Nell received a call from a local church. "We have a young Muslim woman here asking questions about Christianity. Can you visit with her?" She had been searching for spiritual meaning for as long as she could remember. "What does it mean to be a Christian? What is required to follow Jesus? What does it take to be at peace?" One day after attending church with us, she stopped, looked at Butch and said, "I don't want to wait anymore. I want this. What must I do?"

When we first went overseas in 1986, we were told that the missionaries on the field would be our family. And indeed they have been. We are still Aunt Nell and Uncle Butch to many of the children of other missionaries. Some of these MKs are now even serving alongside us. Our children have missionary aunts and uncles, too.

We are Tata and TonTon to those who became part of our family while we were serving in French-speaking countries. Some call us Mere and Pere, acknowledging their gratitude for our role in their lives as they made decisions to follow Christ. We are Mum Nell and Papa to some of the most incredible international students attending the universities. Young people we discipled and shared life with still call for Mother Nell.

And when we thought our family could not get any bigger or our hearts any fuller, we were taken in, cared for and loved by CBF churches—all of this while being free to exercise our gifts and callings as partners in ministry. Just as Harriet's stocking could not hold it all, neither can ours!

We are often asked, "What is the most difficult thing about being a missionary?" We answer that dealing with loneliness and lack of a "home" is by far the most difficult. Gratefully, this has gradually diminished over the years. Why? Because CBF is where we *belong*. CBF is our family. CBF is our *home*.

*Names have been changed to protect privacy.

Butch and Nell Green have served as Cooperative Baptist Fellowship field personnel since 1994. They currently minister in Houston, Texas, where, by providing resources, training opportunities, mentoring and networking, they seek the mobilization of Christians and churches in developing and enhancing ministry among internationals.

After the Fall of the Berlin Wall

By Joyce Cleary

After the Berlin Wall fell in 1989, Tom and I were offered the opportunity to serve a new developing ministry in Poland. In October 1990, we drove from Berlin into Wroclaw, Poland. In those days, the trip took five hours because the border crossing was always slow. We had to show our passports, get entry visas, and wait to have our luggage inspected before we could proceed.

Wroclaw, formerly Breslau, Germany, is a large city. During the communist years, the city became a domain of mundane, high-rise apartment buildings, a few personally owned autos, and small grocery stores with often sparsely filled shelves.

Our first year, we lived in Krakow and studied Polish at Jagellonian University. We often bought fresh vegetables and eggs from street vendors, but our Polish was limited. A funny thing happened one day when Tom mispronounced the word "ten" and, in so doing, asked to buy a thousand eggs. Imagine the shock of the vendor!

At the end of the year, we moved to our apartment in Wroclaw, where our official job was to teach English in the Wroclaw School of Languages. The school was founded by Ruth Kowalczuk, a professor with a solid Baptist heritage. She saw the need for students to learn and become proficient in English. During the Communist years, students were not allowed to study English; thus the need was great, as the Poles longed to enter the "new world" and leave Communism behind.

An advertisement in the city newspaper promoted the school, indicating that it would be in the Baptist Church (the one and only in this city of 800,000). Calls came in from the community inquiring if the language school would be teaching religion. The director assured them the school was strictly for studying English. The locals were so eager to attend that people stood in line overnight to register.

When the school opened, approximately 300 students had registered. Most of them were professionals and college students. Each of our nine teachers, who variously came from the United States, the United Kingdom and New Zealand, was trained and certified to teach English as a second language. Our students studied diligently and also became interested in the Bible studies and English language worship services we held. Each summer, we held two weeklong retreats for the high school and college students, and one year a group of female students in their 40s asked me why we couldn't have a weeklong retreat just for them.

During the retreat, we taught attendees how to study the Bible and how to pray using one's own words—which was a new concept for the Polish Catholics. They loved the experience, and it launched a Bible study ministry to women which continues to this day.

In January 1993, when we were given the opportunity to join the Cooperative Baptist Fellowship, we resigned from the Foreign Mission Board of the Southern Baptist Convention and accepted this new challenge to serve. We always felt that our lives were truly enriched by the experience of living and working in Poland and often said we were glad we did not miss the opportunity to serve in this way.

In 1999, Tom decided he was ready to retire. But it was not to be just yet. We were asked to assist in the Fellowship's ministries of Touching Miami with Love and Open House Ministries in Homestead, Florida. What a blessing it was to serve in both places! We felt God blessed and enriched our lives once more with a new opportunity to serve—this time in our home state of Florida.

Through the years, we encountered many faithful servants of God who gave of themselves in a way that inspired us, encouraged us and motivated us to continue to walk together to serve others.

Joyce Cleary and her late husband, Tom, were part of the first class of Cooperative Baptist Fellowship field personnel. They were commissioned in May 1993 at the CBF General Assembly in Birmingham, Alabama.

Serving Albanians in Athens

By Bob Newell

Near the end of August 2014, we boarded an airplane with one-way tickets, leaving Athens, Greece. This was the first time that we had not purchased round-trip tickets from Athens. After living in the Balkans for more than a decade, we had reached a new threshold. We were relocating, retiring and walking away from the day-to-day oversight of our ministry as Cooperative Baptist Fellowship field personnel.

God had gifted us and CBF with this ministry through PORTA—the Albania House in Athens. But it was time for a change. It was time for indigenous Albanian leaders to take the reins of this ministry, and the time was both right and ripe with possibility.

As the first full-time field personnel sponsored by any group among the half million Albanian immigrants in Athens, we were leaving the meaningful ministry we had founded and joyfully served for years. But we did so with confidence that the God who was working among Albanian immigrants in Athens before we arrived would still be at work, even without us. We were also certain that the concern that had motivated CBF to care for Albanian immigrants in Athens would continue. For this reason, we created the PORTA Tomorrow Fund through the CBF Foundation, where contributions are being given to support PORTA for at least the first five years following our departure.

Bledi and Blerina Mile (pronounced Meelay) trained with us for two months to take the leadership reins of PORTA. They are mature believers—a statistical rarity among Albanians, whose country was ruled for nearly 50 years by a dictatorial Communist regime that declared itself atheistic. The government closed churches, confiscated Bibles and imprisoned or killed clergy. When the dictatorship failed and missionaries were finally allowed into their country, Bledi and Blerina heard the gospel and gave themselves to God in Christ.

In Athens, with its years of Greek/Albanian animosity and its suspicion of evangelical Christianity, they found churches that loved and taught them. They grew in their faith and, with his preaching gifts and commitment, Bledi soon became the recognized leader among the small group of Albanian believers in Athens. In God's providence, Bledi eventually found a good job, working for a wealthy Greek businessman.

Before our departure from Athens, we approached this couple and asked them to pray about taking on PORTA's leadership. The ministry was well-established as a center for education, hospitality, culture, recreation and reconciliation. The art gallery provides Albanian artists a venue to display their works; the library offers Bibles and other reading materials in the Albanian language, as well as classes in English, computers, the Albanian language and culture. An after-school PORTA Enrichment Program (PEP) brings additional education resources, and seminars on parenting, marriage enrichment, money management, leadership development and immigrant rights. An indigenous Albanian church meeting in PORTA's facilities was founded by PORTA participants.

Today, the ministry of PORTA is wide-ranging, offering hope, help and wholeness to Albanian immigrants.

There is a backstory in which we have been privileged to participate. It is inspiring to see how God was and is at work, bringing our lives to a place where we could join God in his care for Albanian people.

Forty-four people gathered in Stockholm, Sweden, in the year 2000. Their purpose was to write accords on ethnic cleansing, indicating that it is wrong to destroy an entire ethnic group and most egregious to do so in the name of God. Included in this group were a Supreme Court justice from the state of Washington, a fiery activist from Northern Ireland, Desmond Tutu's top advisor from South Africa, CBF field personnel in Albania, people of good will from around the world, and me, a former Baptist university professor and administrator turned pastor from Houston, Texas.

Afterward, when I returned to my duties as pastor of Memorial Drive Baptist Church in Houston, the first phone call I received was from the chair of the mission team for our church. She told me that, in the aftermath of the Kosovo conflict, the Catholics had relocated 500 ethnic Albanian families to Houston.

"Did you say Albanian families?" I asked.

When she said "yes," I told her that, thousands of miles away, I had been learning about Albanian people and unrest in the Balkans. In what can only be described as an intervention of God, these people in dire need had shown up in my prosperous, oil-industry, urban backyard of Houston. Our upper-income church began to care for these marginalized people. We learned that CBF had ministry among them, and we became an *adopting* church.

Janice soon had Albanian children in her choirs. We made home visits in their overcrowded apartments, and we focused our caring on this ethnic group, in the name of Jesus.

Shortly thereafter, we resumed a conversation about how we should conclude our careers. We wanted to finish on a high note and keep our sense of calling burning brightly. So we asked God to send us on a cross-cultural ministry journey.

We discovered that the still-young CBF not only cared about Albanians, but had uncovered a pressing need for Albanian ministry in Athens. With the fall of the Communist dictatorship, a half million Albanian immigrants crossed the border into Athens, seeking freedom and a better life. There were no missionaries serving exclusively among diaspora Albanian immigrants in Greece. At the CBF General Assembly in 2003, we were commissioned as field personnel to serve in Athens among these immigrants.

Because of the Fellowship's commitment to language and cultural acquisition, we invested two years in Tirana, Albania, to learn all that we could not only about the way Albanians speak, but how culture shapes their lives. Coming to Athens in 2005, we invested another two years in learning the contemporary Greek language and culture. By early 2007, we were ready to launch our ministry.

As we erected the ministry platform now known as PORTA, we discovered that a group of Albanian believers had been meeting for several years in Athens. They had been praying for God to send someone to work and serve with them. Although there was not yet an indigenous Albanian church, we found evangelical Christians in several churches with a heart for Albanians. These fellow believers accepted us, trusted us and shared our ministry dreams. These Greeks and Albanians immediately became strong partners in the work God was calling us to lead.

Other influential community leaders also shared our concerns. We were fortunate to be sent by CBF, which understood and supported the need to work with partners of all kinds. We quickly discovered our primary local church partner, the Second Greek Evangelical Church of Athens, which also came to be our church home.

Volunteers from CBF churches came to assist us, too. Since PORTA's facilities are located in a neoclassical building next to a hotel in the shadow of the Acropolis, housing short-term volunteers was easy. Over the seven years that we directed PORTA, close to 600 volunteers came to serve with us, including church and student groups from Houston Baptist University, Mercer University, Baylor University and Hardin-Simmons University.

The ongoing story of PORTA is a story of good people in CBF attuned to God's call and being in the right place at the right time, doing the right thing. It is the story of how a concern for unreached, unevangelized and marginalized groups can result in ministry where persons in these ethnic groups come to know Christ and experience a fuller, more meaningful life.

We feel privileged to have been part of this great movement of God. We are grateful that God has allowed us to fulfill our passions in this way. We are grateful to God for this encore opportunity, this finishing capstone to our calling and careers, to serve and to follow our joint passions in partnership with CBF.

Bob and Janice Newell served as Cooperative Baptist Fellowship field personnel from 2003 until 2014, ministering among Albanian immigrants in Athens, Greece. Prior to joining CBF, Bob served as a pastor in Houston and as a professor and administrative dean at Houston Baptist University. Janice, a classically trained organist, taught music and coordinated choirs, and also raised funds for international theological education.

Blessed in Brooklyn

By Taisha Seabolt

I have been connected with the Cooperative Baptist Fellowship since 2003, when I began my academic career at Mercer University's McAfee School of Theology. In fact, I could not help but hear about CBF, since it was then headquartered on the McAfee campus. Though I had read about the work CBF did around the world, it was not until I actually met CBF field personnel firsthand that I truly understood who CBF is.

During my mission immersion trip to Belgium in the spring of 2004, I was blessed to meet CBF field personnel Butch and Nell Green. I still remember that June day, listening to the Greens share about the work they did with internationals in Belgium and their commitment to holistic missions, and then actually meeting one of the individuals with whom they worked. My life was forever changed at that moment, as I felt the Holy Spirit leading me to learn more about the Fellowship.

For me, CBF is more than a network that strives to be the presence of Christ to people all around this world. CBF was the conduit God used to help me live out my life's calling by serving in Brooklyn, New York, through the Global Service Corps program, where participants served for two years as missions personnel. And God definitely knew what God was doing when God told me (like God told Jacob in Gen. 31:3) to go back home.

As an advocate for diversity with a passion to share the love of Christ with all people, I can truly say that being back in my hometown of Brooklyn was one of the greatest blessings in my life. The children and families with whom I worked (and quickly grew to love) genuinely changed my life for the better. Isn't it just like God to take you somewhere and transform you while you serve God's people!

During my time of service, I ministered as the Community Outreach Program Director for Greater Restoration Baptist Church in Crown Heights, Brooklyn. Small in number but with a huge heart and a great love for its community, GRBC is committed to reconciliation and the empowerment of children and youth through education. I assisted the church in its outreach activities, leading afterschool programs and directing two summer camps, building relationships in the community through hosting a Fall Festival for area children and youth, and spearheading a World AIDS Day Sunday service and a memorial service for those affected by HIV/AIDS. I immersed myself in serving the community and loved every minute of my two-year term.

One of the most rewarding aspects of this time was the relationship I developed with the Albany Housing Projects, known at one time to be one of the worst projects in New York City. But I did not see a "bad" neighborhood. Instead, I saw "home" and became a part of a family and community—a place where children just wanted to be loved and cared for. From tutoring children in their afterschool program to providing Christmas presents during the holidays, passing out turkeys at Thanksgiving and bringing mission groups to work with the families throughout the year, I was blessed to share the love of Christ with people so often forgotten.

There was so much potential in the children at Albany and, regardless of the perceptions many people in Crown Heights had about "the projects," good things can and do come out of them. Since I had grown up in the projects in Coney Island in Brooklyn, I felt a special connection to the people of Albany. I was constantly amazed by the beautiful children there who truly touched my heart.

While life and ministry in Brooklyn blessed me tremendously, my experience was also filled with the realities of urban life. Living in a city that was so unpredictable and in such an unstable world, I prayed for the children and youth I worked with and hoped that, in some way, God would use me to make a difference. One person who impacted me was a 15-year-old young man who loved football and caught the eye of college scouts. This "big teddy bear," as we called him because of his lovable nature, was shot nine times in his back and legs while trying to defend his sister. He survived, but his right leg had to be amputated.

In the aftermath, I offered a ministry of presence to him and his family, spending hours alongside them during his recovery and rehabilitation both in the hospital and when he returned home. We joked and laughed. That ministry blessed me more than I could have ever imagined.

After I left Brooklyn, I continued to keep in contact with him and his family. He never ceases to amaze me, as he did not allow his tragic experience to stop him from living his life. He joined an acting club, wrote his own play and even had it performed by his theater group. He went to college and is near graduation. He plans to pursue a master's degree in social work. What a testimony to the power of relational ministry.

As I reflect upon my experiences with CBF Global Missions as a member of the Global Service Corps, I am still amazed that I was actually back home in Brooklyn, serving as an urban missionary. The work God allowed me to do has forever left an imprint on my heart and on my life's calling. I thank God for CBF, and I am blessed to be part of such a wonderful family.

Taisha Seabolt is Assistant Manager for Field Personnel Selection and Training with the Cooperative Baptist Fellowship in Decatur, Georgia. A licensed professional counselor, she served from 2006 to 2008 in Brooklyn, New York, through the Global Service Corps program of CBF Global Missions. She and her husband, Matt, have one son, Jacob.

A Missionary at the United Nations

By David F. D'Amico

The lives of pilgrim servants are guided by divine providence. It was for the "next step in our journey of life" that my wife, Ana, and I dared to move to New York City to minister as Cooperative Baptist Fellowship field personnel at the United Nations in 1996.

"You'll fit like a glove," CBF Global Missions Coordinator Keith Parks told us when Ana and I were considering the move. It seemed like a wild adventure at our "mature age!"

As an "INTJ" on the Myers-Briggs scale, I wrote a three-page document of strategy. Ana, in her irreverent and usual way, said, "We don't need a document, we need presence and trust in God's providence."

The years of service in New York proved her right. Who would have imagined that hosting diplomats in our 37th-floor apartment living room was part of the strategy?

Where else were we to find pilgrims on the journey? Our apartment always seemed to be filled with guests from diverse backgrounds. They included a financial consultant from India, a Japanese couple, a professor from North Africa, a Dominican young man from the Bronx and his white girlfriend from South Carolina, LGBT individuals from Metro Baptist Church, and, of course, our four children, who suddenly felt the urge to visit their missionary parents . . . free lodging included.

We settled into our new life in New York. As an unreconstructed bureaucrat, I kept records and filed reports to CBF's headquarters in Atlanta. Ana invited Church Women United leaders to meet in our spacious apartment, which was the venue for several meetings of friendly nongovernmental organizations.

Then we faced the tragedy of the attacks in our city on September 11, 2001.

The national tragedy rallied Cooperative Baptists across the country to a ministry of compassion, amounting to the distribution of $500,000 in funds and subsidies to more than 30 churches and countless individuals and relief organizations.

The best ministry encounters were unexpected:

- Receiving a package of freshly baked chocolate chip cookies from a mother in Texas, who had baked them for the fire station beside our apartment when we reported that its fire chief had died on 9/11.

- Meeting with a family from Albania to help them settle in New York.
- Being asked by a Communist Cuban diplomat to interpret for him what the Baptist World Alliance would do in Cuba, and using the opportunity to give him a Bible.

How shall I thank the Lord for his amazing grace and his calling to serve him? As the hymn writer put it so well, "To God be the glory!"

David F. D'Amico and his wife, Ana (now deceased), were commissioned as Cooperative Baptist Fellowship field personnel in December 1995. From 1996 to 2004, David served as the official representative of CBF to the United Nations diplomatic community in New York City. In 2004, the couple transferred to Raleigh, North Carolina, where they continued their advocacy ministry with the United Nations. David retired from the mission field in 2006.

Forming Together: A Lifelong Story

By Diann Whisnand

I'm not much of a collector of keepsakes, doodads or thingama-jigs. In fact, one of my favorite hobbies is purging. If it doesn't have a practical use, it's out the door.

That's why I was surprised recently to find a single piece of faded blue paper from my high school days, dated 1972. I'm shocked it survived me. Even after 44 years, I immediately knew what it was: a list of teenagers from the First Baptist Church in Midland, Texas, who were traveling into Mexico to offer a Bible school to Mexican children in border villages. It was my first experience in Christian missions and one that helped to form the rest of my life. I must add that the name of my then-future husband, Phillip, was also on that list.

Fast forward 44 years, and I'm celebrating my 10th year of full-time missions with the Cooperative Baptist Fellowship. This is a real cause for personal celebration, knowing that God placed a seed in my heart all those years ago and that the seed was able to grow, and is still growing. I'm also thankful that my husband's heart for missions was formed from the same seed.

Through the years, Philip and I participated together in on-the-field mission work in Mexico, South America and all along the United States/Mexico border. Through CBF, we've been able to minister directly to poor migrant workers from Central and South America while living in California, Washington and other western states. Although Philip has since retired from CBF, I have come back to the very same place where I started: the Texas/Mexico border. I'm old enough now to be able to look way back and see that God had a hand in all of this from the beginning.

During the formative years of my life—which includes birth through yesterday—I've learned how to do things "the right way" many times over. I've learned how to undo things, then redo them. Formation for me never ends, and it shouldn't. Otherwise, I am presuming to know all there is to know.

So with these thoughts, and in honor of CBF's 25th Anniversary, I write about how my affiliation with CBF has allowed me to participate in the 25-year formation of its Global Missions effort. As one of CBF's field personnel, my assignment is to address the systemic poverty that abounds along the U.S./Mexico border, specifically in the Rio Grande Valley region of Texas. This border area typically wins national blue-ribbon awards in poverty, which is what caught the attention of the Fellowship many years ago.

Issues of social justice and helping the poor are mentioned so often in scripture that I lose count. For me, this Christian mandate is never in question; how to go about helping is the question. What could CBF do to help the poor in the Rio Grande Valley that others weren't already doing? First, CBF could send someone there—long term—to determine how to help. This initial thought was formed by CBF's Latin America Team in 2010 and approved in 2011. I jumped at the chance to do this work, because these are the people and the culture and the place I love. God planted this seed in my heart long ago.

When I accepted this new assignment in 2011, the Rio Grande Valley region had been on the receiving end of Baptist (and other) mission work for decades. Some long-term mission work had taken place through the years, but the majority of the efforts were short-term, much like my own mission trip back in 1972. It was in and out in one week. I quickly observed that these short-term mission teams were still plentiful and were already busy helping the poor in many ways. So my question became, "What can I do long term to help with poverty issues that can't be done short term?

After some research and involvement in the area, it became apparent that low literacy rates and lack of education were having a major impact on systemic poverty in the Rio Grande Valley. These are not short-term issues; they require much time. It also became apparent that God has been forming me and preparing me for this very time and place.

Throughout my life, there had been times when I prayed, "God, why in the world am I doing this?" This question would come when I would find myself in some sort of odd, exasperating situation, like teaching a class about something I knew nothing about or being involved in something big that a friend (or church) had talked me into. Sometimes, it would take years before I'd get the answer to that prayer. Working in the Rio Grande Valley cured me of praying those words because, since 2011, I've used every bit of knowledge, training and experience I ever received.

Once, in 1990, a friend talked me into taking a six-month income tax preparation course with her—"just for fun," she said. Within a week, I was praying, "God, why am I doing this?" I did not find it fun at all, and I didn't see any reason I would ever need that kind of information. I was not an accountant and had never had an accounting class in my life, nor would I ever need to prepare tax returns for anyone. But I finished the class anyway and learned a lot about tax rules and working with the IRS.

Fast forward to 2013. I found myself directing a faith-based nonprofit literacy center in the Rio Grande Valley, which offers English as a Second Language (ESL) and General Educational Development (GED) classes to adults and families struggling with poverty in Hidalgo County. As the director, it became my responsibility to oversee and approve all bookkeeping matters, to transfer all required tax and audit information to the CPA, and to work closely with the IRS on previous and current tax issues. I cannot fathom trying to accomplish this without prior accounting knowledge and tax training.

I began teaching public school in Texas back in 1978, and a few years later, what became known as the "boat refugees" from the Cambodian/Laotian war were making their way to the United States. Some of the families were brought to our town for resettlement, and the Cambodian children were placed in schools—some for the first time. In the middle school where I taught, since I was the only teacher with an open space in her schedule, I ended up teaching a small class of non-English speaking Cambodian refugees for an entire school year. I was totally unprepared. I didn't know a thing about ESL, Cambodia, or how to help refugees. Out came my prayer: "God, why am I doing this? I don't know anything about any of this!" But we all survived the year, and I learned how to work with refugees who flee their homeland in desperation.

During the summer of 2014, my new hometown in the Rio Grande Valley of Texas was inundated with refugees fleeing their homelands in Central America. My mind went back to the refugees from Cambodia and the ways in which I had learned to respond and help. This time it was thousands upon thousands of refugees, many more than my one small class back in 1980. But they all had the same look, the same needs, the same level of utter exhaustion and desperation. I was able to help, and CBF responded in a big way.

When we talk about "forming together," it's a lifelong story for me, one that includes many different surprises and people along the way. But much of my formation has also been intentional, and my relationship with CBF has been with intention. I watched the birth of CBF, the early growth and the ongoing formation. For more than 10 years now,

I've "formed together" with CBF Global Missions, hand-in-hand, to intentionally spread the love and hope of Christ to strangers in our land.

I am profoundly thankful for CBF and for the Fellowship having allowed me to be part of the 25-year formation of CBF Global Missions. To me, it's worth a grand celebration. Praise God!

Diann Whisnand has served as one of the Cooperative Baptist Fellowship's field personnel since 2005. Throughout her 10-year ministry with CBF, she has ministered among Latino populations in the western part of the United States. She currently works to address systemic poverty at the Texas-Mexico border area known as the Rio Grande Valley. Diann and her husband, Phillip, have two grown sons, two daughters-in-law and three grandchildren.

The Answer to a Stranger's Prayer

By Kirk and Suzie

A dozen years ago, we were at the point of giving up. We had been appointed as Cooperative Baptist Fellowship field personnel in 1995, serving jointly with the Wycliffe Bible Translators in Southeast Asia. In 1996, we encountered the "B" people, a small, unreached group. Through prayer and the encouragement of our CBF teammates, we accepted this group's invitation to live among them, learn their language, develop an alphabet and literacy materials in their mother tongue and, eventually, translate scripture. This was all done with the support of the community elders, who asked only that we promise not to "force" them to change their religion or build a church. We bought a bamboo and thatch house in the village and began the task of learning this previously unwritten language and building relationships with the people whom God had brought into our lives.

After about seven years, however, we were becoming discouraged. An alphabet had been created and many children and adults were excited about literacy, yet no one seemed interested in Jesus. There was only one believer in the group—a young blind woman. Who would read the scriptures once they were translated? Were we just wasting our time? Had God really called us to serve the "B" people through Bible translation?

At our lowest point, God parted the veil and let us see what God had been doing all along. We received a phone call from a border town, saying that people from a neighboring country had come to see us—and their language sounded like the B language. This was a big surprise, since up to that point we had not known of B people in that neighboring country. However, the biggest surprise was yet to come.

The next day, we met face to face. They indeed spoke the B language and had not known of the existence of B people in any other country. They shared an incredible testimony of how, 30 years earlier, many of them had come to know Jesus through the witness of other ethnic peoples in their very remote home area. "Since then," they told us, "people in our village have been praying daily for three things: a Bible, a hymnal and a primer, all in our language."

Thirty years of prayer! Our minds went back to our own child-hoods, when we first felt stirrings of a missionary calling through speakers, books and short-term mission experiences. The sovereign God was calling—not just us, but also a team who would send us off with their prayers and support. And in the fullness of time, the puzzle pieces for separate continents came together.

In 2015, we celebrated the printing of the New Testament in the B language. It had been a long and hard process, but by God's grace, it will be worth it. God promised that the Word will not return void, an assurance precious to us and the B believers in the four countries in which they are scattered.

Have you ever had the privilege of being part of the answer to a stranger's prayer? For every believer surrendered to God, the answer is "Yes!" Whether you are called to pray, give or go, you are part of God's work on this earth. As you continue to offer yourself as a living sacrifice to our great and merciful God, you will continue to bless people near and far—whether you realize it or not, and even if (and maybe especially when) you feel inadequate to the task.

Kirk and Suzie serve as Cooperative Baptist Fellowship field personnel living among the B people in Southeast Asia. Commissioned in 1996, their ministry over the past 20 years has been dedicated to creating a written language and resources for this small people group.

Reaching Roma Through Project Ruth

By Ralph and Tammy Stocks

Two mothers and their dressed-up six-year-old children approached Dr. Otniel (Oti) Bunaciu, founder of Project Ruth in Bucharest, Romania, at the opening dedication of the Obed Day Center in September 2010. Oti had to apologize for not recognizing them but was delighted when they stated that they had been students in the very first Ruth School class! Now, a generation later, they were entrusting their young children to the caring hands of Project Ruth.

The miracle that is Project Ruth began in 1992. Conversations between Oti and his father, Dr. Ioan Bunaciu, along with Cooperative Baptist Fellowship field personnel "T" and Kathie Thomas, focused on responding to the local Roma neighborhood which then surrounded the church. Roma kids were playing in the streets rather than going to school. The youth of Providenta Baptist Church invited them in for "Club"—a time for singing, sharing a Bible story and offering a snack.

They quickly realized two things: The kids were always famished, and most of them could not read or write. Roma children face much discrimination in the public schools and often drop out. The initial response of teaching literacy soon developed into a school that would welcome Roma children. The name "Ruth School" was chosen for the biblical Ruth, who was welcomed in a land which was not her own.

With help from CBF and supporters from England, a building was erected on the church premises that included four classrooms, offices, a conference room, a kitchen and cafeteria, and dormitory space for hosting teams. Dedicated in 1998, the Ruth School initially welcomed grades one through four, then each year added a grade up to the eighth grade. Roma students were instructed by caring teachers and enjoyed a hot lunch daily. For many of them, it was the only meal of the day.

Volunteer teams came initially to help construct the building, but soon they were coming to minister to the kids through classroom activities, field trips, music, art and sports. A sponsorship program developed and provided for teachers' salaries, hot lunches, school supplies and operating costs.

The Ruth School quickly established a reputation in the Ferentari neighborhood of Bucharest for caring for impoverished children. Class sizes increased dramatically, and limited classroom space demanded two shifts of classes—morning and afternoon. It became clear that a larger facility was needed. Thus began a drive to purchase a plot of land in the neighborhood and build an adequate school for grades one through eight that would accommodate the demand.

In 2006, the second building was dedicated. School accreditation was granted by the Romanian Ministry of Education. The current Ruth School hosts 220 students in grades one through eight (plus a kindergarten), with a full kitchen and cafeteria, library, IT room, doctor and nurse offices, a sports field and administration space for Project Ruth.

Students attending the Ruth School receive a free education with all school materials provided, a hot lunch each day, seasonal distributions of new clothing and shoes, an annual medical exam by a doctor, library access, and after-school programming that provides homework tutoring and supervision while parents work. There are also field trips to cultural and historical sites and biannual camps in the mountains. Ruth School graduates are assisted in re-entering Romanian public high schools, and free tutoring is provided for their courses. Our success stories include graduates who went on to finish high school and were accepted into university degree programs.

The Obed Day Center welcomes four- and five-year-old children. Most Roma children enter the first grade without having been taught initial skills at home—numbers, colors, alphabet, etc. They often enter the first day already behind Romanian children whose parents encouraged reading before starting school. The half-day program offers the structure for preparing kids for the first grade and greatly improves their success rate.

The church planting movement among the Roma has also been strong in Romania. God has called pastors to lead those churches. However, since few Roma men have more than an eighth grade education, they are unable to attend the Romanian Baptist Seminary. Recognizing that those pastors need training at an adequate level, T Thomas and Oti Bunaciu initiated the Gypsy Smith School for Leadership Training in 1998. Since then, more than 90 students have graduated from a 16-course curriculum that provides much-needed instruction in theological, biblical and practical ministry skills. The students come for four intensive weeks of study each winter for two years and receive a diploma, a Bible and a number of supplementary ministry resource books. They also develop a deep bond with other Roma church leaders.

The Roma mothers of Ferentari often have married young and given birth to many children. Thus they carry a strenuous load that includes heavy housecleaning, shopping and childcare—all on a minimal diet amid impoverished living conditions. The Naomi Counseling Center began in 2011 to provide free counseling for these women. Additionally, sewing classes teach beginning-to-advanced skills, allowing the women to repair family clothing and to create products for sale, with the profits assisting their own families. Childcare is provided so that women may concentrate on learning at the Naomi Center. Job training assists the women to pursue applications and interviews in a chosen field.

The Boaz Second-Chance Program, launched in 2014, allows adults to recapture previous educational opportunities by attending night classes. Classes are held in the Ruth School building, with qualified teachers helping motivated students attain the necessary schooling to function in society.

If you walk through the Project Ruth facilities, you will not find the CBF logo displayed. However, the imprint of CBF is clearly visible, ranging from significant funding of buildings and scholarships to the work of volunteer teams and long-term personnel. The Thomases were members of Providenta Baptist Church and helped to fashion the early vision for the Ruth School and the Gypsy Smith School.

Through the CBF Global Service Corps program, Wes and Susan Craig served full time on the staff of Project Ruth from 2006-2009. Another couple, Skyler and Ronella Daniel, came through Student.Go, CBF's student missions initiative, and served from 2013-2015. Ronella was instrumental in setting up a special needs program that identified students through appropriate testing and developed a curriculum to meet their needs. Skyler became a Ruth School chaplain, leading the weekly chapel services.

We ministered to the Roma in Hungary for more than 15 years, from 1995-2010. In 1996, we started developing a close bond with Project Ruth, and I often took the night train from Budapest to Bucharest to meet teams and Gypsy Smith School professors. We heavily promoted the Ruth School's scholarship program to support the education of Roma children. In September 2010, that passion led us to make a permanent transition to Bucharest.

One of our first efforts was to create a weekly chapel service for Ruth School students. Tammy regularly taught students basic Bible stories, while youth from Providenta led the students in singing.

Students began singing the lyrics during the week and saying the Lord's Prayer prior to their lunch. Greater respect was shown to teachers and other students as biblical values were shared. Most of all, the students came to understand that they are loved by God—not in spite of being Roma, but because they are Roma!

The women coming to the Naomi Center grew to love Tammy as she led weekly Bible studies and created multiple celebration events to let the women know they are valued. In the Roma culture, the women defer to men; yet the Naomi Center boasts a "man-free" zone to allow the women to relax and be nurtured. Even though Tammy despised learning sewing skills while growing up, God has placed her front and center in the lives of women learning those exact skills.

I continued to recruit and prepare Gypsy Smith School professors, and more and more professors were present for the school's sessions. Significant partnerships were established with CBF Heartland, Virginia Baptists and Dutch Baptists. What started in a church basement with a few youth reaching out to Roma children playing in the streets has grown to multiple ministries impacting preschool children, school children, and women and men who otherwise would have been left behind by the local society. The seed planted in that basement blossomed into a ministry that welcomes and nurtures all within its branches!

Ralph and Tammy Stocks have served as Cooperative Baptist Fellowship field personnel since 1994. They are also Area Coordinators for Mission Teams with CBF Global Missions. They currently minister in Bucharest, Romania.

The Legacy of Service in Miami

By Angel Pittman

As the Cooperative Baptist Fellowship celebrates 25 years, it was surprising for me to realize that my husband, Jason, and I have been a part of the story for half that history. We first heard of CBF through Truett Seminary while Jason finished his dual Master of Divinity and Master of Social Work degrees at Baylor University. As Baylor undergrads, we had not traveled far from campus for our first urban ministry experience, volunteering extensively with Mission Waco and then working there after graduating from college. We loved our work, but as graduation from seminary and graduate school was approaching, we sensed God calling us to take our experience and Jason's learning to a place where we could have an even bigger impact.

For seven years, we had been following a model of ministry in which we lived and served in a low-income neighborhood, so Jason and I were immediately drawn to the CBF's mission of holistically serving the most neglected. Our commissioning as field personnel by CBF was a profound moment, and our first term of service took us "out of the pond and into the ocean" of urban need as we lived and served in inner-city Detroit. Those years in Detroit were indeed formative in our ministry experience. As we look back now, we see that God was preparing us for a call to lead the ministry of Touching Miami with Love.

Our story at Touching Miami with Love (TML) can be shared only by also sharing the stories of those CBF field personnel blessed by the Fellowship to lead before us. Butch and Nell Green were the first to answer the call to serve the needs in Miami's urban core in 1994. Having served in West Africa for eight years, they began with a survey to assess the needs of the area. It was also through this process that the name "Touching Miami with Love" was chosen. The Greens began work in the areas for which the surveys had shown the greatest needs: English as a Second Language classes, ministry among homeless persons, international students, and persons living with AIDS, prayer ministry and prison outreach.

After three years in leadership, the Greens sensed their time at TML coming to a close, and Larry and Laquita Wynn took over as TML's second set of directors. It soon became evident during their time of service that for Touching Miami with Love to have a deeper impact in the community, they would need to narrow the focus. A decision was made in 1999 to center specifically on the children, youth and adults in the Overtown community and the homeless population in the downtown corridor of Miami.

With this new focus on the residents of Overtown, another organizational shift came under then Executive Director Steven Porter with a move from the building in the downtown corridor to the neighborhood of Overtown. A new center for ministry was purchased in 2002. Carolyn Anderson, Coordinator of the Cooperative Baptist Fellowship of Florida, helped lead that effort along with Jean Willingham, a member of the Representative Assembly of CBF of Florida.

In 2004, as Steven was looking toward his doctoral studies, Jason and I were approached about assuming the leadership—something we felt called to do. Steven spent the summer months introducing Jason not only to the ministry and work of TML, but just as importantly to the neighbors and friends of TML. As Steven left, Jason and I began to feel we were among family. We were quickly accepted into the community because of the love so many had been pouring into Overtown over the past 10 years. It was affirming to us to continue our call to live among those we served, so we moved into the Overtown community to raise our family.

We have been able to facilitate the growth of the organization as we have built on the rich history we inherited from past CBF field personnel. It has been a great comfort during each hard time or challenge (and there have been plenty), and as we've witnessed tragedies and heartache in an often violent and turbulent community, to know that there are individuals and churches in the Fellowship supporting us and praying for us. As CBF has beautifully told the stories in print, online and through video of the impact we are making together, literally thousands of children, youth and adults in Overtown and West Homestead have experienced the love of the 130-plus churches in the Fellowship who have heard about TML and decided to journey and serve alongside us.

As CBF field personnel, Jason and I have had the support necessary to develop several highly successful programs and projects to serve the Overtown community, including year-round programs for children from kindergarten through 12th grade, multiple parenting programs, case management, and ever-expanding outreach services to the community. Some of the children whose photos were taken years ago at the park across the street during TML Bible Clubs and summer camps now serve on staff with us. Those who were once too young to be in camp and who played on the periphery are now active members of our Today's Leaders Youth Development Program and are making their plans for college.

While we cannot take credit for the rich legacy of ministry at Touching Miami with Love, we are delighted to have a role in it, thanks to the continued faithful support of CBF. This is a story that, under God, is continuing to unfold, not just for Overtown but for another Cooperative Baptist ministry on the other side of Miami-Dade County.

In 2015, we were pleased to be asked to welcome our sister organization, Open House Ministries, under the leadership of Touching Miami with Love as they joined as the West Homestead Site. Open House Ministries began during the same time period as TML, as the Fellowship and CBF of Florida addressed the immense needs in the wake of the destruction of Hurricane Andrew in 1992. Wanda Ashworth-Valencia, Executive Director of Open House Ministries, has poured her heart and soul into the community since 2004. The fruits of her labors are seen not only in the community garden that feeds so many, but in the lives of Martin, Joe, Edith and others who now serve on staff with us.

Through Cooperative Baptist efforts such as the former Global Service Corps program of CBF Global Missions and Student.Go, nearly 100 college students and young people have served over the years in internships at both sites as they have stretched themselves in service. Several have chosen to join our staff because of those experiences, and two of them are still on staff with us.

Keri Spears, our financial director, just celebrated her 13th year with us, having first served through the Global Service Corps program. Amanda Humbert, our lead youth instructor, first came to us as a freshman in high school with her church, Hendricks Avenue Baptist Church in Jacksonville, Florida. This church's commitment to be involved for 11 years provided her the opportunity to be immersed in our community each summer and impacted her college choice of Florida International University, where she remained an active volunteer throughout her years as a student. She has now served on our staff for eight years. Several of our Student.Go summer interns have had life-impacting experiences during their time with us. Their continuing passion for TML and the communities they served are inspiring.

Our vision for TML is to continue to grow, and we believe that it is only one tool to help bring individual life change through Jesus Christ, which will then ultimately effect community change. The seeds of some amazing dreams are already inside the children, youth and adults we serve. We have the joy of helping to bring those dreams to fruition as we seek to inspire, educate and empower the people of Overtown and West Homestead whom we serve. We recognize that leading what has become over the past 10 years a much larger organization, with more than 30 staff serving some 400 children, youth and adults, has been made possible because of those who have served before us. We're so blessed that many of those who have been the recipients of those investments now serve alongside us!

Angel Pittman and her husband, Jason, serve the communities of Overtown and West Homestead as the directors of Touching Miami with Love. They are graduates of Baylor University. Jason also received his Master of Divinity and Master of Social Work from Baylor's Truett Theological Seminary and School of Social Work. They have two sons, Isaac and Lucas.

Love and God in Toronto

By Michelle Norman

When Matt and I began our two-year service as Global Service Corps field personnel in Toronto with the Cooperative Baptist Fellowship, I had no idea of the ways it would change me. Amy Derrick, the manager of CBF's GSC program at the time, often said the goal of the GSC program was to "ruin you forever." In my situation, at least, the program was successful.

We drove into Toronto in 2003 in a "big orange truck" (as our two-year-old called the moving truck), pulling our little green Sentra behind us. Our apartment was in Jane and Finch, a neighborhood known by the intersection of its two major streets. Called the Corner of One Hundred Lands, this neighborhood is one of the most diverse in a city known globally for being extremely multicultural.

Greeted at the apartment by the local Baptist pastor—a Jamaican immigrant—his teenage boys, a West African refugee claimant who served as a community minister, and our CBF colleagues, Marc and Kim Wyatt, we began our service to minister with and among international students.

We served in Toronto at the invitation of Toronto Baptist Intercultural Services. This Canadian Baptist ministry and Canadian Baptist churches were our hosts and guides to learning the landscape of ministry in Toronto. During our time there, we partnered closely not only with the local Baptist churches, but with a Pentecostal congregation, InterVarsity campus ministers and a Christian Reformed church campus minister. The religious, ethnic and cultural diversity was a picture of the family of God at work on earth.

I was continually reminded of Ephesians 3:20: God is able to do "abundantly more than all we ask or imagine." The two years were abundantly more than I ever could have asked for or imagined. The experience was one that shapes my outlook on the world, my understanding of who God is, and the way in which I minister today alongside my husband, Matt, as we serve as CBF field personnel in Barcelona, Spain.

The lessons learned were many, but a few stand out:

Lesson 1: *Thanksgiving isn't just a turkey, dressing and sweet potato casserole.*

For some time before our arrival in Toronto, a group of churches had been working together to minister to at-risk youth in the urban environment of Jane and Finch. They had hoped to begin to connect with students of York University, which was in the same neighborhood as this diverse group of congregations. With our arrival in September, they decided it was the perfect occasion to join together with an Inter-Varsity minister to host a Thanksgiving meal for international students at the university. We stepped in to take a role in organizing the event.

I was excited. Thanksgiving is my favorite holiday and, in Canada, I was going to get to celebrate Thanksgiving twice—once in October for the Canadian holiday and then again in November for the United States holiday. Turkey and dressing with sweet potato casserole—twice!

It was important to me that the students got the "real" Thanksgiving experience. In addition to providing an understanding of the meaning of the holiday, I wanted to make sure we had enough of all the traditional Thanksgiving foods for them to try. Food, I believe, is a great beginning to understanding culture and tradition.

As a local pastor and I worked to coordinate the food for the meal, I told him we should have the "traditional" Thanksgiving foods. His church could provide turkey and dressing and some side dishes. After I went through my spiel about what food should be on the menu, the pastor interjected, "Michelle, our people don't know how to make those dishes. That is *your* Thanksgiving meal. We'll bring a turkey, Chinese noodles and curried goat."

I was taken aback, and disappointed. I wanted the students to experience a "real" Thanksgiving. I had not realized I was imposing my cultural perspective on the event.

On the evening of the Thanksgiving meal, a huge turkey arrived along with the largest pan of Chinese noodles I had ever seen. Other dishes were placed alongside, and the students were treated to an amazing spread of food. Dave, the InterVarsity minister, welcomed the nearly 100 students, and another area pastor shared the history and meaning of the holiday. In the room, with the students gathered around, I was thankful—really thankful. In that room of students from around the world, we experienced Thanksgiving—without the foods I was accustomed to, but in the full sense of the meaning of the holiday.

I was reminded that Thanksgiving is about more than a traditional menu of food. It is a holiday rooted in giving thanks to God for the abundant blessings we experience. Among those blessings on that Canadian Thanksgiving was a broader perspective of culture and tradition.

Lesson 2: *I am not bringing God to anyone. God is already at work.*

One of the ways Matt and I were involved in ministry in Toronto was by participating as conversation partners with international students. I met one-on-one once a week with an international student and engaged in conversation with him or her. It provided me with rich opportunities to discuss culture, foods, family and faith. One of my conversation partners was Chenyu.

I met Chenyu just two weeks after her arrival from China. As mothers of young daughters, we had an instant connection. During our first meeting, we shared tears over the distance that separated her from her daughter and husband, who were both in China. We also discussed her Buddhist faith and her desire to learn more about Christianity. She hoped to get a Bible, she said, so that she could learn more about God.

At our second meeting, I presented Chenyu with a Mandarin Bible. She came with something as well. She came with questions.

"Is Christianity different from Islam and Judaism? How does someone become a Christian?"

And the questions continued. I wasn't prepared for so many questions so quickly. After all, I had not yet done anything more than show up and have tea. As we ended our meeting, Chenyu said that she had two hopes for her time in Canada. One was to improve her English. The second was to learn about the Bible.

After our meeting, my head was reeling. I had not expected these questions so soon. I had underestimated God's work in her life. I had expected that I, the missionary, would be responsible for introducing God into the situation. What I know now is that God is working in places and in lives we could never imagine. Now, as I minister, I don't look to introduce God into a situation. I look for evidence of God at work and say, "Yes. This is God. Did you see it? Did you notice God alongside you? Let's talk about it."

Lesson 3: *God will use unexpected people in amazing ways.*

Halfway into our service in Toronto, we were asked by one of the local pastors to host an Introduction to Christianity course at his small church, which had only 50 to 75 people in attendance each Sunday. The leadership was overworked, and they wondered if we could lend a hand and specifically focus on the student population in the area.

This course was commonly held at churches throughout Toronto, and with great success. A core team would gather and prepare for the 10 weekly meetings, inviting others to participate. Each week would begin with a meal for the participants, followed by a video and discussion.

Step one was to gather a core group. And here is where we experienced the unexpected. The group that gathered to plan the event, prepare flyers and pass them out at the apartment complexes were young adults, including a Filipino who didn't finish high school and had had a difficult youth. He was hoping to enroll in culinary school and agreed to cook the meals each week for a small fee and the cost of the food. Also assisting were two university graduate students. One was Russian from a Russian Orthodox background, and the other was an Egyptian Coptic Christian. Our group was rounded out by a Chinese couple. The husband was working on his doctoral degree. None were Christian.

We were in a unique gathering of individuals from around the world, with vastly different religious backgrounds, coming together to plan and conduct a 10-week course for people to explore the Christian faith. We did it. They eagerly handed out invitations. We met weekly, discovering Christ together with others from Canada, Jamaica, China and other places. Through this group of diverse individuals, God did abundantly more than we could have asked or imagined, as we saw people without any previous understanding of the Christian faith speak amazing theological truth to young women who had grown up in the church but were still struggling to understand who God is. We could see the evidence of the Spirit of God working in each of these young people's lives, and we were amazed at the unexpected journey.

Lesson 4: *We do not take this journey alone.*

GSC field personnel with CBF began with the process of raising a portion of the funds required to support their service. It meant that our young family spent a lot of miles on the road and many Sundays and Wednesday nights in churches as we continued to work our full-time jobs. It was a stressful time. But through the experience, God proved faithful to provide in more than monetary ways.

One of the greatest blessings of the experience was the realization that we did not make this missions journey alone. We were surrounded in prayer and support by individuals and churches from across the Fellowship. The investment these Cooperative Baptists were making financially strengthened our connection.

I remember vividly one weekend that took us to Wingate Baptist Church in Wingate, North Carolina. We were exhausted, and I wondered how I would find the energy to speak at another church. Wingate graciously invited us to stay overnight on the campus of the nearby university prior to our visit on Sunday morning. We left our daughter with grandparents and relished the opportunity to at least have a night away. We shared our story with Wingate, ate delicious food and received an outpouring of love. As we prepared to leave, I received a big hug from one of the women.

"You don't go alone," she told me. "We are like your parents and grandparents. We love you and we go with you. You can be assured of our love and support."

Churches like Wingate demonstrated their support and prayers during our two years in Toronto. We received emails from them and others reminding us of their prayers. When we had our second child in Toronto, families prayed for his health, held baby showers from afar and even made and sent a baby blanket to welcome him. At our first CBF General Assembly after returning to the United States, one prayer partner held our son, just a few months old at the time, and said, "Hello little one. We have prayed you into being. You are so loved!"

Now, some 10 years later, as Matt and I serve in the capacity of CBF field personnel in Spain, I still reflect on our time in Toronto, the people we met and the lessons we learned in ministry there. It is a holy place for me, and a holy period in my journey of faith. I give thanks to God for the opportunity to grow in faith during my time in Toronto— and for CBF and so many Cooperative Baptists who took the journey with us.

Michelle Norman and her husband, Matt, were commissioned as Cooperative Baptist Fellowship field personnel in 2011. They currently serve in Barcelona, Spain, working with refugees, immigrants and international students. The Normans also served in Toronto through CBF's Global Service Corps program from 2003-2005.

Listen. Perceive. Engage.

By Sam Harrell

It was hot. Really hot. The soles on my Tevas seemed like they had melted in the days before as I walked on the roof purlins at midday. Since then, I had learned that "only mad dogs and Englishmen" work between noon and 3 p.m. However much in a hurry I was to complete this school building, local wisdom prevailed, and I had begun to surrender to the rhythms dictated by reality.

Wake up at 6 a.m., arrive at the site by 7:30 a.m., work till noon, crash, work from 3p.m. to 5 p.m. or until the water ran out, head to the borehole with the truck on my way back to camp, and fill up the tanks in the back of the truck for concrete mixing the next day, while not forgetting to drink five liters of water in between it all.

Then—collapse and start it all again.

You may have heard it said about "mission" that it is essentially grounded in God's nature, and that our task as Christ-followers is to perceive God's activity and join in God's work. And you would have heard correctly. Admittedly, since the Spirit is alive and active everywhere, that leaves a lot of ground to cover. God's Spirit precedes us everywhere, so it's less about going to a particular place and more about listening, perceiving and engaging in all the many contexts in which we find ourselves.

We (my wife Melody and I) found ourselves in Kenya. We were second-generation missionaries, working in the land of our birth with people we loved, doing the kind of work that we were made for and had (mostly) been prepared to do. It's no secret that the Christian faith is alive and active in most parts of Africa, adding a much-needed dynamic and perspective to the Global Church and probably taking responsibility for a great deal of its growth. Here also is a region struggling with vulnerability, whether as a result of inaccessible primary healthcare, erratic educational opportunities, environmental challenges, institutional corruption or a biased global economy. With so many challenges, it took us some time to figure out how best to be a part of the solution.

The problem is often one of balance. We can either get caught up in navel gazing (interminable strategic planning) or frantic action in response to the endless needs that present themselves. Not wanting to make that mistake, we took time to plan for a well-researched and considered series of Integrated Child Development Centers and development initiatives. It was a response to the expressed needs of marginalized communities across Kenya for early childhood education and basic health interventions for children under age six.

So here I was with a cadre of local helpers in partnership with an indigenous ministry effort, far from anything you would want to call a road, building a structure that would house a nursery school and outreach center to a community of the Ilchamus people in the central Rift Valley in Kenya. The days stretched into weeks, and we were finally at the point of preparing to lay our first stabilized soil blocks to form the walls of the school. A machine had been imported from South Africa, tests had been done on the soil, appropriate cement mixtures had been determined, 3,000 blocks had been produced and cured, and the day had come.

In the distance I saw a man and his friend approaching, pushing a bicycle. They were walking rather quickly. I let my mind run to what they might possibly be wanting. Likely it had something to do with my pickup truck, which was parked prominently at the job site. Vehicles were rare here, and many folks asked to use the pickup to help with this or that task.

I even began to form a hypothetical response about how busy I was and how I couldn't help just now. In rather cryptic Swahili, one of the men, after the usual introductory pleasantries, said, "I need for you to help me get back what the water has stolen today."

Hmm. I know Swahili well, but this stumped me. Maybe he was saying that someone had stolen his water tank and he needed a ride to the police station to help him get it back. Who knows? Anyway, I was busy building a wall—too busy to try and figure out what this man was trying to say. So I politely, without further inquiry, went with my prepared response, which was to say just how busy I was right now and was not able to help with his water issue. He looked at me for a long moment, shrugged and turned away.

The work site grew quiet, and the mood changed as the men walked away. It was enough for even me to realize that something wasn't right—that perhaps I had not understood. I asked one of the crew to repeat what the man wanted. Sylvester, who was to become foreman on subsequent builds, repeated, "He wanted you to help them get back what the water has taken."

"Do you mean someone stole their water?" I asked.

"No, the water stole from them," Sylvester said.

"What do you mean the water stole from them?" I inquired impatiently.

"Look," said Sylvester, looking down at the ground. "The water took that man's son."

"What?" I asked, stunned.

"The man's son was fishing on the side of the river when he had a seizure, fell in the river and drowned. The men have retrieved the body and were asking you to help transport it to the man's home."

So I was right. It was about the pickup. But was I ever wrong about everything else! Why hadn't I heard the rest of the conversation that had taken place prior to the request?

Because I was busy—building a wall.

I had already predetermined what I would hear. I let my busyness get in the way of other realities unfolding around me. Basically, I had blown it. I caught my breath, and my ears began to ring as I considered my mistake. Looking up, I could still see the two walking off into the distance. I quickly jumped down from my ladder, shouted to Sylvester to make them wait, and jumped in the truck and sped off in their direction.

They heard, and they stopped.

As I pulled up, I profusely apologized for my lack of understanding and added that I would, of course, help them. One of the men hopped in the truck and pointed me in a direction, weaving in between acacia thorn trees toward the canopy of a nearby river. Before long, we came upon a group of four men headed in our direction, carrying the body of the teenage boy. He was held shoulder-high, his feet, with tire sandals still on, prominently extending from underneath the wrap placed over his body.

I stopped the truck. Everyone piled in the back with the body, and we set off to the family's homestead. When we arrived, the boy's father, the one who had come to ask for help, walked calmly around the homestead area as if looking for something.

When I asked what he was doing, I was told he was looking for a suitable place to bury the boy. So before the mother came home from work on the farm, the grave was dug and the boy was buried. The father shed a quiet tear and then thanked me profusely for my help.

I could not speak.

I got in the car and drove away, back to the site. Once there, I stopped the work, left early and went back to camp. I was still stunned, both by my lack of awareness and by the sheer starkness in the way the matter had unfolded. It took me a couple of days before I could go back to the site. My first stop was to the homestead of the burial. On the way, I encountered the father and again expressed my sorrow and offered help in any way I could. He smiled at me, put his hand on my shoulder and said, "The matter is done. We are now beyond it."

It was a great deal longer before I could move beyond it.

Though our efforts eventually expanded to 15 communities in various forms, it was the lessons from this first experience that formed us and framed our subsequent experiences. Even today, this experience serves as a poignant reminder to me of the need for constant mindfulness, even and especially in the midst of good and sometimes frantic activity. I have learned that much of life is lived in the context of struggle, and that eliminating the struggle is not really the point. Rather, we need to be paying attention in the midst of the struggle while doing all we can to bring about change.

God's Spirit is about change—change in us, change in our perceptions, change in our actions and change in the circumstances that impede humanity's becoming who we were created to be.

We have learned much in the 25 years of our existence as the Cooperative Baptist Fellowship. Along the way, hopefully, we've learned to listen. We have much more to learn.

Sam Harrell and his wife, Melody, were born in East Africa to missionary parents and have spent the majority of their lives living and working there, serving as Cooperative Baptist Fellowship field personnel from 1999 to 2015. The Harrells now reside in Atlanta, where Sam is Associate Coordinator of CBF Global Missions.

Student.Go

Student.Go summer interns in 2012 pose together during orientation before traveling across the United States and around the world to serve alongside Cooperative Baptist Fellowship field personnel and partners.

Launched in 2002 and led for many years by CBF Global Missions staff member Amy Derrick, Student.Go is the Fellowship's missions initiative for undergraduate and graduate students wishing to serve for a summer, semester or a year. Student.Go now counts hundreds of alumni with more than 500 mission assignments filled since its inception.

"From the beginning of Student.Go, I began telling students that our goal was for the experience to ruin them forever in that they would never again see the world the same way," explained Derrick. "Their view of poverty, privilege, geopolitics, immigration, refugees, cultures, policy and the power of their own citizenship would be changed forever. Their experience would make them impatient with many situations and passionately committed to people and issues that they have come to love based on their experiences. Issues would no longer be just 'issues' when they have faces, lives and places they have lived and known attached to them. In all of these ways, they are 'ruined' after their experience—and that's the whole point." —**Editor**

Ruin and Renewal

By Ashleigh Bugg

During the orientation for Student.Go, the Cooperative Baptist Fellowship's student missions initiative, leaders and former students often say, "You will be ruined." But the official slogan of the program is, "Beyond Your Culture. Beyond Your Comfort Zone. Beyond Yourself." After having served three internships through Student.Go, I feel empowered, frustrated, furious and hopeful—but not yet ruined.

When something is in ruins, it is abandoned, uninhabited, crumbling. When I look at the situations of the people with whom I've worked, I think, "This isn't right. The way they've been treated isn't right. The way I've tried to help isn't right." Sometimes the world does crumble, and people must hold the pieces and curse the ground. Sometimes we can only live in these crumbled places and attempt to build up from the ruins.

My first Student.Go internship was during the summer of 2013 with Karen Morrow, one of CBF's field personnel serving in Fort Worth, Texas, where I lived in government housing alongside refugees from more than 30 countries. If anyone knew about the earth shaking, it was my neighbors. They had fled from Rwanda, Pakistan, Myanmar, Bhutan, Somalia, Iraq and the Congo. They had escaped ethnic cleansing and political persecution. They had left behind mothers and fathers, children and friends. They had left the beautiful landscapes of their past lives to build something new in the United States.

Kelsey, my Student.Go partner, and I were meant to help refugees assimilate to life in the United States, but they were the ones who welcomed us to the neighborhood, whatever their country of origin, religion or language. We worshiped with a Congolese-Burundian congregation whose members wore bright print dresses and headscarves and danced in the aisles. We stayed up late playing guitar with our neighbors from Bhutan and Nepal who sang for hours on their front steps. We went on family walks with our Iraqi friends who welcomed us like sisters. They taught us how to cook Middle Eastern delicacies such as dolma and biryani rice, and served us coffee on real silver platters. We spent time with Muslims and Christians and with the nicest family in the neighborhood, who were Hindu.

"You girls are ground-shakers," said Chameka, our neighbor. "Sometimes people just need someone to come into their lives and shake them up."

Chameka was right about being moved, but it wasn't because of Kelsey or me. It was our neighbors who taught us the restorative power of community. I learned I could travel without leaving my state. They showed me travel isn't just about visiting other places, but coming to terms with and understanding the complexities of your own places.

The next summer I did leave home, accepting an internship in Slovakia with CBF field personnel Dianne and Shane McNary. I would learn about the history of the Roma people and document their culture through photographs and blog posts. I knew I would be tempted to treat these people like sideshow attractions, coming into their country without knowing anything except stereotypes. I wavered between telling an important story and exploiting a story.

The Roma have been discriminated against for centuries. Their culture has been denigrated and misinterpreted. They've been taught that their ethnic identity is shameful or unimportant. They are still segregated from the majority culture and, when people write about them, it is to show them as pitiful or to call them liars and thieves. In fact, the term "gypsy" translates to "liar" in Slovak, which is why I never use this term.

However, the Roma have a fascinating and resilient history. No matter how hard scholars try, they can't write the Roma off as being one way. Their languages and customs differ from country to country, sometimes even from village to village. They are talented at music and arts but have other interests, including politics, science and math. It's harder for them to get ahead because of discrimination and economic exclusion, but I met dedicated Roma who were working toward change. I ended my internship with a series of photos and a short video. I asked people to donate to the CBF Offering for Global Missions so that a media organization run by Roma could make a documentary about human trafficking in Roma communities. It wasn't a model of charity, but one of art and justice.

I came back from Slovakia after seeing the ruins of slavery and the Porajmos (Romani Holocaust). My stories were snapshots of beauty, resourcefulness and education. They showed Roma children playing at music festivals, Roma priests volunteering in the community, Roma educators teaching children about Roma identity.

After coming home, I wanted to work with communities in my own country who had dealt with xenophobia and exclusion. I was raised in Texas and had friends who were born in Mexico and immigrated to the United States when they were children. I saw their struggle to navigate the immigration system. I saw how they were called names, such as "illegal" and "alien." I've learned that no person is illegal. Actions are illegal, but people are not. I decided to use my minor in Spanish to work with immigrants.

The only available Student.Go placement with Latino and Hispanic immigrants was in Fredericksburg, Virginia, with CBF field personnel Greg and Sue Smith. So I packed up my hiking boots and moved to Virginia. I loved being able to improve my Spanish while meeting people from El Salvador, Guatemala, Honduras, Cuba, Spain, Ecuador, Uruguay and Mexico. Being from Texas, I felt at home among the Hispanic phrases and the wonderful foods like tamales and gallo pinto.

One of my duties was to teach English to a group of Latino adults. On my last day of class, a student shared how she'd never gone to school in her country because she had to walk five hours to get there.

"Besides, it's tradition for the boys to be educated. Girls don't go to school," she said.

I was in awe of my students who came to class despite their long work schedules and the responsibilities of families at home. I was the instructor, but they were the ones who taught me.

Student.Go has taught me to seek out transformative experiences. I understand the bigger picture of the privilege of travel and the importance of going to places as a listener and learner. I am not a savior. But I want to meet people from all walks of life, to learn from them, to see their history and to share a little of my own. I've learned that if I want to be an ally, it's not enough to simply give misrepresented groups a voice. I must listen to the voices already crying, singing and shouting to be heard.

There's a verse in Isaiah that talks about how a servant will come and bring good news to the captives, the prisoners and the broken-hearted. They will be comforted, and they will be seen for how they truly are: beautiful and strong, a planting of the Lord.

"They will rebuild the ancient ruins and restore the places long devastated; they will renew the ruined cities that have been devastated for generations," the verse says.

Student.Go opens us to ruined and crumbled moments and places. But it also shows us how lives are being renewed in the rubble. I am grateful to the communities, families and mentors who have shown me a way to restoration.

At the end of three years, I think back to my Student.Go orientation and wonder if I am "ruined." I don't think "ruined" is my word. I am deconstructed. Student.Go deconstructed my life. I have been taken apart, and I am being put together again with the patience of my friends, family and neighbors. And for that, I am grateful.

Ashleigh Bugg works as a community content producer at the Center for News and Design in Austin, Texas. She has studied and interned in Costa Rica, Nicaragua, Slovakia, Virginia and Texas.

Equipped to Serve

By Carson Foushee

I sat on the Sunday school room floor with my elementary-school classmates at First Baptist Church of Statesville, North Carolina, as we listened to a church member talk about her mission trip to the Philippines. She taught us new words from their language, made a local chicken dish for us to taste, and told us about how she and her friends shared Jesus with the people.

I find myself still learning about God's mission in the world from the floor, only now in a different context alongside my wife, Laura, as Cooperative Baptist Fellowship field personnel in Japan. I find myself sitting on tatami mats, speaking in a foreign language with my friends, engaging culture through my senses to better understand where God is at work here, and sharing the love of Christ with some who have never heard the name of Jesus.

Over the course of my lifetime, God has been shaping me for a life of cross-cultural ministry. Along with the CBF congregations in North Carolina and Georgia that have equipped me with a faith to share, no single entity has been as influential in my missional calling as Student. Go, the Fellowship's student missions initiative.

Like most seniors, my last year of college was spent seeking what would be next in my life and career development. I had thoughts of using my sports management degree to work with a professional sports team in a community relations position, hoping to create better communities through the medium of sports. As I sat with loved ones at my church in Statesville during the Christmas Eve worship service in 2006, I felt a distinct sense of call to serve God in a way that would be different than what I had been studying.

I was being called to take a path that differed from my internships in professional sports. The new path looked more like the homebuilding projects in which I had participated with my church in my hometown and in North Charleston, South Carolina, and more like the Vacation Bible Schools my youth group had led in Tupper Lake, New York and Belize. As I shared this desire with others, I was directed toward Student.Go. My life was changed forever.

My first Student.Go internship, in Nanning, China, occurred the fall after my graduation. I studied Mandarin with students from across

Asia and Europe and assisted my CBF supervisors in teaching English at a government church. It was there that I experienced being a minority for the first time.

I was an ethnic minority and an English speaker in a place where the local language had been developing for thousands of years. Most daunting was living as a religious minority. I experienced the challenge that those who attended worship with me felt each week as they attempted to live an active Christian faith in a place where their devotion was sometimes mocked, and most certainly misunderstood.

It was in China that I was led to another significant life decision—to pursue theological training and continue preparation for long-term cross-cultural ministry. With a few months free in the summer before I began my studies at Mercer University's McAfee School of Theology, I returned to the CBF website to scan the list of potential Student.Go internships. One description stood out to me, and I applied. This time, I joined a team of 13 undergraduate and graduate students focusing on the Millennium Development Goals (MDGs) of the United Nations in six nations through a faith-based lens.

The MDG Special Project Team was comprised of students from various CBF congregations and ministries and from a variety of areas of study, including medicine, policy, communications, environmental science, theology and languages. Each student was drawn to the MDG opportunity for different reasons, creating a beautiful spectrum of perspectives that allowed us to more holistically reflect on the events we experienced together as we faced some of the world's most challenging issues. The group came alongside CBF field personnel and staff, as well as an array of nonprofit organizations scattered across Africa, Europe and North America, to concentrate upon goals that ranged from hunger eradication and child mortality reduction to environmental sustainability and economic development.

Over the course of seven weeks, we learned about becoming advocates on Capitol Hill. We felt the weight of discrimination against the Roma people in educational pursuits in Romania. We thirsted for clean water and hungered for healthy children with villagers in Ethiopia. We danced and praised God with women who had been affected by war and disease in Uganda. We visited the halls of the United Nations in New York. We spoke with villagers who felt the negative effects of free trade agreements between their country and our own. We were inspired by the work of nonprofits from around the globe at the International AIDS Conference in Mexico City. And we wept together as a team in Birmingham, Alabama, as we prepared to separate and take on life beyond our shared experiences.

I was moved by the stories I heard in Uganda of people who had fled war and conflict. I recognized that throughout our travels, there was a daily threat of malaria for many. The disease can be prevented with some basic preparations. I also saw an opportunity to connect people through my passion for sports. An idea emerged that would impact the people of Uganda in many ways—a Student.Go team that would travel to Uganda for one month to distribute mosquito nets, run sports camps and learn alongside CBF field personnel Jade and Shelah Acker.

The goal was to raise enough support to purchase 1,000 nets, in addition to covering other costs associated with the trip. God's people came together to change the lives of their neighbors in Uganda. We received an unexpected response in the form of funds, prayers and sports equipment from family, church friends and strangers. When my team arrived in East Africa, we had enough resources to buy 2,500 nets, more than double the goal.

I will never forget the faces of those to whom we handed the nets as we traveled the roads of the cities and villages, especially those of the widows, orphans and displaced people—the ones whom Christ has called us to serve.

At McAfee, God continued to present me with a larger picture of what it means to do Kingdom work. Once more, Student.Go was there to the guide me in the process—this time in Southeast Asia. There, in poor villages along the rivers, I spent many days working with locals on water filtration systems that would provide clean water to nourish their bodies. At the same time, God was revealing to me what it meant to share the never-ending water of life so that a brother or sister would thirst no more.

On a Christian-managed demonstration farm where neighboring farmers could learn to grow new crops and diversify their fields, scripture came alive in learning to plant good seeds that would cultivate a rich faith. In Bali, Indonesia, as I viewed the beauty of traditional Balinese dance, music and painting, CBF field personnel Jonathan and Tina Bailey demonstrated how the arts connect with the Spirit in a way that can move and transform a person's soul.

It was also during my seminary education where my own role with Student.Go and the Fellowship as a whole began to change. I moved from intern to equipper, working as a Student.Go staff member with

CBF, recruiting and helping to prepare other students for service. Conversations on college campuses, in churches, on the phone and over Skype gave me the chance to encourage and challenge students to use the passions and gifts they had been given to answer God's call on their lives. All the while, my soul was restless, discerning where God was leading me next.

When Laura, whom I met at McAfee, and I eventually married, we discussed how a marriage would work with two seemingly different callings. Laura's focus was on serving the local church, and mine was on global missions. We agreed to take turns but prayed for an opportunity to serve together. What came to pass was a position as CBF field personnel to Japan in partnership with the Japan Baptist Convention, working with congregations in Kanazawa and Toyama. Or put more simply: serving the local church in a global setting.

Not a week goes by without memories of Student.Go internships emerging in my mind. These memories surface in conversations with friends from Africa, Europe, Asia and North America about their home regions when we join in worship together in our English-language ministry at Kanazawa International Baptist Church. They arise when I hear the struggles of Japanese people seeking wholeness and hope, just like so many of those whom I encountered in my internships. They especially came to mind when Laura and I hosted a Student.Go intern as we tried to create a learning environment that would help to prepare another young pilgrim to develop his passions in ministry, much like those that had been developed for me.

Twenty-five years ago, when CBF was born, I was a child sitting on the floor of a Sunday school class, also starting out on a journey on mission with God. Since its founding, our Fellowship has developed and grown, and has so much to celebrate in being the hands and feet of Christ in the world. Student.Go is undoubtedly one of the Fellowship's ministries we should celebrate together.

Carson Foushee has served with his wife, Laura, as Cooperative Baptist Fellowship field personnel in Japan since 2013. He is a graduate of Elon University (Bachelor of Science) and Mercer University's McAfee School of Theology (Master of Divinity).

That's Not What Ships Are For

By Carrie McGuffin

In 2010, I was a college student obsessed with quotes.

The words of famous authors, historical figures, poets, television writers and others littered my journals and blog posts, and graced the covers of my notebooks and the walls of my dorm room. I wanted to live vicariously through these amazing words of people who had really *lived*.

In a personal blog post from that spring, this quote by Presbyterian theologian William G.T. Shedd was a guiding text for the summer upon which I was about to embark: "A ship is safe in harbor, but that's not what ships are for."

To me, a 20-year-old theatre student at a private liberal arts college, I was a ship sitting safe and sound in harbor, and only during storms of life was I going to experience any rough waters or seasickness.

At the time I was nearing the end of one of those storms, trying to figure out if I was docked in the right place. My grandpa, who was one of my greatest friends and mentors, had just passed away, and I was coming to the end of my college career—about to enter my senior year and decide what path to take.

To move forward, I decided to first look back. My experience as a youth at First Baptist Church of Asheville, North Carolina, grounded me and gave me a family that I still hold dear. My time doing missions there and at Passport Camps stuck out as formative experiences.

It was decided. I would be connecting back. I applied to be a Bible study leader at Passport, a place that I knew and loved. I would be safe there and be able to discern a future rhythm for my life. For another summer I would be a ship safe in harbor, or at least on familiar seas.

But that's not the outcome of the story.

I was notified that my application was more tailored to Student.Go, the student missions initiative of the Cooperative Baptist Fellowship—an initiative I had never even heard of. I was told that the Student.Go staff would be getting in touch with me about opportunities to serve.

Open to something new but anchored in CBF and familiar territory, I looked at the available assignments and saw one service location whose description required a creative team that loved the arts and could form a puppet troupe and work with children. This place sounded perfect. I wouldn't be alone, and I could use my gifts and talents to work with kids.

Piece of cake.

So for the summer of 2010, I was bound for Helena-West Helena, Arkansas, a city of 15,000 situated on the Mississippi River, where I would live for 10 weeks with two strangers and do some sort of ministry.

I was no longer looking at being in harbor. I was bound for the sea.

I clung to Shedd's quote and floated on the tagline of Student.Go: "Beyond Your Culture. Beyond Your Comfort Zone. Beyond Yourself." I closed my eyes, took a deep breath, and took a leap of faith beyond my comfort zone into the deep water of ministry in some of the poorest counties in the United States.

Alongside the Together for Hope Arkansas staff, at a site that is part of CBF's rural poverty initiative, I spent a summer learning names and faces of children in Helena-West Helena, Lakeview and Elaine. I found comfort with new friends at Delta Fellowship Church. I found a home in a bus equipped with a library, games and craft supplies. I melted a little in the heat. I experienced a culture of hospitality.

I hosted mission teams and connected with people who would become great friends and a ministry network. I played. I laughed. I prayed. I cried. I went to Wal-Mart at least once a day. I drank buckets of "the best Coke in town." I made jewelry with teenagers. I tried a Kool-Aid pickle. I worked 15-hour days—and went days without feeling that our tasks were work at all.

I was living life in the Delta, and I was doing almost nothing that had been detailed in that job description.

I was confronted daily with poverty and the weight of living in a city that had faced economic collapse. I saw the divide that race still generates in the Deep South—from a McDonald's dining room where people had separated themselves in different areas to the divide between black and white churches and the chasm in the distribution of wealth.

Children that I had the privilege to meet changed before my eyes on a regular basis. Those who had hard-shell exteriors would allow them to melt away to smiles during craft time or while singing silly songs. The joy of reading books lit up little faces. These children found places in my heart and made me want to work hard every day to allow them a little extra fun, comfort and joy. It was not the call for creative arts or puppetry—these children were the reasons I landed in Helena.

I had set sail and could breathe in the humid air, and I found that I was as safe out of harbor as I was in it. In this place, I was able to see myself through the eyes of the children I met and the leaders with whom I worked, and I was able to see myself more clearly—a clarity that could come only from this adventure. I saw myself as a leader, one who could make things happen and take charge of a situation. I saw a more organized and energetic self. I saw someone who could catch a child in the free fall of a life filled with trauma and make him smile. I saw the adult within me that I hadn't yet allowed to surface. I saw the ultimate me. I also saw my flaws. I could see my rough edges, my insecurities, my faltering self-confidence. I could see my immaturity and my fears, and I could name them.

This was where I needed to be. This type of work was what I needed to be doing. The people of Helena and Together for Hope were waves of support pushing me forward, pushing me to be better, pushing me toward a new horizon.

In Helena-West Helena, through Student.Go, in my most unlikely summer, my journey had only just begun.

I was starting to feel the call of the sea—the call of God to dive into the waters of ministry as a vocation. All the floating in safe places that led me to that small Delta town also led me in faith and led me to my calling to continue to be a part of this great Fellowship.

Carrie McGuffin serves as the Communications Assistant Specialist for the Cooperative Baptist Fellowship. She earned her Bachelor of Arts in Theatre Arts from Catawba College in Salisbury, North Carolina, and her Master of Divinity from Candler School of Theology at Emory University in Atlanta.

Hairbows, Hebrews 12 and (a Little) Heresy

By Abigail Pratt

From the time of my birth, I have been surrounded by a beautiful and bold cloud of Baptist witnesses who have served as both shelters and pathways throughout my faith journey. I like to think that the Cooperative Baptist Fellowship and I grew up together and are sort of kin in that our conceptions occurred at just about the same time. While this part of the story is significant to both our beings, my CBF story comes after and is a witness to the vision, dedication, sweat and tears of those Baptists who came before me.

My story begins as a nine-year-old girl squished between Lydia, my sister, and Wendy Jo, our best friend, on a pew at First Baptist Church of Cape Girardeau, Missouri. My grandmother had brought us because my parents were both preaching at different churches in the area that Sunday. Lydia and I had chosen to come to First Baptist because we knew that at the end of the service, the congregation would vote on whether or not to ordain women into our diaconate. As children, we didn't fully understand what that meant or why we even had to vote. What we did know was how our mother, grandmother, Sunday school teachers, and other women who had deeply loved us— and the church —served in the church. With hairbows pinned high on our heads, we raised our hands even higher for the women we loved who had instilled God's love in us.

In May 1998, First Baptist of Cape Girardeau ordained six women as deacons. In the months that followed, our church was asked to leave the local Baptist association. As a child, I could not figure out why women were not able to be blessed and commissioned into the ministries of the church that they were already doing, and doing so well. I also could not grasp why our church was asked to leave the association. To me, this was an indication that we had done something wrong, and it confused me.

At the same time, in observing my church's desire to welcome women into the ministry and its willingness to endure internal issues and external opposition, I grew to have confidence as a young female leader. My cloud of witnesses provided me with a community of faith that extended beyond the local association and offered me refuge and a broader sense of identity.

As I grew up, CBF became more than just a shelter. It was through the Fellowship that I was introduced to pathways that deepened and expanded my faith. When I was 16, I had the opportunity to be a part of a weeklong camp called Echo at Wingate University in North Carolina. The camp focused on the exploration of vocation and calling within the lives of high school students. One of the leaders, Caleb Oladipo, spent a significant amount of time listening to me. He suggested I read I Thessalonians 5:24, with the affirmation that the one who calls me will be faithful. That week shaped my future involvement in church, campus ministries and divinity school. Caleb gifted me with confidence and the tools to explore my calling.

I did not leave with a clear view of my identity, however. I probably left with even more questions. But I knew that within my discernment process, God was present and calling me toward something greater than myself. I continued to explore this calling throughout the rest of my high school and college years by visiting as many different communities as I could. I started out in Helena, Arkansas, with Together for Hope (TFH), CBF's rural poverty initiative launched in 2001 to serve 20 of the poorest counties in the United States for 20 years. CBF field personnel Ben and Leonora Newell welcomed us to the Mississippi Delta and into a new form of missions. They taught us how to partner with struggling communities and challenged us to embrace this transformation.

My church, Second Baptist in Liberty, Missouri, joined in TFH's ministry by going west. We sought partnership with the Lakota people of the Cheyenne River Reservation in South Dakota. Navigating spiders and snakes of extraordinary size—along with broken relationships that were even more daunting —we spent years learning how to be neighbors and, eventually, family. TFH partners Byron and Toni Buffalo spent hours driving back and forth to be with us, and years teaching humility, patience and unconditional love. Robert Francis and the Mid American Indian Fellowship traveled with us from Missouri and introduced us to the spiritual practice of storytelling. In time, we grew to be family. With varying skin colors, ages, abilities, spiritual practices and homes, we shared the burden of suffering, injustice and pain through our love of the Creator.

South Dakota and the Lakota people fostered in me a passion to travel and learn about more cultures and communities in the world. As a student at William Jewell College in Liberty, Missouri, I interviewed Rob Nash, who was then the CBF Global Missions Coordinator, for a class assignment. Rob, a longtime family friend, introduced me to Student.Go, CBF's student missions initiative, and its director, Amy Derrick. The following summer, I traveled to Uganda to work with CBF field personnel Jade and Shelah Acker at Refuge and Hope International. My time in Uganda revealed to me new ways of seeing and acting in the world. As with the Lakota, the people in Uganda challenged me to think beyond myself and my culture to more fully experience God's love and intentions for creation. Student.Go was a formational and foundational pathway within my life that guided me to pursue a vocation in ministry.

After college, I moved to North Carolina to study at Wake Forest University School of Divinity. My Baptist identity, my understanding of self and my cloud of witnesses once again expanded as I sat in classes with professors of many different denominational backgrounds and traditions. I read the words of Elizabeth Johnson, Roger Williams, Marian Wright Edelman, Jürgen Moltmann and others. I worshipped within traditions that varied from my own and found a unique community with young ministers from across the United States. I was honored to be both a CBF Leadership Scholar and a Vestal Scholar during my time at Wake Divinity. Thanks to these scholarships, I had the opportunity to attend CBF General Assembly and Selah Vie, CBF's end-of-summer student retreat. I was able to form relationships with many CBF leaders and to further explore my voice and niche within the Fellowship. During this time, CBF was once again a shelter as I ventured far from home and into vocational ministry.

In October 2013, as a 25-year-old, bright-eyed, passionate seminarian, I once again found myself sitting on a pew awaiting and anticipating transformation. This time it was at Peace Haven Baptist Church in Winston-Salem, North Carolina. A special cloud of witnesses came together to ordain me into the gospel ministry. My council was a tapestry of individuals who had nurtured my faith over many years. My parents, who are both ordained Baptist ministers, held prominent spots on this council. They gave me life and were my first ministers, and they remain my mentors today. I was honored to have my professor, Bill Leonard, who with his wife, Candyce, and daughter, Stephanie, loved, nurtured and taught our family since before I was born. Ka'thy Gore Chappell of the Cooperative Baptist Fellowship of North Carolina was present as someone who had walked alongside me since I was 16 years old at Echo Camp. In addition, I was blessed to have dear members of my community at Wake Divinity, as well as colleagues and congregants at Peace Haven Baptist Church.

We wore red, processed to a trumpet fanfare, and listened to Mumford and Sons' ballad "Below my Feet." Tears were mixed with laughter as stories were shared and blessings overflowed. Prayers written by members of First Baptist Cape Girardeau and Second Baptist Liberty were woven into the service. The communion table was filled with paper beads from Uganda, my grandparents' Bible, my passport, and the sandals I had taken with me on all of my travels. The hands of loved ones touched my head and shoulders and wrapped around me, affirming my ministry and blessing my journey ahead.

My ordination was a humbling, life-changing experience. As I walked through this process, I cherished the cloud of witnesses that included my parents, teachers, mentors, and many other ministers and laypersons who years before had stepped away from a broken tradition to embrace a vision of God's Kingdom that was more whole in its perspective. As part of their vision, I am today a young Baptist minister who has (and will continue) to share in the love of God with all of God's children—Baptist and beyond.

Abigail Pratt serves as Associate Pastor of Youth and Mission at Central Baptist Church in Richmond, Virginia. A native of Missouri, she is a third-generation graduate of William Jewell College, where she studied religion and leadership. In 2014, she received her Master of Divinity from Wake Forest University School of Divinity.

Refuge and Hope in Uganda

By Missy Ward-Angalla

I am always intrigued to hear stories about how God brings people through amazing and different journeys. Each journey is its own unique path, with a different set of turns, curves and potholes. Still more amazing is the way in which God chooses to love and give grace, hope and peace to broken people, redeeming and renewing them.

I have been amazed at the fact of Christ's love for those who are most on the margins of society, whom no one else would love. In my earlier life, I too was, in many ways, on the outskirts of acceptance and love. To come to understand that Jesus' love and grace included even me was a revolutionary experience in my life. It completely transformed me from the inside out.

Shortly after becoming a Christian, I felt called to serve in full-time missions. I wanted to share this love and hope with others who were also on the outskirts of society—those no one else would love. This calling was at times confusing, as I was then part of a church that did not believe that women should be allowed to serve in ministry. Though the path was not yet revealed, the call was clear. I stepped forward in faith, trusting that God would provide direction and clarity.

This journey led me to Wesleyan College, where I had the opportunity to learn about the world's political, social and religious systems. During my studies, I was overwhelmed and dismayed by the state of injustice in our world. I was particularly struck that refugee women who were subjected to the harsh realities of violence, trafficking and exploitation often had nowhere to go. In fact, these women were frequently shunned by their communities, blamed for the injustices that had been done to them.

I was astounded by the lack of services to provide these women with safe places to heal and to empower them with the skills needed to help them rebuild their lives. At that time, I felt God's call on my life to start a new ministry program for refugee women just outside the conflict zones in areas where there were no services.

The summer after my junior year of college, I had the opportunity to serve for the first time with Student.Go, the Cooperative Baptist Fellowship's student missions initiative. As an intern in Fremont, California, I had the unique opportunity to teach English and work alongside CBF field personnel, doing relational ministry among refugee women from Afghanistan. These CBF field personnel, Rick and Lita Sample and Fran Stevenson, quickly became family, friends and mentors to me. They provided direction, wisdom and guidance as I sought to be the presence of Christ to the Afghan refugee women with whom I had the opportunity to minister.

I knew that I had found my missions home. CBF was the first Christian organization I had encountered that focused on doing holistic ministry with the most marginalized and neglected. After working alongside CBF field personnel, I knew that I wanted to serve full time as one of CBF's field personnel. I had the opportunity to continue growing and learning as I returned to California the following summer as a Student.Go intern.

At the end of that summer, I was about to embark on a new part of the journey, growing as a leader and minister at Mercer University's McAfee School of Theology in Atlanta. Even though I knew that McAfee was a supportive environment for female ministers, I still struggled to understand what it meant to serve as a woman.

Rick and Lita helped me process what I was being taught and what it meant in my own personal struggles. They encouraged me in the gifts that they saw God had placed in my life and inspired me to continue using those gifts to minister to hurting refugee women.

My studies at McAfee helped me to discover and further develop my ministerial identity. The staff, professors and students provided a welcoming and nurturing environment in which I could be safe to grow and learn. This supportive environment extended beyond the McAfee community to the wider Fellowship.

In the spring of 2011, I was invited to attend a Baptist Women in Ministry of Georgia meeting to accept a scholarship. I was instantly captivated by the unique group of women that were there. I met a number of amazing and inspiring women, including Pam Durso and the now deceased Gwen Brown, whose friendship, support and love significantly impacted my life. This community provided ongoing support and mentoring as I continued to develop as a leader and minister.

I had the opportunity to once again serve alongside CBF field personnel when I was a Student.Go intern for four months with Jade and Shelah Acker. I arrived in Kampala, Uganda, in August 2010 to begin serving with Refuge and Hope International, the holistic ministry program that the Ackers had started to serve those affected by war and conflict in East Africa. This ministry included a refugee community center. When I arrived, the center had 25 students in two English classes. Within the semester that I was there, the number of students grew to 100. Today, more than 1,000 students pass through this community center every year.

I remember looking out the window after arriving in Uganda and feeling immediately at home. That feeling of home grew and expanded as I began ministering at Refuge and Hope as an English teacher. I immediately connected with the warm and welcoming refugee community and the staff with whom I had the privilege of working. Within my first few months in Uganda, I tutored a young refugee woman named Claire.

One day during class, I found that Claire was in a difficult and complex situation, with no place to go. She was orphaned at a young age and had grown up in a refugee camp where she faced violence and abuse, even where she was living in Kampala.

"Teacher, please help me," she told me. "Please. I just want to be safe and learn. Please help me."

As her teacher, I desperately wanted to help her. Unfortunately, I quickly realized that in Kampala, a city of several thousand refugees and more than 1.5 million people, there were no resources or places for refugee women and girls like Claire.

That day forever changed my life, as I felt God prompting me to start a new program that would offer a place where refugee women who had been through severe trauma could be safe and experience God's healing, transformation and empowerment. Through God's amazing provision, this shelter, the very first for refugee women in Uganda, was opened in 2013. It now provides women like Claire a safe place where they can heal and experience transformation.

I returned to the United States to complete seminary and began applying to serve as one of CBF's field personnel. I knew that CBF was the right fit for me and wanted to remain connected to the larger Fellowship family that had become such a meaningful part of my life. I returned to Uganda the next two summers to continue serving with Refuge and Hope as a Student.Go intern, and I learned, grew and felt even more strongly that I was called to live and work in Uganda.

In June 2012, I was commissioned to serve as one of CBF's field personnel. This moment was the culmination of a long, winding journey which God used to make beauty from ashes in my life. That night in Fort Worth, Texas, I had the privilege of joining the Fellowship in a special and unique way. That moment was an affirmation of my calling to missions and served as a reminder that I was not in the journey alone. This wonderful community that had become a family to me stood alongside me as I began a journey filled with many unknowns: moving to a new country, starting a completely new program, and facing the daily reality of injustice, oppression and complex trauma in the lives of others.

Another moment that reinforced my calling was being ordained into the ministry in November 2012. My church family, friends and professors, as well as many others, gathered to pray and affirm God's calling in my life to serve and minister to refugee women and girls. Looking back on this moment, I remember the distinct feeling of the hands of many people on my shoulders and head as people prayed for me and offered words of encouragement and love. The memories of these moments continue to encourage me on some of my most difficult days serving in Uganda.

Upon completing seminary, I moved to Uganda in 2013. I began the groundwork of starting the Amani Sasa Ministry while beginning to serve families, women and girls in crisis. The shelter officially opened in October 2013, and the programs have grown and expanded since. Currently, we minister to more than 175 families, women and girls each year through our shelter, our vocational training and our education programs. These programs offer refugee women and girls access to crisis social work services, counseling, discipleship, skills training, education and community support.

God has used this ministry in incredible ways to restore and transform the lives of many refugees who were broken and without hope. These women and girls are now leaders, empowered to minister within their own families and community. Their lives offer a tangible picture of a God who is able to give infinitely more than we can ask or imagine, a God who makes beauty from ashes and offers an oil of gladness rather than despair.

Words cannot describe how grateful I am to be a part of God's miraculous work in Uganda. I also continue to be grateful for the loving family of Cooperative Baptists who join us through partnership as we share the love, hope and grace of Christ with refugee women, girls and families.

Missy Ward-Angalla has served as one of Cooperative Baptist Fellowship's field personnel in Kampala, Uganda, since 2012. She directs a social work and women's ministry program of Refuge and Hope International, which ministers to refugee women, girls and families who have experienced severe abuse, exploitation and trafficking.

Fellowship Ministries

United States Army Major Julie Rowan, a CBF-endorsed chaplain (now Lieutenant Colonel), assists an Afghan woman and her child through a line to receive humanitarian supplies at the Egyptian Hospital at Bagram Air Base in Afghanistan in March 2006.

Since January 1998, CBF has endorsed 1,000 chaplains and pastoral counselors who serve in a variety of ministry contexts such as hospitals, jails, prisons, business and industry as well as all branches of the U.S. Armed Services. CBF counts, as of spring 2016, 721 individuals serving as endorsed chaplains and pastoral counselors as of October 2015.

The stories that follow offer a sampling of vital and innovative ministries of the Fellowship, from chaplaincy to collegiate ministry to disaster response to forming missional congregations to advocacy to member care for those on the mission field. These stories give a glimpse of what Cooperative Baptists mean and have meant by "being the presence of Christ" and "forming together." —**Editor**

Seeking Endorsement for Chaplains and Pastoral Counselors

By Ed Beddingfield

We had a general idea of where we were going but barely a clue as to how to get there. Some never doubted that we would succeed. Others weren't so sure. Some wondered if we should even try. But not the retired Air Force general. He had been a career chaplain. I don't remember his name, but I will never forget how he looked: confident and erect at the microphone, secure in his authority, certain of his cause. At several consecutive General Assemblies of the Cooperative Baptist Fellowship in the mid-1990s, he stood during business sessions with the same rousing plea: "CBF should declare itself to be a denomination so we can endorse chaplains!"

Ecclesiastical endorsement certifies that a minister is in good standing with a religious body and is appointed to minister on its behalf. This endorsement is required by groups that employ chaplains in the military and at hospitals or prisons. It is also required for membership in certain ministerial professional organizations.

After the general's first speech, CBF Executive Coordinator Cecil Sherman told a small group offstage, "Denomination? We can't do that." Most CBF churches were "dually aligned"—affiliated with both CBF and the Southern Baptist Convention. For many of those churches, Cecil explained, declaring the Fellowship to be a denomination would represent a forced choice, one they might not want to make.

So dual alignment was a problem. Eventually it would turn out to be the solution. But it would be another year or two before then CBF Moderator Pat Anderson could answer the general, "Sir, we're working on that, and we'll have something for you at our next General Assembly."

In 1994, Judy Powell and I were among the North Carolina representatives elected to the national CBF Coordinating Council. Judy was pastor of Antioch Baptist Church in Enfield, North Carolina, and knew some chaplains at the hospital in Rocky Mount. I was a pastor as well as an endorsed (SBC) pastoral counselor. Many of us wondered whether our existing endorsements were in jeopardy, given the intensifying divisions in Baptist life.

Judy and I were assigned to the Church Resources Ministry Group, one of several Coordinating Council working groups. One particular subcommittee was Ministry to Ministers—"M&Ms" for short. At our first meeting, Judy mentioned the concerns of her chaplain friends. Where in CBF could we go to ask about endorsement?

That very night, I rode on a bus to my hotel with CBF Global Missions Coordinator Keith Parks and his associate, Harlan Spurgeon. I told them some chaplains had asked about CBF endorsement. Would the Missions Ministry Group consider it?

"We can't," they said. "We're not a denomination."

They told us if Church Resources wanted to take it on, they'd help however they could. The next day, I reported back to the M&Ms. Judy didn't hesitate.

"Let's do it," she said.

Church Resources authorized a study group, which met early in 1995 at a hotel near the Atlanta airport. CBF Associate Missions Coordinator Gary Baldridge and CBF Church Resources Coordinator Terry Hamrick were staff representatives. There were a few M&Ms, some local chaplains from the Atlanta area, and several former members from the chaplaincy division of the SBC's Home Mission Board. Later, we would form the core of the first CBF Council on Endorsement.

We all knew what endorsement was and how to do it once it was up and running. What we needed was a national organization to recognize us. But who? After several meetings, we settled on the Congress of Ministry in Specialized Settings (COMISS), an umbrella organization of about 50 groups that either require or provide endorsements. We pitched the idea to newly elected CBF Executive Coordinator Daniel Vestal. We told him COMISS was made up of AFCB (Armed Forces Chaplains Board), AAPC (American Association of Pastoral Counselors), ACPE (Association for Clinical Pastoral Education) and COC (College of Chaplains, today renamed APC—Association of Professional Chaplains). We got as far as NAVAC (National Association of Veterans Affairs Chaplains) and NIBIC (National Association of Business and Industrial Chaplains) before Daniel said, "Enough! It's an alphabet soup!"

He agreed to contact COMISS, who said they had no authority to certify any individual group as an endorsing body. Each professional organization that required endorsement acted on its own. If we wanted to be recognized, they said, we really should go to the military. Get their approval and the others would fall into place.

Meanwhile, we were attracting broader attention. One day, two representatives of the Home Mission Board chaplaincy division drove from Atlanta to my church in the North Carolina mountains to tell me that we had nothing to fear; no endorsement had been or would be rejected because a person belonged to CBF. This was true, at least to that point, so I thanked them for their assurances and promised to pass the word among our constituents. But when they said there was therefore no legitimate reason for the endorsement study group to continue its work, I expressed our concern that their current assurances might not always be honored.

At that point, they insisted forcefully that CBF was not a denomination and had no standing as an endorsing agency. They maintained that just as a person can't be a member of two churches at the same time, neither can a church be covered by two endorsers, and our churches were already represented by the HMB. They said that if we persisted, and especially if we went to the military for recognition, "We'll fight you all the way to the top."

I asked them to say that to our entire study group. Subsequently, we met at Dunwoody Baptist Church in Atlanta and discussed a range of issues. When we talked about biblical interpretation, Hardy Clemons, a former moderator of CBF, asked, "What if I put on my endorsement application, 'I believe the Bible and try to do what it says.' Is that enough?" They told him it was.

"For how much longer?" Hardy asked. We decided to press on.

It finally dawned on us that, in fact, numerous churches actually do belong to more than one ecclesiastical group. Some Southern Baptist churches are also American Baptist. Some National Baptist churches are also Southern Baptist. There's even a term for it—"dual alignment," and chaplains who belong to dually aligned churches can decide which group to go to for endorsement. If others could do it, we could too. Besides that, some churches were becoming uniquely aligned with the Fellowship. What about them?

At the 1997 CBF General Assembly in Louisville, Kentucky, our study group recommended that CBF declare itself to be a "religious endorsing body." We did, without even mentioning the word "denomination." Four months later, in October, the CBF Coordinating Council established the Council on Endorsement. Gary Baldridge and Terry Hamrick stayed on as staff representatives. The council included Robert Duval, a hospital chaplain from Lawrenceville, Georgia; Pat Davis, a retired United States Army chaplain; and Carl Hart, an industrial chaplain from Tucker, Georgia. All were former staffers at the Home Mission Board chaplaincy division. Hart had even been division director. They brought the experience we needed. Pastoral counselor Donna Forrester of Greenville, South Carolina, Alice Combs, a social worker from Niceville, Florida, and Milton Snyder, a retired clinical pastoral education supervisor and mental health chaplain from Milledgeville, Georgia, joined me to complete the group.

By November 1997, CBF had received about 100 inquiries concerning endorsement. In January 1998, we endorsed our first class, which consisted of four people representing four different areas of ministry: Paula Peek, a hospice chaplain in Kentucky; Tim Madison, a hospital chaplain in Texas; Jim Pruett, a pastoral counselor in South Carolina; and Captain Jim Harwood, a chaplain in the United States Navy.

But we still had not been approved by the military or any other group. Harwood became our test case. His current assignment was to the U.S. Navy Chief of Chaplains Office in Washington, D.C., and he was well known by the members of the Armed Forces Chaplain Board who would consider our application.

"It's good to have friends in high places," one member of our council said.

Judy Gooch Strawn, Gary Baldridge's assistant, detailed a package of letters, forms and statistics about CBF and its churches for the board to consider. They accepted Harwood's endorsement and recognized CBF as an endorsing body in June 1998.

Eventually, the HMB (renamed the North American Mission Board or NAMB) began requiring affirmation of the SBC's confessional statement, the Baptist Faith and Message 2000, and restricted the endorsement of women to certain ministry positions. For many, that was the final straw. Among those coming to CBF was George Pickle, a NAMB staff member in the chaplaincy division. George succeeded Gary Baldridge as CBF's endorsing official and served with utmost professionalism, nurturing relationships with endorsees and establishing policies and practices still used today. He retired in 2013 after 12 years of service. Following an interim period by retired Navy chaplain Jim Pope, Gerry Hutchinson, a naval reserve chaplain, became CBF's endorser in 2014.

As of spring 2016, CBF has endorsed a total of 1,000 chaplains and counselors, and 721 are actively serving. For all these endorsees, and for many more to come, CBF represents a safe haven, a family home, "the Fellowship of kindred minds," and a hopeful future. Thanks be to God.

Ed Beddingfield was a member of the Cooperative Baptist Fellowship Coordinating Council from 1994-1997 and was chair of the Endorsement Study Group. From 1998-2001 he served as the founding Chair of the CBF Council on Endorsement. He is a CBF-endorsed pastoral counselor and pastor of Memorial Baptist Church in Buies Creek, North Carolina.

From Chaos to Hope: CBF Disaster Response

By David Harding

Although hard to believe, good often comes out of the shock and pain of the destruction caused by disasters of all kinds. However, the immediate reaction may be one of despair and disbelief that such tragedy could really happen so close to home. A disaster creates upheaval of the usual and familiar ways of life and disorients victims with a sense of bewilderment. The suffering of personal and communal loss and the death of loved ones plunges them into uncharted territory.

Paradoxically, the chaos may prompt an awakening to the reality that God has not abandoned God's children, despite the seeming appearance of wrath and judgment. Strangers begin to show up to take the first steps needed to restore order and begin repairs. The care and kindness received in the early days gives a taste of hope that God really does care. For 25 years, Cooperative Baptists have been those strangers who come alongside people in pain to help reorient and kindle new beginnings.

The actual beginning of disaster response efforts by Cooperative Baptists was the bold response in the aftermath of Hurricane Andrew in August 1992, led by the Cooperative Baptist Fellowship of Florida under the leadership of its coordinators, Carolyn and Pat Anderson.

The journey from relief to reconstruction to development can be a long and tortuous path that takes many turns. Each response is different, based on the nature of the event and the resources that are available. Unbelievable damage was done to homes and lives in South Florida. CBF of Florida mobilized money and volunteers to help rebuild the city of Homestead in Miami-Dade County—an effort that ultimately gave birth to the Fellowship's community-based ministries of Touching Miami with Love and Open House Ministries, which merged in 2015. This is an excellent example of transitioning from relief to long-term transformational development.

Perhaps a more formal beginning for CBF's disaster response efforts started after the terrorist attacks on September 11, 2001. CBF Global Missions Coordinators Barbara and Gary Baldridge created a position for a disaster response coordinator, and my wife, Merrie, and I were transferred from our posts as CBF field personnel in the Middle

East to the United States to fill this new position. A plan was created to address both the domestic and international needs generated by the 9/11 attacks and the ensuing war in Afghanistan.

John Derrick, who served as Volunteer Coordinator for CBF Global Missions, took the lead to implement the domestic response. This included working with field personnel such as Ronnie Adams, based in New York City, and establishing partnerships with area churches as well as with organizations like the Red Cross.

For the international response, CBF formed a relationship with World Vision that enabled the Fellowship to work actively among the poor and vulnerable in Afghanistan. Just four months after 9/11, in January 2002, the first CBF international disaster response team was deployed to Pakistan and Afghanistan. The team was comprised of Jim Jennings of Conscience International, Dr. Don Meier, a CBF medical volunteer, and me.

Since 9/11, the Fellowship has engaged in an array of responses to rapid onset disasters such as fires, tornadoes, hurricanes (typhoons), earthquakes and tsunamis. CBF also engages in slow-onset disasters, from extreme poverty to water crisis to famine, as well as complex humanitarian emergencies like the Syrian refugee crisis. In all engagements, the Fellowship pursues a holistic response with victims that includes the spiritual, emotional, social and physical dimensions that lead to personal, social and cultural transformation.

During 2004, Hurricanes Charles, Frances, Ivan and Jeanne ravaged the Florida peninsula over the course of just six weeks, beginning in August. These hurricanes initiated a training program with protocols to help CBF churches develop disaster preparedness plans and become frontline responders.

Then, the day after Christmas in 2004, only a few short months after the series of hurricanes struck Florida, an earthquake off the coast of Sumatra, an island in Southeast Asia, resulted in tsunamis that killed 230,000 people. CBF responded with a multimillion dollar effort in Indonesia, Thailand, India and Sri Lanka. The devastation opened incredible opportunities to restore livelihoods and live into our commitment to be the presence of Christ. CBF formed strong partnerships that remain vibrant today with groups such as Asia Pacific Baptist Aid and Transform Aid Australia. CBF field personnel like Eddy Ruble emerged as regional leaders to support the network of partnerships.

Hurricane Katrina led to the next major disaster response effort in 2005. The generous support of Cooperative Baptists and a large number of CBF volunteers helped launch a coordinated domestic disaster response program.

In 2010, an earthquake devastated the Caribbean country of Haiti. CBF was able to send numerous volunteers to rebuild homes, churches and orphanages. Haiti has a long history of chronic and acute poverty and dependence on charity. To address this debilitating mindset and create behavior change, CBF started a small savings and credit movement called Sustainable Living Groups. SLGs are mutual support community groups for the poor to organize and learn about saving money and how to generate income. They build the dignity of individuals while growing the sense of responsibility and accountability needed to address pressing community issues, such as poor sanitation and hygiene. There are now more than 150 SLGs in Haiti that are transforming countless lives.

Other international disaster response efforts followed an earthquake in Chile (2010), an earthquake and tsunami in Japan (2011), a typhoon in the Philippines (2013), and an earthquake in Nepal (2015).

CBF also considers the world water crisis, extreme poverty and hunger as global disasters. They are silent tsunamis that kill millions each year. The Fellowship engages in programs such as "Water is Life" in Ethiopia to construct wells and establish SLGs. CBF has established more than 500 SLGs in southern Ethiopia, representing approximately 10,000 members (80,000 beneficiaries) who have saved their own money to build capital of about $132,000. Small loans are made from this capital for income-generating activities that support families with food, medicine and education. They address the root causes of global challenges, like extreme poverty, hunger and environmental issues.

The experience of loss, emptiness and bewilderment in a disaster leads to exhaustion. CBF has long invited the hurting to go beyond the boundaries of pain and suffering to enter into a new way of knowing how to traverse the path given to them. We as Cooperative Baptists engaged in disaster response ministry have shared and continue to share Christ as the One who puts devastation in perspective and enables us to move on to new beginnings with thanksgiving, enthusiasm and encouragement.

Hope emerges out of the chaos. God has not forgotten us. For responder and victim alike, the goal is to be re-membered with God

out of the disaster to a new and living way of faith that ultimately transforms communities.

David Harding and his wife, Merrie, are International Coordinators for Disaster Response and Transformational Development for the Cooperative Baptist Fellowship. The Hardings have coordinated the Fellowship's responses to chronic and acute disasters abroad since 2001 in their roles as CBF field personnel. Prior to this assignment, they served with CBF in the Middle East for five years. They reside in Orlando, Florida, and have three adult children.

Missional Conversations

By Bo Prosser

In 1998, Darrell Guder published a groundbreaking book titled *The Missional Church: A Vision for the Sending of the Church in North America.* Guder and a group of six leaders within the Gospel and Our Culture Network challenged church leaders to move beyond the grip of the "institutional church" that was stifling ministry and mission in the local congregation. Their work introduced the term "missional church" in response to "missionary church." They challenged pastoral leaders to discover where God was at work "glocally" (globally and locally) and to join in God's work with purpose.

This book, and others that would follow, would have a huge impact on parish ministry. Alan Roxburgh, David Bosch, Justo Gonzales, Phyllis Tickle, Brian McLaren, Craig van Gelder, Craig Dykstra, Dallas Willard and others wrote about the missional stance and challenged congregations to make the shift toward intentional missional ministries.

The missional approach is more about reaching people than drawing a crowd, more about immersing in cultures than avoiding the world, more about empowerment, process and collaboration than competition and programming. As the missional challenge gained traction, the Cooperative Baptist Fellowship also responded.

CBF began the conversation in earnest around the year 2000, when Terry Hamrick formed the CBF Missional Church Task Force. Dennis Faust, Michael Tutterow, Greg Hunt, Doris Nelms and Karen Gilbert held regular conversations and began brainstorming to bring missional principles to the Fellowship. This foundational work would set the tone for deepening the conversation among CBF pastoral leaders.

They first wrestled with the basic understanding of *missio Dei*, and the task force clearly articulated that God's mission was central to the church's being. The more the church participated in this mission, the more clarity it would have as to its identity. Most churches were inventing and reinventing their own missions, hoping these activities fit with the mission of God.

To assist congregations, the task force developed "The Missional Journey Guide." This notebook was a detailed guide for helping churches embrace the missional terminology and the thought processes involved in shifting toward a more missional mindset. It clearly unpacked the missional conversation, shared other resources that were being added to the body of literature, and gave suggestions as to how to embrace missional approaches.

The task force set as a goal to move the missional conversation deep into the Fellowship. Their work was instrumental in calling awareness to missional ministries and intentional processes to become more missional.

In 2002, upon being called to CBF as the Coordinator for Congregational Life, I joined the task force. While the missional conversation was not new to me, the learning curve was still steep. The members of the task force engaged me and helped get me up to speed quickly. During this period, the importance of one's personal story emerged, as did the need for more resources to help churches and church leaders.

The task force began to challenge clergy and lay leaders to develop their personal stories of missional engagement. This challenge was certainly helped by the publication of two books: Brian McLaren's *A New Kind of Christian* and Daniel Vestal's *It's Time: A Journey Toward Missional Faithfulness*. Both authors challenged Christians to think about their personal stories of faith and how these stories have helped shape them.

The task force picked up on these ideas and published a "field guide" for the missional journey. We affectionately named this the "Brown Book." The resource included an overview of missional terms, space for journaling along the missional journey, and a DVD with video clips unpacking the ideas of the missional journey. On the heels of this resource, we developed the "Green Book" companion to the field guide. "Glimpses of the Missional Faithfulness" was a compilation of stories from CBF churches illustrating what God was doing in their communities and how they were joining in ministry and mission.

Moving into 2004-2005, the missional conversation ramped up. Using Vestal's book as the foundation, a resource called *It's Time!* was developed. This resource included a copy of the book, a leader's guide, and publicity materials. Members' guides were also provided. The *It's Time!* resource was designed for church-wide studies to deepen the missional conversation throughout the Fellowship. More than 500 churches participated in the study in some fashion. Missional weekends were held by many churches either as a kickoff of the study or in celebration of completing the study. CBF staff were engaged in presentations, preaching and leading missional journey retreats.

As further incentive for participation in the *It's Time!* study, missional grants were developed and made available for churches that completed the study and were ready for missional ministry. Grant awards for up to $25,000 were given to more than 100 churches over a three-year period. Churches were eager to dream, to think missionally and to implement those dreams.

A further outgrowth of the missional study and missional grants was a call back to scripture. The *You've Got the Time!* Bible listening program was introduced to encourage listening to the Bible for 20 minutes each day. In partnership with Faith Comes by Hearing, and thanks to a most gracious gift to CBF, audio Bibles of the New Testament were provided free of charge to Fellowship churches. More than 500 churches participated in the program, and many more stories of missional faithfulness emerged. Audio Bibles were shared in small group gatherings, Sunday school classes and worship services. These audio Bibles were also shared in mission efforts, providing God's Word to people who could not read, had no access to a Bible, or were in hospital and nursing home settings. As a result, the missional conversation continued to reach deeper into the work of the Fellowship.

To keep up with the growing demands of churches and the many voices sharing varying thoughts about missional ministry, the Missional Team was formed from the staff of the Fellowship. The challenges facing this staff team were to foster collaboration across all areas of the CBF Resource Center in Atlanta to bring clarity to the missional conversation, to engage pastors in missional ministry, and to train other leaders in helping foster the missional conversation.

The team developed a series of tools to help local congregations identify their missional passions and to implement missional ministries. Four areas of the missional journey were visualized in the missional church logo: Missional Engagement, Sustaining and Nurturing Church, Spiritual Formation and "Glocal" Visioning. Missional studies, a church visioning process, short-term engagement opportunities, prayer retreats, a speakers bureau and opportunities for missional leader development were a few of the resources provided for our churches. This was a very rich time in the formative conversations within the Fellowship and among our churches.

Because there were so many voices among the Fellowship and outside the Fellowship teaching "missional" approaches, the word "missional" suddenly began losing some of its impact. The institutional church was clamoring for a definition of "missional" and more clarity for its members. The Missional Team at CBF was also feeling this push from Fellowship churches. While we resisted the demand for a "missional definition," many of us tried to give word pictures to help churches visualize the missional possibilities. Finally, however, I began to share my working definition to help others understand the term:

The missional church is about empowering people to use their passions on purpose to be the presence of Christ in the world—whether anyone joins our church or not!

While some embraced this, many pushed back on my definition. Many church leaders could not fathom doing ministry without calling people to church membership. Many church leaders did not embrace my definition as "attractional" enough to encourage church growth.

However, I continue to share this as my understanding of a call to a missional lifestyle. My point is this: When we talk church growth, most of us think that this means we will reach people for our church who are like us. That is not missional; it is institutional. When we do ministry so that someone will then respond to us, we are merely Christian salespeople.

Missional Christians love simply because God loves. And here is the key: When we are on God's mission, simply loving, we are going to have more people in our churches than we know what to do with. Acts 2 gives evidence to that. Bringing people into church membership is still important, but it cannot be the only focus of our ministries. I understand that not everyone shares my opinion!

To bring consistency to the missional movement within CBF, a design team was formed. Rob Nash, then Coordinator of Global Missions, and I put together a collaborative team to develop a uniform presentation that everyone could use in teaching and training. Rick Bennett, Devita Parnell, Steve Graham, Matt Norman and Harry Rowland began working on a retreat model that could produce further clarity and deeper understanding. Phil Christopher, Terry Hamrick, Brian Foreman, Jill Jenkins, Brian Harfst, Kevin Ritter and Kevin Meadows were also instrumental in helping us refine this process. The result of their study was the Dawnings initiative, a process leading to church renewal.

Dawnings is not another program but a series of spiritual conversations that seek to clarify vision, deepen formation and bring about purposeful engagement. Through these conversations, spiritual discernment emerges. The result is three to four ministry opportunities that lead a church to missional ministry. As God's people share their passions on purpose, a sense of renewed call and depth of ministry emerges.

The missional conversation will continue to permeate the ministries and missions of our churches for years to come. At some point, history tells us, we will move into the next conversation. Until then, CBF will continue standing on the shoulders of the missional pioneers who have helped shape us and guide us. I'm grateful to be a voice in the conversation.

I'm thankful for the many colleagues who have guided these conversations, given us feedback and participated with us. I'm especially grateful to Daniel Vestal and Suzii Paynter for the trust and support to keep dreaming. When this conversation started, I imagined a retreat and maybe a resource or two. The Dawnings initiative is the culmination of the many missional conversations that have occurred over the last 15 years. Most of us never dreamed we would still be impacting congregations all around the world with this call to missional work. Thanks be to God, who continues to bless us in ways beyond our own imaginings.

Bo Prosser is Coordinator of Organizational Relationships for the Cooperative Baptist Fellowship and has served on the senior leadership team of CBF since joining the staff in August 2002. A graduate of Southern Baptist Theological Seminary (Master of Religious Education and Master of Divinity) and North Carolina State University (Doctor of Education), he is a sought-after speaker, improvisational trainer and professional coach. He has authored and contributed to more than 15 books and hundreds of articles.

Exploring "Call" Through Collegiate Ministry

By Wanda Kidd

From the inception of the Cooperative Baptist Fellowship, there have been passionate voices at the table speaking to the importance and value of collegiate ministry. Many Fellowship leaders, past and present, have spoken about the impact their collegiate experience through the Baptist Student Union had on their lives and the lives of others. It was in those groups that they learned to be leaders and how to engage in missions. It was there that they were introduced to the concepts of soul freedom and religious freedom, and the understanding that God could and does call both men and women to serve Christ. Many believed that offering these possibilities to young adults at the crossroads of their lives was the future of this new movement. The value and impact of their involvement compelled them to ask CBF to offer future generations the same possibilities they had been afforded by the Baptists of their youth.

While there were few who disagreed with the importance of equipping young adults to serve, the early CBF organization had limited financial resources and many voices vying for specific areas of ministry to be launched. The triage of ministries was a complicated process for the fledgling Fellowship. Several areas of ministry were in crisis and needed immediate attention. Many Baptist campus ministries were still intact and offering balanced opportunities to explore call and to serve through summer missions. Another issue to consider was that Baptist collegiate ministry was not a centralized organization, like missions and theological education. To address collegiate ministry through a new Baptist lens would be complicated and expensive. For those reasons, the development of CBF's role in collegiate ministry has been a slow process. But it has always been important and remains a valuable work-in-progress.

The historical philosophy and theology of Baptist collegiate ministry were congruent with the direction that was in the DNA of the Fellowship. Some common watermarks for both CBF and historical Baptist campus ministry are the beliefs that all people have the freedom to respond to God's call and that there is a need to provide mission opportunities for both lay people and long-term missionaries, and the idea of empowering all people to use their spiritual gifts for the building of God's Kingdom.

During the Fellowship's founding years, four of its state and regional groups were led by former campus ministry leaders: Tom Logue, the first Coordinator of the Cooperative Baptist Fellowship of Arkansas, was the past Director of BSU in Arkansas; Ircel Harrison, the Coordinator for Tennessee Cooperative Baptist Fellowship, was the past BSU Director in Tennessee; Sandy and Ken Hale were both CBF coordinators and campus ministers at Dartmouth College; and Lynn Hawkins, the first Coordinator of the Cooperative Baptist Fellowship of Louisiana, was a longtime campus minister at Louisiana Tech.

Those leaders and many others wanted to make sure that Baptist campus ministry provided the freedom, space and opportunities needed for our students. They understood that young Cooperative Baptists needed mentors to help them develop as leaders and grow in their Christian faith. Campus ministry was the natural and appropriate place for that process to begin. People gathered on many occasions to make their concerns known to the CBF leadership. In addition to the state leaders, supporters such as Becky Matheny, David Weatherspoon, Bruce Gourley, Ruth Perkins Lee, Scott Lee, Mike Young, Devita Parnell, Tim Willis, Leslie Limbaugh, Wanda Kidd, Amy Derrick and John Derrick spoke often in public forums and in private meetings about the need to look for ways to provide college ministry congruent with CBF's ethos.

One of the first ways that CBF responded to those concerned about shaping young adults was to launch a program called Student. Go, a missions initiative for college and seminary students. A pilot project in 2001 sent one student to Southeast Asia. The following year, Student.Go was instituted under the leadership of Amy Derrick. Over the past 14 years, hundreds of students have served for a summer or a semester alongside CBF field personnel around the world.

During the early 2000s, CBF formed a partnership with the Lilly Endowment, a foundation whose grants funded initiatives to help young adults explore areas of call and leadership. The first grant received was awarded to both CBF and Baptist Theological Seminary at Richmond. It provided smaller grants to other groups, but a significant amount was set aside to host a retreat for college students and seminarians called "Antiphony," to be sponsored by CBF and Passport Camps.

Antiphony was designed to be a time for students to join together and have conversations "about things that mattered." The grant and supplemental funds provided for two events. One was held in Birmingham, Alabama, the week between Christmas and New Year's in 2004. The keynote speakers were Julie Pennington-Russell and Colleen Burroughs. More than 250 young adults participated. Two years later, the second and final Antiphony retreat was held in Atlanta.

During the summer of 2007, a team of people interested in engaging college and seminary students met at the Passport Camps office in Birmingham to formulate a new proposal to submit to the Lilly Endowment to begin an internship initiative that would offer young adults the opportunity to serve in local churches so that they could explore call through congregational engagement.

The proposal also requested funds to hold an end-of-summer retreat debriefing for students who served with Student.Go, Collegiate Congregational Internships and Passport Camps. This event was called Selah Vie, and the inaugural retreat was held in Shocco Springs, Alabama. The grant provided retreat funds for three years.

Beyond the events and programs CBF provided on a national level, states and regions began to respond to local collegiate ministry needs. The first local CBF student ministry began in South Carolina at Clemson University in August 2004. First Baptist Church of Clemson provided the group with a space and funding to begin the ministry, and campus minister Tim Willis guided the start-up of the group, with the students naming it Cooperative Student Fellowship.

That name and the idea for beginning more groups took hold on other campuses. In South Carolina, a group began at Winthrop University through Oakland Baptist Church, with David Brown as the campus minister. Another group started at Furman University and was directed by Joe Farry. Early on, these groups began to offer a fall retreat in the mountains of North Carolina to provide an opportunity for students to study, reflect and build an identity for Cooperative Student Fellowships. These retreats were (and are) open to all students, regardless of whether they belonged to or had access to a CSF group on their campus. The Cooperative Baptist Fellowship of Georgia was the next state to foster student ministry, with CSF groups starting at Mercer University and the University of Georgia.

This movement inspired Dr. Walter Shurden, then Callaway Professor of Christianity at Mercer University, to lead Mercer and CBF to partner together to sponsor a two-day event at First Baptist Church in Decatur, Georgia, on May 4-5, 2006. This meeting brought together CBF state and regional staff, representatives from historically Baptist colleges and universities, and others with a vested interest in ministry to college students. The desire was to examine the value of collegiate ministry, the state of collegiate ministry in Baptist life, and the role of local congregations in fostering ministry to students. At the meeting, Dr. Shurden credited Bruce Gourley, a church historian with whom he had worked at Mercer, with encouraging him to see the shifting sands of collegiate ministry as an issue in which CBF and others should be investing time and energy. This two-day meeting served as a galvanizing call to action for CBF.

Because of that meeting, Rick Jordan and I began to envision a ministry to students for the Cooperative Baptist Fellowship of North Carolina. In 2008, I was named the Coordinator for Collegiate Ministry for CBFNC. A campus ministry was formed at the University of North Carolina at Chapel Hill in the fall of 2008, with Amy Canosa as the campus minister. There is now a CBF presence on nine state campuses and a partnership with the six historically Baptist colleges and universities in North Carolina. Since 2009, these campus ministries have offered a mid-winter retreat that is open to all students and congregations.

Since 2008, CBF Heartland (formerly CBF of Missouri) has sponsored an annual conversation about collegiate ministry in its region. People from across the region come together to strategize ways for CBF Heartland to grow collegiate ministry. Since 2012, CBF Heartland has also sponsored a statewide retreat for college students. Alabama CBF, CBF of Oklahoma and CBF of Florida are also exploring ways to promote new collegiate groups in their states

CBF has several ongoing collegiate events that are building an identity and offering opportunities for college-age students. One of those events is called Sessions, which has occurred each year at the CBF General Assembly since 2008. Students gather at the annual meeting to discuss a specific topic through a theological lens. This event began with a planning meeting at First Baptist Church in Chattanooga, Tennessee, in October 2007. The goal of the event was to connect students to the larger CBF body, to provide students a way to meet other students, and to engage them in conversations about complex theological issues. Topics discussed have included human trafficking, prison reform, race, mental health and poverty.

In 2014, CBF decided to put both summer and semester service opportunities under one umbrella to provide a unified identity. Since 2002, Student.Go has allowed students to serve through Global

Missions alongside our field personnel. As of 2009, the Collegiate Congregational Internships initiative has placed students in local congregations to give them an understanding and appreciation of ministry in the local church. For clarity and promotion, it was decided to blend the two programs into the Student Dot initiatives.

Another event that grew beyond the Lilly grant to find its own place in collegiate ministry is the Selah Vie retreat at the end of summer. It matured from a simple debriefing event for our students on assignments to a place for all students to come together and recharge for the upcoming school year. Seeing the need and value of such an event, CBF has invested in the retreat for the foreseeable future.

In 2014, at the CBF ChurchWorks conference in Atlanta, Fellowship leaders officially launched the CBF Collegiate Ministry Network. Its goal is to foster community and provide resources for people invested in collegiate ministry.

Collegiate ministry is a complex and often diverse endeavor, but one that the Fellowship continues to engage by exploring ways to enhance the spiritual lives of young adults.

Wanda Hardee Kidd is the Collegiate Ministry Specialist for CBF and the Collegiate Engagement Coordinator for the Cooperative Baptist Fellowship of North Carolina. She earned her Master of Divinity and Master of Religious Education degrees from Southeastern Baptist Theological Seminary and her Doctor of Ministry from Drew School of Theology.

Being a Voice for the Voiceless

By Katie Ferguson Murray

I grew up within the "denomi-network" that is the Cooperative Baptist Fellowship, although I'm not sure I knew what that meant until I accepted my call to ministry. I was only five years old when CBF was formed, and I spent my childhood being nurtured in the faith by First Baptist Church in Austin, Texas. My mom was a deacon, and I saw women preach from the pulpit with regularity. I was taught how to ask questions of my faith, how to dialogue with people whose opinions differed from mine, and how to appreciate diversity.

These experiences and others significantly shaped my faith and the way I view the world, most notably with the understanding that I have a vital role to play in God's transformative work here on earth. The Fellowship was integral in shaping my identity in such a way that I could readily say "yes" when God called me to ministry. I consider it a great joy to partner with CBF.

One of my favorite quotes, attributed to Francis of Assisi, is, "Preach the gospel at all times; when necessary, use words." The introvert in me resonates with the message that our actions are, at times, a stronger indicator of our faith than empty words disconnected from action. I still believe strongly in the power of action. But in these past few years, I have started to look at this message in a new way, asking, "At what point are words necessary?"

As people of faith, we are well aware of the power associated with words. The first action in our Scriptures is God voicing creation into being. Christ himself was described in the Gospel of John as the "Word." We see it through the prophets—the mouthpieces of God to the Israelites—who spoke the truth with fearless passion. People of faith have long been in the business of speaking truth to power.

How, then, do we join this chorus? How can we use our voices to proclaim the gospel truth of transformation, reconciliation and redemption?

In my current context, I have the distinct joy of exploring the role of using our voices as people of faith in the work of advocacy. This work is often met with varying responses, from excitement to hesitation. But when we look at scripture, this divine call to advocacy becomes clearer. "Advocacy" is a word that is deeply rooted in the Christian faith. Both the Holy Spirit and Jesus are described as our advocates in the Scriptures (John 14:15-17; 1 John 2:1-2), and we see throughout the Old Testament that God calls the Israelite people to speak out in action and word against systems that oppress widows, orphans, immigrants and the poor. Love of neighbor is a prominent theme in this work as well, and our love for others propels us to speak up when they are hurting and to join our voices with theirs in solidarity.

Perhaps the most unique element of Christian advocacy is that this work is not motivated by self-interest, but instead is directed by God's movement in the world. In a culture that tells us to be concerned with our own needs, the act of lifting up the concerns of another points to God's love lived out in beloved community. God has called the Church to the margins of society and requires that the Church use her voice to speak out against injustice.

So while, for some, advocacy is a newer word in CBF life, it is clearly not a new practice. CBF churches and field personnel have been engaging in the work of advocacy for the past 25 years, using their voices to speak up for the needs of others and to proclaim the good news of a God who liberates those who live under systems of oppression. When we look at this emphasis more deeply, we see that in the Fellowship's focused commitment and dedication to advocacy, we have developed our unique voice not only on the local level, but nationally and internationally.

This voice is firmly rooted in the gospel and is informed by local congregations who are being a voice for the voiceless and working so that every person's voice is heard, particularly among the marginalized within society who are so often silenced by stronger powers.

Katie Ferguson Murray serves as Christian Advocacy Specialist at Wilshire Baptist Church in Dallas, Texas, where she is working with CBF to create a model for congregational advocacy. She is a graduate of the George W. Truett Theological Seminary and the Diana R. Garland School of Social Work at Baylor University.

CBF Member Care: Embodying the Love of God

By Tere Tyner Canzoneri

What does it mean to embody the love of God?

For our Cooperative Baptist Fellowship field personnel, embodying God's love means following God's call to live a life of cultivating beloved community, bearing witness to Jesus Christ, and seeking transformational development of individuals and communities in the context of global poverty, global migration and the global church.

For those called to be part of CBF's member care team, embodying God's love means coming alongside these field personnel and asking, "And how are you?" Our purpose is to facilitate physical, mental, emotional, spiritual and relational wellness for the field personnel and their families as they embody God's love, doing the work that God has called them to do in the place where God has called them to do it.

One of our CBF field personnel serving in a remote part of the world found himself increasingly discouraged. Though he and his wife are people of prayer who clearly felt called to their place of service, the work was different from what they had expected, and they were experiencing significant problems with colleagues. The man became depressed and saw no solution other than leaving the field and returning to the United States.

A CBF member care provider traveled to be with the couple. During several days of talking together, they experienced wisdom, compassion and encouragement—and began to see new possibilities. It was also determined that the man would benefit from several months of antidepressant medication, which he took as part of his ongoing care. Because of this embodiment of God's grace, the couple stayed on the field and witnessed God at work, changing many lives.

While checking Facebook one night, I received a message from one of our CBF field personnel serving on the other side of the world. She told me she was increasingly worried about her father in the United States who was trying to care for her mother, who suffered from dementia. I contacted a CBF member care volunteer who lived near the family. The volunteer knew a chaplain at a memory care facility and made a connection for the father. The daughter was moved that people cared for her by caring for her parents, and she was able to continue her work.

Another of our field personnel had had emergency surgery in the country where he was living. There were complications, and his wife worried about the treatment and whether it would be different if he were in the States. A physician who volunteers with CBF member care called and talked to the field personnel on the phone, looked at the X-rays and test results she sent him, and was able to provide assurance that her husband was receiving quality treatment and didn't need to return home.

The trust needed for all of this to happen develops over time through visits the member care counselors make to see where the field personnel work and what their lives are really like. It develops through regular conversations using Skype, FaceTime, Google Hangouts, email and sometimes even the telephone.

The counselor gets to know the field personnel by asking lots of questions, listening attentively, reading newsletters and monthly reports, offering encouragement and resources, and praying for the field personnel and all those they touch. When a need arises, the field personnel know they can reach out to their member care counselor.

Member care conversations include topics such as physical health, stress management, prayer life, spiritual and emotional well-being, personal development and growth, rest, how the marriage is, how the children are doing, concerns about family back home, finances, safety in politically unstable situations, relationships with co-workers, frustration with work, celebration of successes, dreams of the future, getting away and having fun. The responses might mean making a referral for medical care or counseling, or helping find resources the field personnel might need.

When invited, member care providers offer workshops, retreats or seminars at field team meetings. Recent offerings have included a marriage retreat, seminars on caring for aging parents who are far away, secondary PTSD, mind-body wellness and stress management.

The member care providers are counselors, therapists, chaplains, pastors with training in pastoral care, physicians and nurses. They are all volunteers and do this work out of their sense of calling. There would be no member care program without them.

"Being member care counselors for the last two years has been a humbling experience," one volunteer told me. "As we see God's work being done around the world, we feel extremely blessed to be able to love, to listen to and to encourage our field personnel. Having worked with college students for the last 31 years, especially international students, our church has gained a broader worldview. As we share about our travel to and visits with CBF field personnel, our church feels like it is an extension of what we have been doing for years."

CBF's commitment to its field personnel includes providing the structure as well as financial support for member care. This starts with an exploratory conference where people are invited to begin knowing themselves and their strengths and vulnerabilities while having conversations about their call and where it might best be lived out. It continues during orientation, when we use a variety of resources in helping people prepare strategies to stay healthy in their particular new setting.

Global Missions supervisors encourage field personnel to check in with their member care providers. These providers report to the member care manager any member care-related concerns that come to their attention.

For me, as manager of CBF's member care and wellness program, embodying the love of God means bringing a lifetime of experience as an MK/TCK (missionary kid/third culture kid), pastoral counselor, spiritual director and social worker to overseeing all this. It includes finding and training volunteer member care providers. It means checking in with field personnel (as well as the providers) to see how the relationship and care are going. It means being part of field personnel selection and training. It means being a resource for member care providers and being available for any field personnel who need or want to talk with me. It means participating in Global Missions conversations to represent how field personnel are likely to be impacted by decisions and policies.

We also provide a camp every July for the teenage children of our field personnel. Helping to staff this camp are other adults and some of our college-aged TCKs. At camp, our TCKs have a chance to be "normal." As one of my adult MKs said, "I get to hear people talk about their lives and say, 'Me too!'"

We create a safe space for them to be together, support each other, have fun, and learn about themselves and about issues facing adolescents everywhere. We talk about TCK distinctives, worship together, study together, and provide a place where they experience God's love for them. On the last night of our time together, we have a prom. For most of these kids, it's the only prom they will have.

I have an agreement with the parents to post a photo of each camper each day we are at camp. Parents report how encouraged they are to see their teens laughing, engaged, happy. One mother wrote: "I know this camp has been very important to our 16-year-old son, who even asked if he could skip his grandparents' 50th anniversary celebration in Hawaii last summer to attend. I've long said I don't know what happens at the retreat, but I know that camp is a safe, nurturing environment that feeds these kids' souls like no other church camp or retreat experience can. It's such a joy to see the kids reconnect and build lifelong friendships."

Many mission organizations have begun member care programs that offer something akin to what employee assistance programs offer here in the United States. At CBF, our commitment is beyond crisis intervention or responding to problems. We are committed to the wellness of our field personnel and to supporting them in their physical, mental, emotional, spiritual, and relational health and well-being. We want them to live out their calling of embodying God's gracious redemptive love to the world. We support them by embodying that love to them as well.

Jesus suggested we should love our neighbor (which, for Jesus, included everybody) as we love ourselves. Through the member care and wellness program, we support our CBF field personnel so that their love might be as healthy and whole and reflective of God as is humanly possible.

Tere Tyner Canzoneri has served as manager of CBF's Member Care and Wellness program since 2010. She grew up in the Philippines, where her parents were missionaries. A graduate of Mercer University (Bachelor of Arts), Candler School of Theology at Emory University (Master of Divinity) and the University of Georgia (Master of Social Work). She has been a counselor, spiritual director, marriage and family therapist and clinical supervisor in the metro Atlanta area for more than 30 years.

Waiting Patiently

By Jim Pope

It was a dark and stormy night. Really, it was. Southern California was in the grip of a severe El Nino weather system, with flooding all around us and with the hillsides along the Pacific Coast Highway sliding toward the sea. I had just returned from checking on damage to the base chapel and helping to mitigate the impact of water-soaked floors throughout the building. That was the low point in what had been a spiritually depressing year in my life as a Navy chaplain.

Our house sat on a small rise and was, for the time being, unaffected by the water that had turned our street into a creek. As I walked into the house, bone-tired and waterlogged, Judy was waiting with a cup of hot coffee. We began to talk about the preceding two years. Our pain poured out, and we decided that early winter evening in 1998 that I could not continue to straddle the broken fence of denominational loyalty. I had to do something.

We had returned to the United States in 1996 after nearly four years with forward-deployed United States Marines in Okinawa, Japan. Eager to reconnect with our Baptist roots, we had hoped to receive orders to one of the several Navy or Marine bases in the Southeast. Instead, I was assigned as Command Chaplain at a naval air station in Southern California. We settled in quickly and invested our lives in the life of NAS Point Mugu. That chapel, made up of active-duty sailors and family members, was a special place and the focus of my work and worship life.

While our worship needs were fulfilled at the base chapel where I was the Protestant pastor, I found opportunities to become involved in the area Southern Baptist Ministers Conference. My colleagues, pastors and other professional ministers of churches in Ventura County, were more than a little suspicious at the presence of a military chaplain in their company, but most were accommodating and accepting. The theology and practice of the group seemed more provincial and restrictive than this North Carolina-born-and-bred Baptist had generally experienced, but I knew the songs and understood identity markers like Cooperative Program, Lottie Moon and Annie Armstrong. It felt good to be somewhat "connected" again.

Judy and I started making plans to attend the 1997 meeting of the Southern Baptist Convention in Dallas. The convention would be a time of renewal for us. Well, that was the plan. Instead, it became our wake-up call. Rather than regaining a sense of connection to our larger Baptist family, we felt isolated, alone and embarrassed to be part of the group.

In a rude awakening, I realized that, as a Baptist chaplain, I had been hunkered down within the relative security of the military community where we employed a different language, where most were attentive to levels of acceptable and unacceptable behavior, and where we found integrity to be an invaluable currency. Decorum and integrity were certainly not present at that meeting in Dallas.

I was trapped. Ecclesiastical endorsement was a requirement for service as a military chaplain, and I was endorsed for chaplain ministry by the SBC. I loved being a chaplain. God had called me to that work. I could not quit, even when my Scots-Irish notions of honor seemed to demand it. The issue became, "How can I remain true to God's call on my life and maintain my own personal and spiritual integrity?"

I fussed and stewed over what to do for weeks, not daring to discuss my misgivings with the brothers at the pastors conference. I tried to forget about it, to keep my head down and focus on my chapel. Soon, I discovered that another Navy chaplain in Southern California, Chuck McGathy, was experiencing a similar struggle. We began to talk regularly by phone and email.

That October, we went to Birmingham to attend a Baptist Center for Ethics conference and to meet with Cooperative Baptist Fellowship Executive Coordinator Daniel Vestal to discuss possible endorsement. Dr. Vestal was kind and gracious, and I left the meeting in high spirits, believing approval for endorsement of military chaplains would be forthcoming.

Chuck and I decided to attend the fall meeting of CBF West the following month. In many ways, that meeting was the spiritual life preserver that kept me afloat for the next several months. There was an attitude of community and trust that I had not witnessed among Baptists in a very long time. When we sang "There's A Sweet, Sweet Spirit in This Place," I cried. It was as if a dam had burst; I was refreshed and freed. Thank God, I could breathe again! These were my kind of Baptists. These were Cooperative Baptists.

Still, there was no word on endorsing military chaplains. Earlier in the summer, the CBF Coordinating Council had approved the concept of chaplain endorsement, but much work was needed to gain the approval of the Department of Defense Armed Forces Chaplains Board for CBF to become a recognized endorsing body for military chaplains. Chuck and I were encouraged to be patient. This was a tall order for me. All who know me know patience is not a virtue I possess in great quantity.

"Be patient . . ."

Those words were playing over and over in my head as I went to my desk that February night, towel around my shoulders, coffee mug in hand, with some mail from the kitchen counter. I found an unopened letter from CBF. It had come in the household mail and had been overlooked for several days. When I opened it, I found the "Application for Endorsement."

That application form was the product of the hard work of many early champions of CBF chaplaincy and pastoral counseling, but it was Jim Harwood, a fellow Navy chaplain assigned to the Office of the Chief of Navy Chaplains, who had moved the process along. He worked in Washington, D.C., and kept a steady hand on the wheel to ensure every question or concern of the Armed Forces Chaplains Board was adequately addressed. Finally, CBF was officially recognized as an ecclesiastical endorsing body by the Department of Defense. Capt. Jim Harwood, CHC, USN, became the first military chaplain endorsed by the Fellowship.

A few weeks later, I wrote a letter to my endorser at the North American Mission Board, as is required of all chaplains seeking a change of ecclesiastical endorsement, informing him of my decision to seek endorsement through CBF. I shall never forget the feeling of complete relief and release I experienced when that letter was dropped into the mailbox.

Much has happened since then. I had the privilege of continuing to serve as a Navy chaplain and, by God's grace, attained the rank of captain (0-6). Throughout my career, I was privileged to interact with thousands and thousands of young men and women from every conceivable faith/spiritual background, in times of joy and seasons of sorrow. Long before the end of "Don't Ask, Don't Tell," sailors and Marines "told" me. I kept their confidences and honored the privileged communication that we chaplains hold sacred.

When Wiccan sailors insisted on being able to exercise their religious freedom along with all the other religious groups on our base, I surprised the commanding officer by offering to make space available to them. It was never again an issue. You did not see a story of religious bigotry and intolerance spun on the evening news or laid out in the press because none occurred. It was a non-issue.

During the early days of Operation Iraqi Freedom, I was asked by a reporter, "Why does the military have chaplains? What do they do?" I said this to him:

We are always mindful of our role as peacemakers in the world. Our role is not to bless bombs and bullets, but to buttress the young men and women the nation has called to the service of arms. Our mission is to stand with our sailors, Marines, soldiers, airmen and Coast Guardians in difficult, lonely or dangerous times and help them as they try to make sense of the insensible, to remind them of the infinite mercy of God, and to help them maintain their humanity surrounded by life's most inhumane experiences.

Of course, there is much more one could say about the roles and responsibilities of chaplains: how they advise command, nurture the living, care for the wounded and honor the dead. It is unsettling to talk with frightened sailors in a violent storm at sea or during a real "general quarters," when inbound enemy missiles are reported. It is energizing to help Marines, sailors, soldiers and airmen prepare for combat, and it is humbling to sit with one who has just learned of the death of her father.

Nothing else in ministry comes close to the feeling experienced when standing before an entire ship's company to conduct a burial at sea, or in blowing sand and searing heat to offer a final memorial for fallen comrades. Sometimes the simple act of sharing a cup of coffee with a medical team, following hours of complex surgery, is what it means to be a military chaplain. In all those situations, I believe my initial statement about the "why" of military chaplains remains sound.

I have sailed the waters of or set foot upon all but two of the world's continents. My family and I have lived in two foreign countries and traveled to many more. Our lives have been enriched by those among whom we have lived and whose paths we have crossed. I am a better person; my ministry is richer, my marriage is stronger, my family is healthier, and my children are more accommodating of others because we lived our lives as a Navy chaplain family.

I am incredibly grateful for the opportunity to have served as a CBF-endorsed military chaplain, as a member of the Council on Endorsement, and as staff in the CBF Office of Chaplaincy and Pastoral Counseling. That was great work. I will always treasure it. Following a "turnover" of about three months, my ministry within CBF concluded on May 30, 2014. I am most blessed. Thanks be to God!

James H. (Jim) Pope is a graduate of Southeastern Baptist Theological Seminary and Duke Divinity School. Jim and his wife, Judy, are the proud parents of three children and seven grandchildren.

A Different Kind of Baptist

By Angela Lowe

The last conversation I had with my maternal grandmother occurred on Christmas Eve of 1967. I was 12 years old, and my grandma had colon cancer. For several months, she had endured the pain from the cobalt radiation treatments.

As her grandchildren gathered around her wheelchair in the waiting room of St. Mary's Hospital, the presents she had previously wrapped were on a table beside her. She would call out the name of each grandchild, one by one, offering a warm hug and voicing some loving words before giving us our respective gifts. She knew that it would be her last Christmas with us. In those moments, I realized my beloved Mama was dying. Her transition to the next life occurred three weeks later—the day after her birthday, to be exact. What a celebration she must have had! Yet I will always remember how my first "sting of death" experience felt. It did not feel like a grand banquet. My grandparents' home felt so empty without Mama's presence, her warm hugs and her big pot of white beans on the stove.

Years later, as a Cooperative Baptist Fellowship-endorsed board-certified chaplain, I am sensitive to the needs of family members, and especially those of the children who are expressing their goodbyes to a dying loved one. It a humbling experience to be the presence of Christ in the midst of sorrow and release. Patients have lingered on until the final "amen" at the close of a prayer, or until the last words of *Amazing Grace* are sung, or until a great-grandbaby's chatter resounds as if on cue as Great Grandpa breathes his last breath. It is the silent transition from one life to another and the inevitable passing of one generation to the next. These times are sacred spaces that are filled with much grace, tender love and resurrection hope.

I will always be grateful that the vision and mission of CBF include endorsing chaplains and pastoral counselors—a process required by institutions where chaplains serve. CBF's Council on Endorsement is a duly appointed group of eight persons who review applications and make the determination as to whether or not CBF will grant endorsement, attesting that the candidate is in good standing with his or her faith group. Seven of the members are endorsed CBF chaplains and/or pastoral counselors, and one is an individual who serves in a local church ministry and is knowledgeable about ministry in specialized settings.

Our chaplains and pastoral counselors minister in workplace settings and locations around the globe. We have the privilege of being in various circumstances in which congregational ministers would never be allowed to enter. Yet we are present in all the vulnerable stages of life, responding to all the *Codes* that reverberate through the public address systems of hospitals. I have stood beside an anxious young father in the midst of the mother/baby operating room as his wife was having an emergency Caesarean section. I have offered *shalom* to a Jewish patient whose lips were blue minutes after his abdominal aortic aneurysm and moments before he was whisked away by the helicopter medical crew. I have embraced a young mother who was traumatized by the near drowning of her child.

Several years ago, in the middle of the night, I was called back to the hospital where I am a chaplain. A young Muslim mother had just died after struggling with cancer for several years. When I arrived at the hospital, I was immediately surrounded by the grieving family and the patient's mother, who spoke only Arabic. Her beloved daughter had just died, and she wanted the body to be shipped to Saudi Arabia to be buried in the family plot. The leaders of the local Islamic Center had gathered, too. This council of 12 men was to decide where the young woman would be buried. I escorted them to a large community room and had no sooner shut the door when one of the council members called me by name and said, "Pastor, you must come and meet with us. You are the spiritual advisor. You must tell us what to do."

I was thinking, "Dear God, it's 2 a.m. What am I supposed to do?" I listened as each council member voiced his opinion. Then, I stated that the consensus was to have the woman buried at the local Muslim cemetery so that her husband and children could visit her grave. I looked around the table at this all-male council and said, "Before you leave, please offer your sincere condolences to the grieving mother, because her heart is broken." So, one by one, the men graciously offered their hugs and condolences to the mother, who accepted the council's decision.

I often hear staff and patients state, "You're a different kind of Baptist. You have listened to us, you have walked beside us, and we feel as though we have been heard." I am personally grateful to have had the opportunity to attend and graduate from a CBF-partner theological school—Central Baptist Theological Seminary in Shawnee, Kansas, where both women and men are encouraged to follow their ministry calling. I am grateful to have had the opportunity to serve on the CBF Council on Endorsement, first as a member and later as the chairperson.

I am grateful to have had the opportunity to work with George Pickle, the Fellowship's former and longtime endorser of chaplains and pastoral counselors, who frequently called me just to offer a blessing for my ministry. I am grateful to have had the opportunity to serve on the search committee that recommended Gerry Hutchinson to be our new endorser after George's retirement. And I'm grateful to have had the opportunity to consult with CBF Executive Coordinator Suzii Paynter regarding the inclusion of newly endorsed chaplains and pastoral counselors in the commissioning service at the annual CBF General Assembly.

Christ's love compels us to allow the Spirit to work in and through us. My prayer is that I will continue to hold God's people in my heart until my transition to that place of safekeeping, where my Mama's bowl of white beans will be served at the table prepared for me. Amen.

Angela Lowe serves as Director of Chaplain Services at Lawrence Memorial Hospital in Lawrence, Kansas. A native of Colorado, she is a Cooperative Baptist Fellowship-endorsed chaplain, former Chair of the CBF Council on Endorsement, and board-certified chaplain with the Association of Professional Chaplains. She is a graduate of Oklahoma Baptist University (Bachelor of Arts), Midwestern Baptist Theological Seminary (Master of Religious Education) and Central Baptist Theological Seminary (Master of Divinity).

Cooperative Baptists on Mission

Cooperative Baptists on mission in South Florida during the summer of 1994, serving victims of Hurricane Andrew and assisting in the Fellowship's first coordinated disaster response effort.

In the aftermath of Hurricane Andrew in August 1992, first responders rushed to South Florida to offer relief. Two years later, most of these relief workers were gone, but Cooperative Baptist volunteers remained as CBF field personnel David and Tracy Bengtson coordinated the Fellowship's relief ministries, helping restore hope to still-recovering communities ravaged by Hurricane Andrew. The story of the volunteers pictured above is but one example of Cooperative Baptists on mission, serving the almost-forgotten and meeting their physical and spiritual needs.

The pages that follow feature additional stories of Cooperative Baptists on mission over the past 25 years. Pastors and mission ministers share their stories of being on mission in diverse ways, from providing relief in the aftermath of Hurricane Katrina to working together for community transformation in the rural Mississippi Delta and an urban neighborhood in Shreveport, Louisiana, to mentoring the next generation and serving alongside long-term partners abroad via short-term missions in China, Slovakia and South Africa. —**Editor**

The Why and the What: A Reflection on Hurricane Katrina

By Chris Ellis

"Disaster. Storm of the century. Incompetence. Levee. Lower Ninth Ward. Refugee. Displaced. Superdome. Flooding."

All of these words are now fully associated with the historic Hurricane Katrina that came ashore in New Orleans and on the Gulf Coast August 29, 2005. It wiped away an assumption that something like this happens only "over there somewhere else"—or as Jesus' disciples might have said, "on the other side of the lake." Katrina showed us that no matter how far we as a country have come, there are those who are left behind to fend for themselves—sometimes on bridges, on roofs and in water-filled streets. It showed that we're not always in control of nor exempt from the wrath of nature, no matter how many times we tell ourselves we are. It showed that no matter how much we think we can control things, control is often a mere illusion that can be easily washed away by wind and rain.

Of course, this wasn't the first storm, nor will it be the last. But as with many storms, we ask why. Why didn't God stop it? Why did God allow us to experience this in the first place?

I'm sure the disciples probably found themselves asking the same thing as they were being tossed up and down, side-to-side, on the Sea of Galilee. "Why is Jesus sleeping?" "Why is God allowing us to go through this?" Afraid they were going to drown, they awakened a slumbering Jesus, who calmed the storm and elicited bewilderment from the disciples as to who exactly he was.

I wonder how many of those who experienced Katrina firsthand found themselves with the disciples in asking, "Does God care that we are perishing?" Many who try to answer such questions end up making fools of themselves. As important as it is to struggle with the *why* questions, it's as important, if not more important, to answer the *what* questions.

For those of us at Second Baptist Church in Little Rock, Arkansas, our question was, "What is God calling us to do to be the presence of Christ among one of the worst natural disasters to befall the United States?"

Second Baptist's answer didn't start with a church-wide discernment process. It started with two faithful people asking, "What should we do?" and expecting a tangible answer. Ten days after the storm, Robert Sproles and Roy Peterson found themselves driving to Hattiesburg, Mississippi, where the eye of Katrina had passed within one mile. They were assigned chainsaw duty at the home of an elderly gentleman with Alzheimer's. After they arrived, Robert and Roy soon realized that the hurricane had not only passed by but had spawned a strong tornado that snapped off the tops of trees and left behind a mangled mess. Over the next five days they were assigned to six different homes, each home with a different story of how the residents survived. Some fled, and some sheltered in place. All were affected, and all asked some variation of the question, "Why did this happen?"

As Robert and Roy were answering their *what* question, faith communities across the United States, including Second Baptist, were beginning to answer it, too. It wouldn't take long before the flood of refugees, many with nothing but the clothes on their backs and a bus pass, began making their way to Dallas, Atlanta, Houston and every small town in between where a bed and warm food could be found.

Churches opened their doors and lives to those who had lost everything. Little Rock was no exception. Over the coming days, weeks and months, Second Baptist hosted about 40 displaced folks at our Lake Nixon retreat camp. The needs those 40 individuals brought with them were immense and couldn't be addressed by just one or two people. They had to be resolved by the entire congregation. Teams were created to make sure that basic necessities like food, transportation, clothes and laundry were taken care of.

We couldn't answer the evacuees' questions of "Why did this happen?" But we did our best to be present with them and to answer their questions of "What do we do now?" and "What can you do for me?" Once the immediate needs were met, we began brainstorming about how to move individuals to a more permanent situation. During the course of the next few weeks, our church would raise more than $30,000 for relief efforts.

However, we didn't feel absolved of the *what* questions. So we began sending teams back to the Gulf Coast to help others rebuild. In partnership with the Cooperative Baptist Fellowship, Cooperative Baptist Fellowship of Arkansas and local churches, over the next year we would send more than seven different teams to various places impacted by Katrina.

We worked on everything, from reshingling roofs and hanging drywall to framing doors and clearing debris. Two of our members answered the what question by living in their RV for five weeks, helping others reclaim what the storm had washed away. Longtime member Charles Ray answered the *what* question by organizing relief teams and becoming CBF's first disaster response coordinator.

As Katrina relief efforts began to subside, Second Baptist still did not feel absolved of the *what* question with regard to natural disasters. Our response to Katrina stirred something in us that we did not know existed. Since Katrina, we've responded to more than 30 natural disasters in such places as Haiti, Texas, Oklahoma, Missouri and others.

We created a "Churches United" group that consists of downtown churches from various denominations who respond together to disasters that occur within an hour of Little Rock. We even have a church member who serves on the National VOAD (Volunteer Organizations Active in Disasters). Our *what* became an integral part of how we would participate in mission and understand the "God of Mission."

Yes, words like "disaster, storm of the century, incompetence, levee, Lower Ninth Ward, refugee, displaced, Superdome and flooding" are all associated with Katrina. But because of the response of Christ-followers—including countless Cooperative Baptists—from throughout the United States, there are some other words that should be associated with Katrina: "love, sacrifice, hard work, life changing, hospitality, presence and calling."

Second Baptist will never be able to answer the questions related to *why* something like this happens. But we always have to be ready to answer the question of *what* God is calling us to do to be the presence of Christ now.

Chris Ellis is Minister of Mission and Outreach at Second Baptist Church in Little Rock, Arkansas. A graduate of George W. Truett Theological Seminary at Baylor University, he is a co-founder of the CBF South Africa Ministry Network.

Hands for Hope
in the Mississippi Delta

By K. Jason Coker

At every turn, we have bumped into God.

I think that is the best way to begin telling the story of Delta Hands for Hope in Shaw, Mississippi. While the organization was incorporated in the state of Mississippi in 2013, there were several years (if not decades) of prayer and activity that laid the foundations for what became Delta Hands for Hope. What follows is our story of origin, which includes a vast array of networks and partnerships. But most of it—if not all of it—is a Cooperative Baptist Fellowship story.

It is a fact that Delta Hands for Hope would not be where it is organizationally or financially without the overriding and enthusiastic support of the Fellowship, which also includes the local expressions in CBF of Mississippi and the Baptist Fellowship of the Northeast. Particularly, Together for Hope, CBF's rural poverty initiative, gives us a place to live and breathe with others who are committed to transforming rural poverty in America. These partnerships are not simply helpful to Delta Hands for Hope; they are integral to our existence.

Our story starts as a sincerely personal one. Shaw, Mississippi, is my hometown, and the people there shaped the person I have become in profound ways. I'm a Delta boy, which means more in Mississippi than in most other places. The Delta in Mississippi is known throughout the state for poverty and racial tensions. It is a tough place economically, socially, educationally and beyond. Within that crucible, I am somewhat of an enigma—a fact that is neither self-debasing nor self-aggrandizing.

In the racial discourse of the Mississippi Delta, I am white. White people make up the numerical minority in the Delta but hold the vast majority of wealth, land and property. There are some whites, however, who do not enjoy this economic privilege or pedigree. I grew up in this latter group of poor whites, which meant that I did not go to private (all white) schools. I went to public schools, which were predominantly black.

In many ways, I am the product of the African American community in Shaw. This personal experience gave us a fundamentally different starting place when exploring the idea of creating an organization in

Shaw. When I came back to my hometown, I returned to the relationships that had always been there. It was a starting place of trust rather than skepticism. We never had to establish roots as an organization; our roots were already there.

From 2009-2011, the church where I serve, Wilton Baptist Church in Wilton, Connecticut, started taking short-term mission trips to Shaw. We worked with local churches, tearing down dilapidated houses, cleaning decades of debris from downtown Shaw, co-hosting Vacation Bible Schools and hosting town-wide carnivals. Those trips solidified relationships between our church and local leaders in Shaw.

Out of these relationships, we all (both local leaders and members of our church) felt that we needed to establish a long-term partnership that focused on the children. During one of these trips to Shaw with leaders from our church, I noticed a little old lady walking into the old drug store that had been closed for years. She was white, but I didn't know her, which was unusual. I went in and told those in the building that I was originally from Shaw and was wondering what they were doing in the old drug store. This sounds crazy, but it's a very small town where this kind of thing is not uncommon. One of the women—there were three—told me that they had just started a tutoring center for children.

It was even more remarkable because she spoke with a thick Irish brogue! They confirmed that they were from Ireland, and I immediately asked how they got to Shaw.

"Well, the Holy Spirit brought us here," Sister Una said softly, with a smile.

It was that moment I knew we were about to be part of something special!

After establishing a wonderful relationship with the Presentation Sisters of the Blessed Virgin Mary, I connected with student Christine Browder from Baylor University's School of Social Work and George W. Truett Theological Seminary, who wanted to do her fieldwork with Wilton Baptist's involvement in Shaw. Christine helped lead a town hall meeting in Shaw where she put her social work concentration of community practice into action. With more than 60 local people in attendance, including African Americans and whites, Christine led the group in a process called asset mapping. Rather than asking the community what they needed, which would have forced them to focus on all the negative aspects of their area, Christine asked them to list all of the assets in the community.

"Where are your strengths? What educational assets exist here? What governmental assets do you have?" When, after the asset mapping exercise, the community looked around and saw all the assets that existed in Shaw, they were stunned! They were so excited about all that their little town had going for it that everyone left energized and excited about what we all would do next.

We took the information we gained and met with a small group of recognized local leaders. We worked together to narrow our focus, using the results of the asset mapping. The local leaders told us that we had to start with the children. Everyone in town wanted something better for their children. Through a strategic-focus exercise led by one of our church members (who used his experience as a president of a large international corporation), Shaw's local leaders recognized that they wanted an organization that worked with children and youth and focused on four areas: education, recreation, health and spiritual development. This was the point of no return.

In November 2013, Delta Hands for Hope became an incorporated nonprofit organization in the state of Mississippi with the purpose of establishing and enhancing local assets for children and youth in the areas of education, recreation, health and spiritual development. Even before our incorporation, Together for Hope voted to accept us as one of its rural poverty initiative sites. Bob Anderson, an attorney from Jackson, Mississippi, with whom I worked on the CBF Coordinating Council, filed the necessary papers for us *pro bono*. Our incorporation would have never happened—or, at least, would never have happened as fast—without Bob's generous help. Things seemed to be moving fast. We were an organization with a purpose but with no budget and no staff! Within months this would all change.

Local leaders were volunteering to host CBF churches across the country for mission trips. First Baptist Church in Waco, Texas, made a commitment to Delta Hands for Hope, coming to serve several times and generously giving resources to the organization. South Main Baptist Church in Houston brought nearly 100 youth to Shaw in the summer of 2013 and hosted a Vacation Bible School, which became the first racially integrated VBS in Shaw's history—thanks to the openness of Shaw Methodist Church.

Rev. Leroy Woods, pastor of United Rock of Ages Missionary Baptist Church in Shaw and a member of our board of directors, became the first African American to preach at Shaw Methodist Church. Other churches that came and participated included Trinity

Baptist Church of Moultrie, Georgia; Cliff Temple Baptist Church of Dallas; First Baptist Church of Memphis, Tennessee; Northminster Baptist Church of Jackson, Mississippi; University Baptist Church of Hattiesburg, Mississippi; and Wilshire Baptist Church of Dallas. Some are still coming today.

The energy—or the Spirit—that was being generated created a sense of FOMO (fear of missing out). One of our younger members at Wilton, Lane Riley, who had come to us from First Baptist Church in Greenwood, South Carolina, a sister CBF church, told me that she wanted to do something more meaningful with her life than being a nanny. At first, she was thinking about going abroad as a missionary. When I asked her how she would finance her work, she said that she had saved up some money and that her parents were very supportive. In awe of her faith, I jokingly told her she could go to Mississippi and work for nothing at Delta Hands for Hope.

Two weeks later, Lane asked me how serious I was. By the spring of 2014, Wilton Baptist had commissioned Lane to be the first Program Director for Delta Hands for Hope. Before she arrived, Christian Byrd, the Coordinator for the Cooperative Baptist Fellowship of Mississippi, and Jill Hatcher, a contract grant writer for CBF, conspired together to write a U.S. Department of Agriculture grant to offer a summer feeding program in Shaw. By a miracle of God, we secured the grant. One week after Lane landed in Shaw, she was administrating a USDA grant that provided hundreds of meals to children that summer.

In October of that same year, we were able to purchase a 7,100-square-foot building in the middle of Main Street in Shaw. It now functions as our office space and community center. This purchase was another miracle of God. To make a long story short, no bank would seriously consider giving us a loan. An inspired donor from a CBF church in Mississippi, not knowing that we were being turned down by banks, volunteered to give us a major gift and finance the rest with a personal loan. In the same month, CBF of Mississippi hosted its annual General Assembly in our new facility, bringing dozens of CBF people from across the state to Shaw. It even brought CBF Executive Coordinator Suzii Paynter as the guest speaker.

By the beginning of the summer of 2015, Lane and Christian had established six other sites in which to sponsor a summer feeding program. By the summer's end, Delta Hands for Hope and CBF of Mississippi had provided more than 10,000 meals to children across Mississippi. With Lane's leadership, we are in the process of writing other grant proposals to fund another staff person and expand the footprint of Delta Hands for Hope to other towns throughout the Delta and beyond.

Our story is one of the stories of the Cooperative Baptist Fellowship. We are just one example of what can happen when individuals, churches and organizations inside—and sometimes outside—CBF come together with a single focus. I can't wait to see what our future holds as we continue forming together.

K. Jason Coker is the pastor of Wilton Baptist Church in Wilton, Connecticut, and the founder of Delta Hands for Hope in Shaw, Mississippi. He has served on the CBF Coordinating Council (2009-2012) and was the first Recorder for the CBF Governing Board (2013-2015). He continues to serve as a council member for Together for Hope, CBF's rural poverty initiative.

A Church Undangled

By John Henson

It all started with a preposition—"for," to be precise. That's the one we spent most of our time on in one of our first core group meetings as we discussed next steps for launching a new church together.

It came up as we tossed possible names for our church back and forth. While most of the founding members had extensive experience going to church, none of them had ever named one. It was a joyful exercise, one much like any brainstorming session, where ideas are to be shared freely without judgment, doubts and chuckles. I recall that the last of those was the only one that went unviolated, as chuckles erupted when one of our leaders thought I was joking as I offered a name—one I was sure would stick and would brand us as the cool, hip church everyone would want to join.

We kept working with it until we decided on "Church of the Highlands," which still did not sound quite right. We knew we wanted to be in the Highland neighborhood where our heart and missional ministry work had been throughout the years, but some of us lived in South Highlands and some in North Highlands. We came to the conclusion that we didn't want to just be *of* the Highlands, but *for* it— for the people, organizations, schools, businesses and well-being of our neighborhood. The preposition gelled with our collective vision for our community, rolled nicely off our tongues as we began saying it aloud, secured our required Baptist consensus, and quickly found its home in our founding documents, beginning with our mission statement: *We exist to bless the Highland neighborhood with the love of Jesus through Volunteers of America and other community partnerships.*

After our initial celebration of being able to nail down a name— and without a church split or the creation of a duly nominated and assigned subcommittee/task force—we began to explore what exactly being "for" the neighborhood would mean. The founding members sought to be a church in keeping with the approach of the Cooperative Baptist Fellowship, to be "the presence of Christ" in the world. Most of us had already served in various ways in the neighborhood with church mission outreach and in the programs of Volunteers of America, and we had experienced some of the "for" already.

More "for" would come as we set out in our first year.

Church for the Highlands began and continues to meet at the Highland Center at 520 Olive Street in Shreveport, Louisiana, sharing a building with Volunteers of America of North Louisiana and Highland Center Ministries. The building, large and historic, was the church building for Highland Baptist Church before it merged with another church in Shreveport in 1996 after years of decline and a decision that it could no longer minister effectively to the changing population in the Highland neighborhood.

The Highland Center is located at a crossroads between downtown Shreveport and an affluent neighborhood to the south, intersecting with a major road leading to a hospital to the west and a major highway to the east. It is also the site of two prominent bus stops, coming and going from the main bus terminal downtown. The location enhances our mission by providing us with visibility and accessibility to the people of our neighborhood. Even though not everyone in the neighborhood is aware of all the Highland Center's programs and services, they see it as a safe haven and a resource for help with everything from assistance with utilities to providing a hot meal.

The location's accessibility to Highland's mobile residents and city transportation riders provides our church with a myriad of opportunities to serve the people coming in and out of the building. Even though members are involved in missions activity throughout the neighborhood, they can engage in missions activity without ever leaving the building.

The diversity of the neighborhood enhances our mission as well. Our church's mission to be radically inclusive of all people is a welcoming draw to people in Highland. Though such diversity could be a liability for more homogeneous churches in some neighborhoods in Shreveport, it is a true asset for Church for the Highlands. Highland residents, accustomed to the random mixture of races, ideas, architecture, restaurants, music and art of their neighborhood, can find these things reflected in the worship, programs, community and values of Church for the Highlands.

As a result, our church has earned a reputation as a caring and loving member of the community, enabling us to carry out our mission more effectively. The tremendous needs—poverty, substance abuse, incarceration, family crises, unemployment, educational inadequacies—provide Church for the Highlands with unlimited opportunities to carry out the "blessing" part of our mission and the "for" in our name as we exist "to bless the Highland neighborhood with the love of Jesus."

One of the first efforts at being "for" the neighborhood grew out of CBF's *It's Time* missional study for churches. Our core group went through the study, learning that we could then apply for a grant to be used on a sustainable missional ministry project. Randy Scoggin, a local businessman and one of our founding members, had a burden for the systems that entrap the working poor and shared a vision for a financial services program to give community residents the tools and resources necessary for breaking free from these traps and into greater financial independence.

The working poor of Highland are typically skating on thin ice when it comes to an economic crisis. One flat tire, broken-down car, medical bill or lost job can quickly send them into a rapid downward spiral. Such crises can lead to unemployment, hunger, homelessness and substance abuse.

Church for the Highlands has a great opportunity to help people in Highland achieve some financial stability and progress through its Christian Financial Services—free tax preparation, one-on-one credit counseling, credit union partnership and first time homebuyers program. Our church loved Randy's idea! CBF approved the project and grant, and our financial services soon began with the purchase of an ATM machine (with only a 50-cent charge) to provide unbanked people with a safe point of access. It continued with the offering of free tax preparation, credit counseling and a credit union partnership to give an alternative to payday loans/predatory lending in our neighborhood. The ministry continues to provide these programs and more for the working poor, now in collaboration with other churches and organizations in our neighborhood who provide the oversight and funding.

We soon saw the blessings that come from partnerships, especially since the Highland neighborhood contains more nonprofit and social service organizations than any other neighborhood in Shreveport. They provide our church with a plethora of opportunities for collaborating to accomplish our mission. The Highland neighborhood has wonderful assets and the powerful potential to be healthy and thriving. The desire for improvement that already exists among many neighbors and neighborhood groups, combined with the mission of Church for the Highlands and its partners, can result in renewal in our neighborhood, leading to a reduction in crime, an increase in the self-esteem of

Highland, an improvement in the quality of schools, and the creation of neighborhood businesses and jobs.

As we set out to be "for" the neighborhood, the "what" of our existence began to form and develop. Now, five years later, we are able to look back and see who we have become: a missional community of people following Jesus, seeking to continue the work of Jesus in our local urban setting. We are a Baptist church (we like to say "a different kind of Baptist church"), rooted in historic Baptist principles of freedom and affiliated with the Cooperative Baptist Fellowship. We are a church that values partnerships with organizations already working for the good of the Highland area.

We are diverse, enjoying the rich blessing diversity provides as we extend the radical inclusion of Jesus to everyone we encounter. We are ecumenical, seeking to collaborate with other churches, denominations and faith groups in our community and around the world. We are a group of people learning to balance contemplative spiritual practices with community action, going deeper within ourselves while expanding outward to others. We are missional, focusing our attention on living out our callings and vocations outside of church gatherings as we share the love and good news of Jesus with our world. We have become a diverse congregation, increasingly reflecting the diversity of the Highland neighborhood. We are black (23 percent), white (76 percent), other (1 percent), Republican, Democrat, straight, gay, rich, poor, Catholic, agnostic, Cooperative Baptist, interdenominational, old, young, baptized, unbaptized, housed, homeless, fixed, broken, churched, unchurched, introverts, extroverts and more.

Five years later, we continue with our preposition, seeking to keep it from dangling as the final word of our existence, for there is so much more to come after "for" as we look to the future.

John Henson is the founding pastor of Church for the Highlands in Shreveport, Louisiana, and a Cooperative Baptist Fellowship church starter. He serves as a chaplain for Volunteers of America of North Louisiana. He and his wife, Jinny (along with their son, Jack), work together in Maggie Lee for Good, a nonprofit organization they started in name and memory of their daughter, who died in 2009.

Family Ties

By Michael Cheuk

When I first heard that Rob Fox, then Coordinator of the Cooperative Baptist Fellowship of Virginia, was leading a team to Macau and Hong Kong for a mission immersion experience in May of 2013, I was instantly intrigued. The idea of this trip captured my heart not only because of the mission aspect, but also because I saw it as an opportunity to visit Hong Kong, my birth city.

My family emigrated from Hong Kong to Shreveport, Louisiana, in 1973, and I had been back only once, in 1995. I still have relatives living in Hong Kong. Yes, going on this trip was an opportunity for me to see and learn about the ministries of Cooperative Baptist Fellowship field personnel in China, but it was also a rare opportunity for me to visit my childhood home.

I flew to Hong Kong a couple of days ahead of the team. My uncle Kevin picked me up from the airport and took me to a restaurant where I was greeted by two aunts, another uncle and a cousin. There, I was also introduced to another cousin, Almon, and his wife. After a delicious meal, we went to visit my 100-year-old grandfather. Even though he didn't recognize me, it was heartwarming to see him again, and memories of times with him during my childhood came flooding back.

During those first hours in Hong Kong, something resonated deep within me. Half a world away from Virginia, I felt at "home." I felt a deep connection with people whom I hadn't seen for years (and two of whom I had never met) because we were related by blood, descendants of a common grandfather.

After my time with family in Hong Kong, I thought Macau might be anticlimactic. I was wrong. In Macau, CBF field personnel Larry and Sarah Ballew and members of their Hospitality Industry English class overwhelmed us with their welcome. They acted as our personal tour guides around the city and hosted and served amazing meals at the restaurants where they worked.

Members of Macau Baptist Church also extended hospitality. Together we sang hymns, laughed, baked cookies, ate, learned Chinese and English, shared testimonies and worshipped. Through all this, I was inspired by the Ballews and their ministry. One cannot underestimate the sacrifices and challenges they face in sharing the Gospel of Jesus Christ in Macau and China. But they serve with an abiding faith and a contagious joy.

And during those days in Macau, something resonated deep within me. I felt a deep connection with people whom I'd never met because we were related by Spirit, descendants of a common Heavenly Father. Beautiful souls like pastor Peter Chan and his wife Lilian, Cecilia Dell'Immagine, Winnie, Yuki, Cory, Jenny, Gary, CBF field personnel Brenda Lisenby and many others captured my heart.

After our time in Macau, we traveled back to Hong Kong to spend one more day there before flying back to the United States. That last night, my uncle Kevin met me and the whole mission immersion team and took us to a restaurant near our hotel. At the restaurant, Kevin played host and ordered for the whole group, choosing favorites like crispy noodles, roast pork, and steamed fish with scallions and soy sauce. He also introduced us to a sweet red bean soup dessert and showed us how to eat it. We had a wonderful time.

When the meal was over, we went back to the hotel. I was tired, said goodbye to my uncle, and returned to my room to pack and go to bed. The next morning, as I went downstairs to the hotel lobby, several of the team members told me how much they enjoyed spending time with "Uncle Kevin." (Apparently, he became an uncle to them too!)

It was then that I found out that my uncle and several of our team members stayed in the hotel lobby late into the night talking, making song requests to the hotel piano player and capping off the night singing John Denver's classic "Leaving on a Jet Plane."

It was a strange and wonderful feeling knowing that a member of my extended family from Hong Kong shared such a time of connection and fellowship with members of my faith family from the United States. That night at the restaurant and at the hotel, my heart was captured by experiencing the gift of mutual hospitality. Our team was blessed by the gracious and fun-loving hospitality of my uncle. My uncle was likewise blessed by an opportunity to enjoy a night of respite from caring for his centenarian father, by eating and singing with a bunch of fun-loving Americans.

My grandfather died in November that year, and I can't describe how blessed I am to have had an opportunity to see him one last time. I also can't describe how "at home" I felt seeing and experiencing the mutual joy of my uncle and our mission immersion team together during our final night in Hong Kong.

Because of this mission experience with fellow Cooperative Baptists, I can honestly say that Hong Kong *and* Macau now both pull at my heart because I have family ties there—family related by blood and family related by God's Holy Spirit. Thank you, CBF, for making this deeply personal and spiritual journey possible!

Thank you, CBF, for giving me a spiritual home. As we celebrate the 25th Anniversary of our Fellowship, may we give thanks to God for birthing this movement through courageous men and women, and for providing a home for so many. As we look toward the next 25 years, may we strengthen and widen our family ties in Christ to include many, many more, spanning all ages and all nationalities.

Michael Cheuk is the former senior minister at University Baptist Church in Charlottesville, Virginia. He is a graduate of Rice University (Bachelor of Arts), Southwestern Baptist Theological Seminary (Master of Divinity) and the University of Virginia (Doctor of Philosophy in Religious Ethics). He served as Chair of the CBF Ministries Council from 2013-2015.

Realizing My Connection
With God's Mission

By Kathy Shereda

The opportunity to join Cooperative Baptist Fellowship field personnel Jon and Tanya Parks in Slovakia came through an invitation from the Cooperative Baptist Fellowship of Virginia, where I was serving as Moderator-Elect. The church where I serve as pastor, Purdy Baptist Church in Emporia, Virginia, was becoming increasingly involved in the mission and ministry of the Fellowship.

I had not traveled internationally since my mission immersion experience to Kenya in 2005 with the Baptist Theological Seminary at Richmond. Košice, Slovakia, was a different kind of mission encounter. While Slovakia is not a third world country, there are poor and marginalized people everywhere. Learning about the lives of the Roma people in Slovakia opened my mind to yet another group of people who are struggling for survival and inclusion.

Jon and Tanya introduced our team to the history, architecture, religion, politics, industry and daily life of the Roma in Košice. We went on walking tours, met interesting people, ate different foods, and experienced the bustle and excitement of the outdoor market. While we were there, an event called "Košice Days" was in full swing in the city square. There were vendors with handcrafted items to sell, as well as live music and plenty of friendly faces, so we were able to see and experience Slovak culture.

The Roma people have been a part of the mission of CBF from the beginning. Everywhere they exist, they are marginalized. More often called "gypsies"—a cultural/racial slur—Roma experience discrimination across Europe. Slovakia is no exception. Jon and Tanya do a great job of communicating love to both the Slovak and Roma people, which helps bridge the gap between the two groups and opens up communication and understanding.

We began our mission experience with tutorials in the living room of the Parks' home. Their young daughters, Kaitlyn and Abigail, taught us basic Slovak phrases, and Jon and Tanya helped us understand the challenges of daily living for the Roma. One of the first places we encountered these challenges was at a school in a neighboring town,

Kezmarok. The building was an abandoned car dealership office, refitted to accommodate classrooms. It was spare but worked well for them.

Our next encounter was in an English as a Second Language class at the Roma church in Košice. The church members greeted us with much warmth and kindness. Their hospitality and affection made it seem as if we had always known each other. That is how it is when we are in Christ. When the Spirit brings us together, we already know each other.

We met a young man named Leo, an accomplished pianist and vocalist, who was studying at the music conservatory, something which distinguished him from other Roma. Jon taught the group the English lessons using word games and conversation, and we dispersed ourselves among the students to help them as they learned to say new words. They taught us a few words in Romani as we helped them with English.

We traveled to the far outskirts of town, to a village where some of the Roma lived in community. We had a cookout with church members, worshipped together in a home church service, and enjoyed an evening of fellowship. We were invited inside to sit with others while a Bible study was held, with at least 30 people in attendance. Leo was there and played his guitar while the group sang. A woman named Christina preached while an interpreter translated for us in English. At the end of her sermon, two women came to her for prayer and to accept Christ. Another woman picked up the guitar and began playing while everyone sang. Even though we did not understand the language, we understood the love and acceptance that had just taken place in the name of Christ.

When the service was over, we adjourned for our cookout. Jon and the Roma men cooked chicken, sausages, peppers and onions on a charcoal fire. The women played music and everyone danced, first in a large circle holding hands, then in lines with the children, much like square dancing at home. It was very festive and upbeat. It doesn't matter what part of the world you are in, when church folks get together, they like to eat.

Our group was divided into pairs, and we were guests in different homes. These "home stays" were a more personal way for us to experience how the people lived and to enter into a closer relationship with them.

Our first home stay was with a Slovak family. Victor and Lenka and their four-year-old son, Matthew, were welcoming and hospitable.

Victor made homemade rolls for our breakfast the next morning, and Lenka gave me a halušky maker. Our gift to them was a large tin box of chocolates with all kinds of American symbols on it. I mentioned that our family also loved to eat halušky, small dumplings made by dropping an egg-rich potato and flour dough in boiling water. She showed me her device for dropping the dough, basically a plastic plate with holes. I couldn't believe she gave it to me. What a treasure!

We had American gifts for the Roma family we stayed with on the second night as well. The mother, Denisa, had multiple sclerosis and was in a wheelchair. Her teenage son, Mario, enjoyed playing the drum box at church, and her 17-year-old daughter, Nikola, gave up her bedroom so we would have a place to sleep. After a good night's rest, we were invited to a breakfast of bread, butter, a slice of deli meat, sliced tomatoes, yogurt, and coffee or hot tea. Nikola and Mario were interested to learn what American teenagers were like. They wanted to know what phrases were popular and what kids did for fun. After breakfast, we all left for worship at the Roma church. The service was lively, with Shane McNary, one of CBF's other field personnel in Slovakia, as guest preacher. Someone interpreted from English to Slovak and also Romani. The songs we sang were in both Romani and Slovak.

We were expecting special guests at the church, as Lubos Dzuriak and his family planned to join us. The Dzuriaks were Slovak Baptists who lived in Košice. Years before, the building now occupied by the Roma church had once belonged to the Slovak Baptist church where the Dzuriaks worshiped. The Slovak congregation had grown, moved and rebuilt elsewhere. The Roma were now using it as their worship space. The significance of Lubos being there had several meanings.

Lubos had attended seminary with me and others on the team. My relationship with him was also tied to my home church, Poplar Springs Baptist in Richmond, Virginia, where my husband's father, Rev. Joseph J. Shereda, was pastor for 27 years.

Rev. Joe Shereda and his wife, Rose, were first-generation Americans whose parents immigrated from Domažlice, Czechoslovakia. My father-in-law was called to become a Baptist pastor as a young man. In July of 1930, the Czechoslovak Baptist Convention commissioned Joe and Rose as missionaries to Czechoslovakia. After a few months, he was called to Zlin, Czechoslovakia, to help grow a church where eight believers were gathering in homes. His work as a Baptist minister was not always easy, as many Baptists were persecuted in a largely Catholic environment.

Then the whole world changed with the advancement of Hitler in Eastern Europe. When the threats of war began, the United States called home its citizens, including missionaries. Saying goodbye to their beloved congregation, the Sheredas boarded the SS Manhattan on Thanksgiving Day, 1938, the last ship out before the ultimate invasion by Hitler in 1939. Their third child, Paul, my husband, was three years old at the time. Paul and I had been married just shy of 25 years when he died of cancer on July 23, 2010. This was his story. It became part of my story.

Paul's church became my church when we married in 1985. It was there I found my calling to ministry and began my Christian educational journey with Bluefield College in Virginia and then with Baptist Theological Seminary at Richmond. The church supported me both spiritually and financially. It was from there I was called to my first full-time ministry position as minister of outreach at the First Baptist Church of Petersburg, Virginia. It was also while there that Paul was diagnosed with cancer and given five to seven years to live. Within that time, I was called to my first pastorate at High Hills Baptist Church in Jarratt, Virginia. I was ministering there when Paul died, almost six years to the day of his diagnosis.

During those last years, we talked about what he wanted to do before he died. I asked him if he wanted to return to Zlin and visit the place where he was born and first lived. He was too frail and declined to take the trip, but asked that perhaps someday some of his ashes could be laid to rest there. I promised to do so, without knowing how I would ever accomplish this task.

Fast forward to the CBFVA Mission Immersion Experience to Slovakia in May 2014. My first thought was of the Roma people and our "Step By Step" missions emphasis with Jon and Tanya through CBFVA. But, as I thought through the process, I wondered if there might be a possibility that I could take a quick side trip to the Czech Republic, spread my husband's ashes where his father had served and where Paul was born, and return to the group without so much as 24 hours passing. But how could this be done?

The answer: Lubos Dzuriak.

If Lubos could accompany me and take me to places where he was familiar, to navigate through territory unknown to me, it could be accomplished. So here he was, my friend from seminary, a Slovak with know-how in Eastern Europe, ready and willing to take me on this trek of closure. Lubos became my link to finalizing something important to Paul and to me in our life's journey.

Lubos made all the arrangements. I left the group with their blessing after the worship service with the Roma church. We left for the Czech Republic early the next morning. It was a journey of about four or five hours from Lubos' home near Vienna, Austria. It was so surreal to see the reading on Lubos' GPS that read "Zlin." I could not believe that I was in the place of Paul's birth.

We arrived in Zlin, found accommodations and ate some traditional Czech food, like my in-law family had always prepared after church on Sunday. I felt so at home. The next day, we met with the pastor of Bratrská jednota Baptistů (Brotherhood Baptist Church). This church is a continuation of the church my father-in-law helped plant. Pastor Marek Titěra was there to greet us. It was there I discovered something significant.

Rev. Titěra took us upstairs to the church worship space and offices and explained the renovations being done to bring the building up to date. There, hanging in the hallway upstairs, was a photograph of the original congregation taken in 1938 on the occasion of the departure of their pastor, Rev. Joseph J. Shereda, for the United States. My family was in that photo, including my husband, Paul, who was just three years old. I had seen a copy of that photo in Joe Shereda's keepsakes. The connection was more than I could fathom, because my sole mission was to spread ashes, not to realize my own connection with God's mission. I was there on God's terms, not my own. I was there to realize the marginalization of people of all kinds, all cultures, all regions, no matter where they were from or who they were. God sent me there for more than one reason. And I learned much from the experience.

After Lubos and I left Rev. Titěra's home, we went to two places. One was a music hall where Rev. Shereda had done Bible studies for seekers. The other was the Zlin Castle, as it was called, which was a large, three-story building used by the city for multiple reasons. Rev. Shereda was given a meeting room by the city for his growing congregation. Years later, the congregation moved to the building where Marek Titera is now the pastor.

It was on the grounds of the Zlin Castle that I decided to spread some of Paul's ashes. Lubos and I found a peaceful spot to have our memorial service. I chose Paul's favorite psalm—Psalm 24—to read as I began to spread his ashes. "The earth is the Lord's, and all that is within it," I read as I considered the entirety of all we borrow from

God. Paul was, among other things, a farmer. He borrowed from God as he worked the earth with crops and cattle. He knew that all he had belonged to God, and everything he produced was because of God. I let go of a portion of his ashes during this reading. They were spread on ground he likely had played upon during his childhood.

Leaving was difficult, but as the plane set down on the tarmac in Richmond, I felt a sense of mission. We had been to Slovakia to meet our CBF field personnel in Košice, Jon and Tanya Parks. Their mission became our mission. We, as a church, learned more about our world.

Kathy S. Shereda is the senior pastor of Purdy Baptist Church in Emporia, Virginia. A graduate of Baptist Theological Seminary at Richmond, Kathy was ordained in 2002 and has served Virginia churches in Henrico, Petersburg, Jarratt and Emporia. She has also served on the Coordinating Council and as Moderator of the Cooperative Baptist Fellowship of Virginia.

A Sacred Moment at General Assembly

By C. Franklin Granger

Reflecting on my 25-years-and-counting journey with the Cooperative Baptist Fellowship revealed a photo album of mental images that was like standing in the center of one of those 360-degree theaters. The sensory experience is complex and inspiring, and more is available for reviewing than can be observed at any given moment. While the constantly moving images and scenes circled around, it was, oddly, a recent image that continued to hold my attention. This new addition to the memory album incorporated the varied ministry and mission experiences of this journey with a depth and breadth of meaning.

That recent image is from the 2015 CBF General Assembly in Dallas, Texas. Following the Wednesday evening worship, many of us were, as would be expected, talking with friends, hugging those we hadn't seen in years, meeting new people, sharing ideas and opinions, and looking to see who else was present. I had just finished catching up with a college classmate and was starting to make my way across the crowd, looking to see whom else I knew. A young adult stepped over, extended her hand and said, "This may be a bit awkward . . ." Not recognizing her, I was unsure how to respond and certainly had no way of knowing what she was about to say. We shook hands, and I waited. There was no more than a second or two between the silent shake and her next comment, although it seemed as if time had been momentarily suspended.

Honestly, I expected her to say she was the daughter of someone with whom I went to school. However, she didn't introduce herself; nor did she give one of those "you might not remember me, but" introductions. Before I had any more time to speculate or to linger in suspense, she went straight to the punch line: "I wanted to tell you that . . . you are part of the reason I am now in ministry."

Wow! Really! How? When? Who are you? Those were the thoughts running through my mind. Still, I couldn't place this person, so I had no reference point for having had any influence on her, much less something that would result in a career. She continued to tell me about her time at Camp PRISM (Preparing and Reaching Individuals in Spirit and Mind). This was a children's camp that First Baptist

Church in Athens, Georgia (where I serve) and about six other Baptist churches from North Carolina and South Carolina coordinated together in the 1990s and 2000s. She recounted remembering Kenney Standley and me as leaders, and she credited Camp PRISM with her faith formation. Teary-eyed, I made my own awkward move at this point and asked her to tell me her name.

"Judith Myers," she said, adding that she grew up at Fernwood Baptist Church in Spartanburg, South Carolina. "Yes, of course!" I said. "I remember you."

Judith's message changed the course of my whole experience at the 2015 CBF General Assembly. That moment also provided a new, multidimensional lens through which to view the past quarter-century journey with CBF. Initially, it was what could be termed a delayed confirmation. We ministers believed that what we were doing in all of our planning, preparation, hopes and craziness at Camp PRISM would have meaning for the children of our churches. But hearing it confirmed in this way made all the difference.

More impactful than that was the confirmation that each of us touches people in ways that we never know. The working of God's spirit through us is more fluid and less encumbered when we are unknowing conduits and vessels. Nonetheless, hearing in retrospect of a time of inspiration touches those lingering doubts we carry with a hand of blessing and confirmation. What to her was an awkward moment became for me a sacred moment of blessing and grace. Sometimes, entering the presence of the sacred is awkward. Judith dared to risk the awkwardness, which became for me a holy and sacred moment.

In that sacred space, when time and distance intersected, everything from every day of every year of those camps converged—every goofy song and serious song, all the Bible studies and mission projects, the conversations while walking to the dining hall, the afternoons at the pool, the camp fires and recreation games. With these, all the faces of the children and the adults surrounded me like a great cloud of witnesses. But there was more in that moment: the realization of what was yet to be accomplished in mission and ministry from that point forward. For as much as it was a moment of confirmation, it was equally full of promise and the calling of what was yet to come.

Remembering is like that. Remembering provides the opportunity to confirm and to celebrate. But there also is something about the act of remembering that generates newness of life. It is the echo of the two as they reflected on their Emmaus journey one fateful morn—"did not our hearts burn within us." Remembering calls us forward.

Camp PRISM was but one example of how our congregation has partnered with other churches in the Fellowship for the work of ministry and missions. A few local congregations from three states partnered together to provide summer camp eyepieces for their children. The ministers on the staffs of these churches pooled their gifts to plan, organize and lead. Men and women and college students chaperoned and provided leadership, teaching, guidance and love. This story expresses what we do, week after week, year after year, season after season, from generation to generation. Our congregations engage in the work of ministry. The ministry we do as a congregation and the missions in which we engage produce relationships that are faith-forming and investments that are identity-shaping. Relationships and faithful service go together, and this is the basis of our lives as a Fellowship.

I remain awed by that experience on Wednesday evening at CBF General Assembly. That one brief exchange was filled with years of ministry. And within that holy space was contained both the past CBF experiences of people, trips and ministries, and all that is still to come, all that which is yet to transpire. It was life-giving as well as faith-forming. It was confirmation as well as calling. In the affirmation of the past attempts at faithful and meaningful ministry came also the calling and the challenge to continue, to forge ahead, because it does matter. It does make a difference.

My 25-year journey in the Fellowship suddenly is no longer just a quarter of a century of mission projects, ministry experiences, meetings, conversations and initiatives. No longer is it only a memory book of people, places and events. This point of remembrance has become a revelatory point of beginning. We are linked together through our ministry and mission relationships in ways that transcend our conscious awareness.

When we experience that internal nudge to speak a word of gratitude to another, or to share with someone how he or she has made a lasting impact on our lives, we need to pay attention. It is an opportunity to embrace the grace of past experiences and allow it to become a moment of sacred blessing. What we anticipate as awkward may actually be the movement of the Spirit, pulling us toward the promise of God which is yet to be fulfilled.

C. Franklin Granger is Minister of Christian Community at First Baptist Church in Athens, Georgia, having served there since 1989. A native of Greenville, South Carolina, he is a graduate of Furman University (Bachelor of Arts), Southern Baptist Theological Seminary (Master of Divinity) and the University of Georgia (Doctor of Philosophy in Adult Education).

Ubuntu:
South Africa Ministry Network

By Matt Cook

In the days leading up to his election as president of South Africa, Nelson Mandela was asked about his political philosophy. To answer the question, he told a story. "In the old days in our country, a person on a journey would set out from one place to another and would travel light and easy, carrying little, but with no worries, for the person knew that at the end of each day's walk he would reach a village. In that village he would be received with food, and shelter and all manner of hospitality. That is what my people called *Ubuntu*. As a nation, we have to reclaim that spirit for we will not rise as a nation unless we all rise together."

Ubuntu means "I am because we are."

As Baptists, we love our freedom. We cherish the idea of the priesthood of the believer and the autonomy of the local church. Those are good expressions of our identity, but they also display the Baptist tendency toward rugged individualism, on both a personal and organizational level.

Sometimes, however, Baptists come together, and the task that has brought us together more than anything else is sharing Jesus with people around the world. For more than two centuries, Baptists have come together for the cause of mission, and because working together makes it possible for us to accomplish far more than any of us could do alone.

In 2009, Second Baptist Church in Little Rock, Arkansas, was coming off its second mission trip to South Africa. Most of the congregation's work had been alongside organizations and people that were focusing on those impacted by the HIV/AIDS crisis that had been raging through sub-Saharan Africa for more than a decade. Door of Hope is a nonprofit organization that arose out of a local church's abandoned baby ministry. Refilwe is kind of like a South African version of a Baptist children's home. Musa was a pastor in Kwa-Zulu-Natal province whose church and preschool acted as a community center for families, many of whom had lost loved ones to the epidemic.

After each trip, the church members came home both energized and overwhelmed—energized by the opportunity to work alongside

South African brothers and sisters, but overwhelmed by the combined problems of poverty, the HIV/AIDS crisis, and the aftermath of apartheid.

The church had sent two teams to work alongside CBF Global Service Corps field personnel and their South African partners. But only two years into the work, they found themselves unexpectedly at a crossroads. The desire for impact was great but the work was huge, and Josh and Caroline Smith, the field personnel who were facilitating the work, didn't know if they could go back. The dilemma for Second Baptist was trying to support the work in South Africa and the Smiths without abandoning their commitments to other mission opportunities, especially at home in Little Rock.

And so the idea for a network was born. The staff at Second Baptist had a hunch that other churches like theirs wanted to have a hands-on connection to global mission and wanted their work to have real impact, but would have to figure out a way to make it happen with limited resources. So the staff at Second Baptist got on the phone and started calling ministry friends and colleagues who might be on the lookout for an opportunity to partner globally. They offered to underwrite the cost of a discovery trip to South Africa, asking only for one thing in return—a genuine openness to the idea that God might be calling their church to partner in South Africa. No promises, just openness.

It worked. The first church to jump on board was First Baptist in Abilene, Texas—the church where Caroline Smith grew up. FBC Abilene was already doing a lot missionally around the world, but the church was open to partnering in South Africa as well. Soon after, the folks at Broadway Baptist Church in Fort Worth became interested. Broadway was deeply invested in homeless ministry in Fort Worth but was looking for a place to engage globally.

Over the next couple of years, other churches jumped on board: Gaston Oaks Baptist Church in Dallas, Texas; First Baptist Church in Knoxville, Tennessee; First Baptist Church in Wilmington, North Carolina. A critical expansion of the network resulted when an existing partnership between Second Baptist Little Rock and Second Baptist Church in Memphis, Tennessee, expanded into a global partnership. The people at Second Baptist Memphis decided to make a long-term commitment to mission work in South Africa and soon began to bring other nearby partners to the network. First Baptist Church in Chattanooga and the Tennessee Cooperative Baptist Fellowship soon joined up.

And then, at almost the same time that Josh and Caroline Smith began to raise support to go to South Africa, another couple, Mark and Sara Williams, also felt the call. Josh and Caroline were planning on working at Refilwe in Johannesburg, while Mark and Sara hoped to work in a rural region of Kwa-Zulu Natal.

In a very short time, the "network" of one church and two field personnel became a real network of four field personnel, eight churches and multiple organizations, not to mention the anchor organizations and individuals in South Africa whose work we were going to support.

And so, in the months that followed, things began to happen. First, the network came together to provide funding to support the CBF field personnel. Second, the network came together to fund the construction of a volunteer housing block at Refilwe. Volunteer groups paid to stay at Refilwe but saved money on gas and housing costs, while Refilwe gained a source of revenue and a training opportunity for people wanting jobs in the tourist industry.

Before long, each of the churches began to include a fee in their trip costs to help provide financial support for two medical caregivers at the Refilwe medical clinic. A couple of months later, the Tennessee churches came together to buy a truck for the clinic to aid with visits and medical supply deliveries.

Broadway Baptist Church in Fort Worth, Texas, provided funding for a weekly community meal patterned after the *agape* meal served every week at Broadway for hungry and homeless people. Gaston Oaks Baptist Church, a multi-congregational church with six different ethnic congregations meeting under one roof, sent two of its pastors (one from Africa) to lead an ecumenical training workshop for Zulu pastors in Winterton, South Africa.

But if there's any story that symbolizes the surprising and organic ways in which the birth of a mission network came to have an impact, that story probably happened at a restaurant in downtown Little Rock. During the fall of 2009, Second Baptist Little Rock held what it called a South Africa Mission Summit, inviting churches from all over the country to come and hear how they might get involved. A grand total of three churches sent people. It seemed like a massive failure. But two South African ministry leaders had flown in for the event—Jaco Van Schalkwyk, the Executive Director at Refilwe, and Cheryl Allen, the Executive Director at Door of Hope. They had never met.

Over lunch one day, they told each other about their respective organizations, and an idea was launched: Maybe Refilwe could open its own baby house with some help from the folks at Door of Hope. And so three years later, on a warm and sunny September morning, two CBF field personnel and people from three CBF congregations in three different states came together with local South African business leaders and the staffs of two different South African nonprofit organizations to celebrate as the El Roi Baby Home opened on the Refilwe campus. The lives of orphans and abandoned children would literally be saved, all because God brought a group of people together to do far more than any of them could have accomplished alone. Ubuntu!

Matt Cook serves as the senior pastor of First Baptist Church in Wilmington, North Carolina, and as the CBF Moderator for 2015-2016. He is also one of the founders of the CBF South Africa Ministry Network. A graduate of Samford University (Bachelor of Arts) and Baylor University (Master of Divinity, Doctor of Philosophy), Matt and his wife, Allyson, have two children, Nathaniel and Caroline.

2013 Caravan for Women participants pose in front of Al Akhwayn University in Ifrane, Morocco where Karen Thomas Smith, a pastor in Morocco and Kentucky native, serves as chaplain.

In 2005, the Kentucky Baptist Fellowship formed a partnership with EEAM (Église Évangélique au Maroc), an association of Protestant churches in Morocco. With a church-to-church partnership model, nine CBF congregations in the Bluegrass State have enjoyed unique and fulfilling relationships with their sister churches in the EEAM. Each church-to-church partnership has the goal to develop and sustain transformative, long-term relationships that help develop leaders and contribute to improved cultural and social understanding between the two groups.

The Morocco Partnership is one of the many exemplary partnerships that exist across the Fellowship. Since the birthing of the Cooperative Baptist Fellowship at the 1991 Convocation in Atlanta, partnerships have played a central role in the life of the Fellowship. With different types of partnerships focused on the areas of missions, theological education and congregational resources, CBF continues to partner with nearly 50 organizations. The following pages share the stories of just a small sampling of the Fellowship's partners over the past 25 years. —**Editor**

CBF and Passport: A Perfect Match

By Colleen Burroughs

In 1993, sitting in the basement apartment of the guest house at Southern Baptist Theological Seminary in Louisville, Kentucky, with embarrassing hairstyles and heads full of larger-than-life dreams, my husband, David, and I prayed about how to answer one question. Pat Anderson was the Coordinator of the Cooperative Baptist Fellowship of Florida, and his question was simple enough: Would David and I create a camping program for moderate Baptist youth in the state of Florida? How could we possibly know then that the answer would forever change the direction of our lives?

After a conversation with our band of bright-eyed idealists—Rev. James Bush, a brilliant youth minister, and Nathan Hanson, our Lutheran saxophonist—our answer was: "As long as anyone who wants to is free to come."

At the time, that response was meant to ensure that our camps would be open to Nathan's Lutheran audience and anyone else who wanted to attend. However, the idea that *everyone is welcome* became a fundamental principle of Passport Camps.

Pat and his wife, Carolyn, who served as CBF of Florida's Associate Coordinator (they always worked in tandem), said "yes" to our request. CBF of Florida financially backed Passport for its first two summers of existence.

From its inception in 1993, Passport was a place where everyone was welcome and where women could freely preach the word from the Lord. This automatically made Passport a perfect fit for moderate Baptist churches hungry for a safe and inviting option for their children.

We would often field calls from curious ministers looking for more information, and we would engage in almost a theological secret handshake of sorts. We would tell them three things:

1) "We do mission work at camp." This made people smile, as all Baptists celebrate missions!
2) "We have a dance." And, if they didn't hang up on us at this point, we would say . . .
3) "Sometimes our pastor at camp is a woman."

At this point, we would either hear the dial tone or the sound of a wide smile. It was a special code that identified a field of theological freedom in which someone could practice faith, dance for no reason and worship without restriction. From the very beginning, Passport and the Cooperative Baptist Fellowship have been a perfect match.

As the moderate Baptist family was reinventing itself in every direction, CBF churches were rethinking ways to do missions more thoughtfully. CBF churches resonated with Passport's novelty of being the first summer youth program to invite students to *be* the hands and feet of Christ at a discipleship camp.

Our first camp mission project was to build hurricane shutters for the people of Homestead, Florida, which had been hit hard by Hurricane Andrew. A truck was sent to carry the new shutters back to Homestead, and on the door of the truck were painted these words: "The Cooperative Baptist Fellowship of Florida." It was literally the first time we had seen our new Baptist name inked onto the side of anything. All the campers cheered: "We own a truck! We are real!"

As CBF Global Missions took form, Passport's mission focus grew wider. David remembers the surreal reality of unpacking our tiny exhibitor booth at state meetings right next to our mission strategist giant, new CBF Global Missions Coordinator Keith Parks. David asked Dr. Parks about where our small summer camp missions offering might be used in 1997.

Laughing in his big Texas way, Dr. Parks said, "Well, we need to build 10 huts in Thailand." So we raised the offering and presented him with the check at a CBF Coordinating Council meeting.

Those huts, built to help the work of then field personnel Rick and Ellen Burnett, may be gone by now, but they represented a way to participate in CBF's new approach to doing missions in a world without borders. We were so excited to be a part of it and to tell our students about it. Our first international camp was on the edge of the Black Sea in the Republic of Georgia in 1996. We have since held international Passport experiences in Canada, Kenya, Korea, Liberia and Malawi.

When Dr. Parks' successor, Dr. Gary Baldridge, introduced Passport to the World Vision organization, a visioning trip to Malawi was planned. That introduction opened a new door that resulted in the birth of Passport's water poverty initiatives. "Watering Malawi" continues to fund access to clean water, sanitation and hygiene in the landlocked country in southeast Africa.

Twenty-four years later, Passport campers have contributed $1.9 million to Global Missions causes, the majority of which has been given to CBF field personnel and to partner projects in Kenya, India, Romania, China, Indonesia, Vietnam, Liberia, Ethiopia, Hungary, Afghanistan, Kosovo, Ukraine, Jordan and the United States.

In 2001, Daniel Vestal visited the grand opening of our new office building in Birmingham, Alabama. He challenged us to consider a camp for children. PASSPORT*kids!* was created with the help of a three-year investment from CBF. Thousands of children have now been introduced to the work of CBF field personnel, thanks to the visionary direction of Dr. Vestal.

Passport's mission education and mission offering gifts to Fellowship causes remain an intentional choice in respect to our longstanding partnership. We are still so excited to participate in giving to and teaching our students about CBF Global Missions.

As an independent partner with CBF, we have enjoyed creative conversations and collaborative projects all along the way. These include Mission Exchange—a five-year project, the brainchild of Dr. Tom Prevost—to help facilitate young volunteer teams wishing to work with brand new CBF field personnel, and Student.Go, CBF's student missions initiative, which was created in the Passport office and initially co-facilitated by John Mitchell and CBF's Amy Derrick. Passport also worked in partnership with Amy and with Wanda Kidd to develop collegiate events called "Antiphony" and "Selah Vie." Faith in 3D, born in 2006, is an event made possible through a conversation with CBF's Bo Prosser and through Passport's participation on a standing committee of the National Council of Churches. Faith in 3D has become a magical weekend at Walt Disney World, celebrating the ecumenical diversity of the family of God with 2,000 multidenominational students.

After the attacks on September 11, 2001, John Derrick of CBF, knowing that the traditional themes of peace, love, joy and hope had in that instant taken on a new meaning, voiced a wish that someone could create new devotions for the coming Advent season. Passport quickly assembled a team and, in just 28 days, created an online devotional website, d365.org, to help youth find a place of holy refuge and comfort. From that humble beginning, d365 now logs more than two million visitors annually. It is produced by Passport and sponsored by CBF, the Episcopal Church and the Presbyterian Church (USA).

Now, some two decades later, our young Passport campers have grown up. More than 1,000 churches have joined us, volunteering more than one million mission service hours. As of this writing, Passport has trained 608 summer staffers who have invested more than 900,000 discipleship hours into the lives of 100,000 children and youth. One in three of those summer staffers are now serving in ministry, and more than half of those ministers are women.

Those former campers, turned staffers and now ministers, are leading the next generation of Cooperative Baptists, far beyond the borders of Florida. They are serving at every level of church ministry, in CBF state and national leadership, and as CBF field personnel. They are sitting on committees in CBF churches (hiring women pastors) and serving as thoughtful Christians in an increasingly complicated world.

Passport has chosen to be a life partner with CBF from its inception, trying to make sure that whoever wants to participate with us is welcome. We are looking forward to future possibilities of creative partnerships as we continue growing old together.

Colleen Walker Burroughs is co-founder and Vice President of Passport, Inc., and served as Moderator of the Cooperative Baptist Fellowship from 2012-2013. She and her husband, David, are parents to twins, Milligan and Walker.

The Whitsitt Society: Celebrating Baptist Courage

By Doug Weaver

The William H. Whitsitt Baptist Heritage Society was born in 1992 out of the debris of the Southern Baptist Convention controversy. On October 9, 1992, respected Baptist historian Walter Shurden hosted a gathering of concerned Baptists at Mercer University to discuss the preservation of historic Baptist identity and the accurate telling of recent Baptist events. At the conference—"The History of the Moderate Movement"—those present developed an energy and enthusiasm for the creation of a heritage society that would honor and promote historic commitments such as soul freedom, separation of church and state, local church autonomy, and resistance to the creedalism that had become so evident in SBC circles.

Conference attendees, who included both clergy and laity, were regarded as charter members of the society. They declared their purpose to be "fostering the study of the Baptist heritage and raising consciousness of Baptists by honoring, preserving and affirming a treasured and threatened heritage." The Society was named after William H. Whitsitt, the Baptist seminary president who was forced out of his position in 1899 after courageously defending his research that Baptists originated in the 17th century, even though most Baptists traced Baptist history back to the New Testament.

As a heritage society, the Whitsitt Society was not intended to be an organization for historians but for all concerned Baptists. The election of a journalist, Walker Knight, as the society's first president reflected this vision. Key players in the early years were Knight, Shurden and Loyd Allen. In 1996, Allen, a professor of church history and spiritual formation at Mercer's McAfee School of Theology, became Executive Director and Treasurer. Two years later, in 1998, I was named Editor of *The Whitsitt Journal*, which Knight had edited its first four years. Allen and I would remain in these positions for the rest of the society's history.

The Whitsitt Society developed a Board of Directors and elected annual presidents who reflected the deep riches of recent Baptist heritage and the promise of broader and more inclusive leadership in the future. Presidents included a roll call of Baptist movers and shakers: Loyd Allen, Carolyn Blevins, James Dunn, Pam Durso, John Finley, Kirby Godsey, Glenn Hinson, Fisher Humphreys, Marv Knox, Bill Leonard, June McEwen, Suzii Paynter, John Pierce, Robert Nash, Melissa Rogers and Walter Shurden. In its later years, the Whitsitt Society incorporated younger Baptists like Bruce Gourley, Julie Whidden Long and Aaron Weaver in its planning.

Board meetings were held annually at the home of Walter and Kay Shurden in Macon, Georgia. For me, sitting in a living room with executive board members Walter Shurden, Loyd Allen and Rob Nash, along with other Baptists like James Dunn, Suzii Paynter and John Pierce, was reason to believe the heritage would not only survive but would flourish.

While the Whitsitt Society was always an autonomous organization, most of its supporters were deeply invested in the Cooperative Baptist Fellowship. Annual meetings were held in conjunction with the CBF General Assembly and included presentation of a Courage Award and a Penrose St. Amant-endowed lecture. In the early years of the Fellowship, the Whitsitt Society's program was one of the most well-attended meetings at the annual General Assembly.

In 2001, the theme of the Whitsitt Society's meeting was "A Decade of Destiny: Ten Years of the CBF." In addition to written reflections by CBF pioneers Cecil Sherman and Keith Parks, Walter Shurden presented an important address titled "Six Words for the First Ten Years of CBF."

In response to the calls that CBF had not defined itself adequately, Shurden reminded the audience that the Fellowship had always been committed to diversity. Its reasons for formation were diverse: the need for a new missions outlet and new theological education options, the preservation of Baptist distinctives, and the need for greater engagement in justice issues and providing religious liberty for all. Shurden noted that the Fellowship partnered with the Baptist Joint Committee for Religious Liberty (and others) and encouraged shared leadership, both male and female and laity and clergy.

"We are Baptists who have resisted thus far a tightly drawn doctrinal or ethical statement," he said. "[And we] are Baptists who want to honor the self-government of congregations." Shurden challenged the room full of Cooperative Baptists to even greater study of the Bible and to more ecumenical activity.

The most distinctive element of the Whitsitt Society's ministry was its annual presentation of a Courage Award to Baptists who had demonstrated unusual courage of conscience. Coined by Shurden, the motto of the award was: "Whitsitt's name and this award stand as monuments to Baptist bravery of Baptist individuals who have lived out the gospel ideals of freedom and faith in the face of any and all would-be tyrannies."

Since the society emerged in the aftermath of denominational controversy, award recipients naturally included some Baptists who were heavily involved in the Baptist battles: Ralph Elliott (1994), Cecil Sherman (1996), Ken Chafin (1998), James Dunn (2000) and Jimmy Allen (2005). Many of the recipients provided important leadership in CBF (Sherman, CBF's founding Coordinator) or among its partners (Dunn, Executive Director of the Baptist Joint Committee, and Kirby Godsey, President of Mercer University).

President Jimmy Carter was honored with the Courage Award during a plenary session of the 2001 General Assembly in Atlanta. Shurden, who received the Courage Award in 2009, was a key figure in the Fellowship's founding. In 1991 he delivered the "Address to the Public," which outlined the reasons and commitments of the newly formed Fellowship and graced CBF with the language and exposition of the "Four Fragile Freedoms" (soul freedom, Bible freedom, church freedom, religious freedom) that still anchor the identity of Cooperative Baptists.

The Whitsitt Society's goal was never to be a new "historical commission" for Cooperative Baptists, but to be a voice that acknowledged and honored the wider "treasured" yet "threatened" heritage of Baptists as a guide for the future. African American Baptists who played key roles in the Civil Rights Movement were honored with the Courage Award: John Porter (1999) and Fred Shuttlesworth (2008). Women were also honored for their courage, including Carolyn Weatherford Crumpler (2010), Molly Marshall (2004) and Lauran Bethell (2007).

The presentation of the Courage Award often offered a progressive voice to Fellowship audiences. Programs highlighting the contributions of Porter and Shuttlesworth focused on Baptists and race relations. Social justice was emphasized with Bethell's ministry combating sex trafficking. Other programs honored ethicist Henlee Barnette (1997; speech by Ken Sehested of the Baptist Peace Fellowship) and social gospel proponent Walter Rauschenbusch (2003; speech by activist Tony Campolo).

Recipients of the Courage Award affirmed but often challenged Cooperative Baptists.

"The goal of gender-inclusive, multicultural churches, schools and communities is worthy of intentional pursuit . . . for of such is the reign of God," exhorted Molly Marshall, president of Central Baptist Theological Seminary in Shawnee, Kansas.

Glenn Hinson, professor at Baptist Theological Seminary at Richmond, used blunt language to caution against complacency: "The Baptist tradition may not survive among people called Baptist but may live more vitally among people who do not bear the name because that tradition of the voluntary principle in religion has been of God."

The Whitsitt Society's most eye-opening program occurred in 1995, when the well-known civil rights activist Will Campbell urged the audience to act on the radical possibilities of Baptist identity. Speaking to the largest crowd ever at a society meeting, Campbell said that Baptists no longer followed Jesus the radical. Asked to speak on the struggle of personal soul freedom, he bluntly declared that institutions were evil and were the death of soul freedom. Campbell asked what Baptists had done to advocate for women who were seeking equality, and what had they done to side with conscientious objectors in the 1960s. Baptists will apologize to them one day, he said.

"We joined the Civil Rights Movement when the prophets were safely dead," Campbell said, poking again at his audience when he said that Baptists will also one day apologize for their homophobia.

Year-in and year-out, the meeting of the Whitsitt Society prodded audiences to remember their historic heritage but never to be satisfied with the status quo as they sought to be free and faithful to a radical gospel. Whitsitt meetings presented an audacious Baptist identity to CBF listeners, from Campbell to Barnette (both called heretics for believing the Word of God) to Dunn (who claimed he was not courageous but stubborn).

"Never in the Baptist wars of the past 20 years did I consider courage, risk, daring or danger, not for a minute," Dunn proclaimed upon receiving the society's Courage Award. "I'll be jiggered if a batch of neo-pharisaical, power-mad politicians, frazzling fundamentalists trapped in a truncated theology, were going to redefine religious liberty."

Just one year prior to his retirement, in 2011, Daniel Vestal, CBF's Executive Coordinator from 1996-2012, received the Whitsitt Society's Courage Award, a fitting honor as the Fellowship celebrated its

20th anniversary. The following year, in 2012, the society ceased active operations. The Whitsitt Society gave endowed monies to *Baptists Today* to continue the society's legacy through annual articles in its news journal, written especially by younger Baptists, on Baptist principles, with an emphasis on freedom of conscience.

Baptist courage is alive and well.

Doug Weaver serves as Professor of Religion and Director of Undergraduate Studies in the Department of Religion at Baylor University. He also directs Baylor's J.M. Dawson Institute of Church-State Studies.

CBF and BJC: Partners for Religious Liberty

By J. Brent Walker

The ministry of the Cooperative Baptist Fellowship and the mission of the Baptist Joint Committee for Religious Liberty (BJC) have been inextricably linked over the past 25 years.

The BJC, in a real sense, has been the face of CBF in the nation's capital. We continue to provide expression to the Fellowship's embrace of the crucial Baptist distinctives of soul freedom and religious liberty for all, as well as the constitutional separation of church and state.

This partnership began in the summer of 1990 when the Southern Baptist Convention consummated its effort to emasculate the BJC by massively defunding the BJC's annual budget. In August of that same summer, other disaffected Southern Baptist exiles assembled in Atlanta, a conclave that would later blossom into CBF.

Initially, the BJC/CBF partnership involved mutual wound-licking, but it soon turned to matters fiscal. With the BJC's annual budget cut in half, then BJC Executive Director James Dunn scrambled to right the BJC's financial position. In the Fellowship's fragile infancy, it made funding the BJC a priority, restoring a healthy percentage of the approximate $400,000 loss.

Yes, others helped, too: individual friends, churches, state conventions and other Baptist bodies. But CBF's rescue effort was pivotal. Over the years, because of the firm footing CBF provided, the BJC has been able to rely less on the financial support of our 15 Baptist bodies and has focused on building an ever stronger, more diversified base of support.

This initial coming together of the BJC and CBF, based on shared grief and fiscal exigency, has blossomed into an affectionate, mutually beneficial, bilateral partnership focused on Baptist distinctives and the fight for religious freedom for all of God's children.

When CBF held the 1991 Convocation in Atlanta, the BJC started a new gathering in conjunction with it. Today, our annual Religious Liberty Council Luncheon has grown to become a marquee event at the annual General Assembly, bringing together more than 600 religious liberty supporters from across the country.

In 1996, the generous support and partnership of the Christian Education Mission Group of CBF allowed the BJC to publish *Citizens of Two Kingdoms: Lessons for Youth in Baptist History and Religious Liberty*—a curriculum tailored for use in the local church. This resource was a widely distributed and wildly popular effort to teach and train the next generation of religious liberty advocates.

The BJC/CBF partnership includes Cooperative Baptists on the BJC Board. In 2005, Kay Shurden and Pam Durso joined, providing a CBF voice and establishing a personal link between the two bodies. Today, Pam Durso, David Cooke and Suzii Paynter are BJC Board members.

Incarnational participation goes both ways. The BJC's General Counsel, Holly Hollman, served on the Fellowship's highly successful 2012 Task Force, whose work has and will continue to inform CBF's identity and mission.

CBF's Advocacy in Action conference is another example of collaboration between our organizations. Stephen Reeves, a former BJC staff member now on the CBF staff, brings laity and clergy to Washington, D.C., to explore advocacy as a faithful expression of Christian mission and to learn how to be effective advocates. As part of that journey, participants have the opportunity to visit the BJC to learn about religious liberty, church-state separation and our advocacy efforts.

Finally, the Fellowship's core mission as a "denomi-network" is to serve local churches. The BJC is similarly committed, providing helpful information on our website and serving as a resource for pastors, laypeople, and both local and national CBF bodies when religious liberty questions arise. Speaking, teaching and rendering legal advice on current church-state issues are key elements of the BJC's work. Recent events include Holly Hollman's meeting with a group of pastors in Georgia about a troubling bill in the state legislature, Staff Counsel Jennifer Hawks' presentation on current issues to a CBF of North Carolina group visiting Colonial Williamsburg, and my participation in the 2016 CBF of Arkansas meeting. Dozens of churches and ministerial groups also visit our offices each year.

Many challenges to religious liberty continue to arise. The commitment of CBF and BJC to religious liberty and education are shaping a new generation of Baptists who can continue to stand up for this Baptist distinctive, as well as for the rights of their neighbors. We relish this partnership to promote religious liberty that I pray will be as vital and integral to both bodies 25 years hence as it is today.

J. Brent Walker is Executive Director of the Baptist Joint Committee for Religious Liberty. He is a member of the Supreme Court Bar and an ordained minister. Published widely, he routinely speaks in churches, educational institutions and denominational gatherings and provides commentary on church-state issues in the national media.

BJC: Religious Liberty and the Next Generation

Charles Watson, Jr.

What do you mean Baptist ministers were once thrown in prison in this country for preaching without a license? Why does the Baptist Joint Committee care about the rights of a Muslim prisoner? So, your organization *really* doesn't protect your own beliefs over the beliefs of other religions? You *actually* fight for their rights just as much as you do your own?

These are just a few of the questions I have been asked in my time as the Education and Outreach Specialist for the Baptist Joint Committee for Religious Liberty (BJC) in Washington, D.C. With each question, I see students, congregants and clergy wrestle with the idea of religious freedom and what "separation of church and state" means. It is a special pleasure to watch people learn about the history of Baptists in this country and our forebears' struggle for religious liberty. These revelations can impact someone's life, creating a new sense of Baptist connection and commitment to make sure our heritage is protected. I know how it feels; it is how I was introduced to the work of the BJC, and it is why I am proud to work there today.

For 80 years, the BJC has fought to uphold the historic Baptist principle of religious freedom. We engage in various arenas to defend and extend religious liberty for all people. These arenas include the courts, Congress and the executive branch of the federal government. Of course, our work does not end in the marble halls of government buildings in Washington; it extends through our efforts in educating others and equipping advocates to stand up in their communities and raise their voices to protect this freedom. The BJC's education efforts are at the core of our everyday activities, where we provide resources and opportunities for each generation of advocates. For 25 years, the Cooperative Baptist Fellowship has been a linchpin of this work.

Religious liberty is always only one generation away from extinction. Protecting it demands the utmost vigilance, including a targeted approach to the education of young people.

At the BJC, one of my tasks is to cultivate the same level of commitment to our mission in the next generation as was exhibited by previous generations of advocates. Fortunately, through its churches, universities and seminaries, CBF has provided the BJC with fertile grounds in which to nourish the seed of religious liberty. Not only does the Fellowship undergird our work, but it provides a vital connection with advocates who want to deepen their understanding of religious liberty and learn how they can make a greater impact on the world around us.

The BJC understands that our high expectations for the next generation must be matched with new ways of reaching them. With the opening of our Center for Religious Liberty on Capitol Hill in 2012, our capabilities for religious liberty education increased dramatically. We now host groups who visit Washington, D.C., in our own state-of-the-art facility. Since we opened the Center, hundreds of individuals connected to CBF churches and partner seminaries and divinity schools have visited for educational programs.

One of our most distinct educational partnerships comes with CBF's Advocacy in Action conference. Each year, CBF organizes a trip to Washington, D.C., to allow Cooperative Baptists a chance to explore advocacy as a faithful expression of Christian mission. While the participants of Advocacy in Action are developing a biblical basis for advocacy and learning how to be effective, they meet with members of Congress and with CBF partners that are actively involved in the work, including the BJC. This face-to-face time with Cooperative Baptists in various roles and from communities across the country allows us not only to help them understand this cause for which we fight each day, but also to provide a unique opportunity for them to engage our staff with questions and concerns. As they return to their communities, we know they are equipped to speak up and speak out for religious liberty in the historic Baptist tradition.

Our internship program has been an integral part of involving college students in our mission at the BJC. Each spring, summer and fall, the BJC offers internship positions to undergraduate and graduate students who want to work in our Washington, D.C. offices. The interns work alongside our legal, communications, education and development staff members to carry out the day-to-day mission of the BJC. They help us provide resources for our constituents while also developing skills that will aid them in their future careers. Our CBF connection increasingly provides us with quality applicants, raising the standards for our competitive internship program. We are proud that CBF has strong representation among the interns we have selected over the years. We have seen former interns go on to lead colleges, hold political office and work in CBF church and organizational positions.

Just as CBF is a part of our work at the Center for Religious Liberty, it impacts each of our educational programs outside of Washington, D.C. Our annual Religious Liberty Essay Scholarship Contest challenges high school juniors and seniors to research and evaluate a specific religious liberty issue. The contest allows the BJC to connect with students far and wide while providing them the opportunity to write on a subject with which they may or may not be familiar and challenging them to think deeply and intentionally about what religious freedom truly means. Hundreds of students submit entries each year. This high level of participation is thanks in large part to CBF regional and state organizations that promote the contest online and through their newsletters or magazines. We strive to give our partners ways in which they can provide students opportunities to learn more about the issues that impact our country every day. The essay contest continues to be one of our strongest connections to the next generation.

The BJC also reaches future advocates with various lecture programs, including our annual Walter B. and Kay W. Shurden Lectures on Religious Liberty and Separation of Church and State. The event brings a speaker to a university, law school or seminary campus who can inspire and call others to an ardent commitment to religious freedom. The Shurden Lectures have been hosted by five CBF partner schools and have enriched future Fellowship leaders with a robust understanding of religious liberty and why its continuation is crucial.

Our education efforts with the next generation achieve a deeper level with our BJC Fellows Program. Launched in 2015, this initiative provides young professionals with an opportunity to build their historical, theological and legal understanding of religious liberty and to develop skills to advocate for the cause throughout their careers. BJC Fellows are selected each year to attend an intensive multi-day seminar in Colonial Williamsburg which gives them the tools they need for public engagement. The program creates a network of leaders who can work independently for religious liberty in their communities and who can serve as liaisons to our work in Washington. The BJC Fellows do not have to be Baptist or even Christian, but they must be committed to the cause of religious freedom for all people. We are pleased that several of our inaugural fellows were connected to CBF churches or to CBF partner schools.

As a person of faith, I see these educational programs as more than just ways to promote the BJC. They speak to the well-being of our society. It is not about my faith versus someone else's faith. It is about "justice" for my faith and "justice" for the thoughts and freedom of conscience for those who think and believe differently from me. Religious liberty is a social justice issue. In many of the next-generation advocates I meet, a passion for justice and freedom is not something we have to create. It already exists.

Our goal is to engage the energy and passion for justice of younger generations and unite it with the enduring heritage of religious liberty. I believe wholeheartedly that the result of this union will be the empowerment of future advocates in our churches, our courts, our community and our government, ensuring that the Baptist tradition of religious freedom continues today and tomorrow.

I know the result of this union because it is my own story. I was once one of those students hearing about the BJC for the first time during a class at Mercer University's McAfee School of Theology through a presentation by BJC General Counsel Holly Hollman. I was inspired to ask the same questions that I now receive on a daily basis: "So, your organization *really* doesn't protect your own beliefs over the beliefs of other religions? You *actually* fight for their rights just as much as you do your own?"

I'm proud to answer those questions with a resounding, "Yes, our mission is to defend and extend God-given religious liberty for all!" The BJC's partnership with CBF gives me confidence that our answer will always be "yes," and that our mission will be successful for the next 25 years and beyond.

Charles Watson, Jr., is the Education and Outreach Specialist for the Baptist Joint Committee for Religious Liberty. His work is focused on expanding the base of support for religious liberty and engaging the next generation of advocates. A graduate of The Citadel, he earned a Master of Divinity degree at Mercer University's McAfee School of Theology.

Fellowship in Fes:
The Morocco Partnership

By Alice Wright Mull

We are sitting on a bench along the Avenue Hassam II, the main thoroughfare as you enter Fes. One of the four "imperial cities" of Morocco and at one time the capital, Fes is two cities in one—the Ville Nouvelle, the new modern city, and the old walled Medina, one of the best preserved in the Arab world. We are, of course, in the new city. We watch the city work crew as they remove the flags that have lined both sides of the boulevard. As an imperial city, Fes is often host to the king, who maintains a residence here as well as in the other three imperial cities—Meknes, Marrakesh and the current capital, Rabat.

Since the king's wife is from Fes, it's not surprising that he visits this city often. But when the king leaves, the flags must come down. However, this thoroughfare is not bereft of beauty. Along this magnificent entryway to the city are several reflecting pools and many gardens of flowers. They remain and decorate the city long after the king has returned to Rabat.

As we sit here in the early October afternoon, enjoying the sunshine and gentle breeze on our last day in Fes, my husband and I are approached by several children on their way back to school from their lunch break. They spot our camera and are eager to pose. Then, of course, they want to see themselves among the saved pictures in the camera. While enjoying the evening, our thoughts go back to the beginning of our visit to this country.

Our plane landed at the Casablanca airport. It was there that we met Cooperative Baptist field personnel David and Julie Brown, who first introduced us to Moroccan food (spicy and heavy on root vegetables, both delicious and filling). They also introduced us to the refugee ministry that would become an important part of the Cooperative Baptist Fellowship's presence in Morocco through the Kentucky Baptist Fellowship (KBF).

We went to Morocco for a special reason: to visit our partner church in Fes. It is among 10 churches that make up the EEAM—the Église Évangélique Au Maroc. This unique conglomerate of churches is the only Protestant group in Morocco that is recognized by the government. Because of this recognition, there is an unusual amount of freedom for the worshipers in this Islamic country—and also an unusual amount of freedom for us to visit and be involved with these congregations.

The EEAM was established in 1958 by the Reformed Church of France. Many Swiss, German, French and Scandinavian expatriates, as well as local Christians—mostly students from sub-Saharan Africa who traveled to the cities to study at universities—needed a church where their faith could be strengthened.

Our involvement began in August 2005, when the missions work group I chaired met at Georgetown College to consider our next step. Rhonda Abbott Blevins, then KBF's Missions Coordinator, pointed out that we had met all our immediate goals for mission and ministry and needed to look elsewhere. The result was a yearning for a global mission partnership. Of two suggested locations, Morocco quickly became our focus.

My church, Living Faith Baptist Fellowship in Elizabethtown, already had a partnership with Karen Smith. Her husband's family had settled in our county after years on the mission field, and when our new church began to look for a mission partner, Karen was our logical choice. The partnership with Karen resulted in Living Faith giving support to three of her projects: a wheelchair ministry in Fes, which matches donated wheelchairs to those who need them; the women of the small Berber community of Tarmilot, who learn to weave rugs and other products to sell while the men in the community are out shepherding their flocks; and the school for deaf children in Immouzer.

KBF contacted Karen and later sent a "discovery team" to Morocco to flesh out what a partnership in Morocco might look like. The result was partnerships between CBF churches in Kentucky and the churches of the EEAM, as well as with the Browns and others who worked with the refugees who came to Morocco from sub-Saharan Africa seeking to gain entrance into Europe and, they hoped, a better life.

Living Faith was partnered with the church in Fes, a congregation largely of students. We helped by sending money monthly to fund their pastor-in-training, by sharing worship experiences and by developing communication with their membership. Our purpose was not to build or paint; it was simply to get to know and understand the people and to establish friendships with them.

Our first full day in Fes, we gathered items we brought with us and walked the several blocks to the church. Our first task: help decorate the church for a wedding the next day! Taking direction from church members who had also come to decorate, we pitched in with our flowers and festoons to add color to the church walls and to prepare a floral archway through which the young couple would walk. Working together in this way gave us an opportunity to begin forming friendships. Although most church members were French-speaking, several spoke fluent English. We soon learned that some came from countries established by the French, and others from countries established by the British.

At the wedding the next evening, we were given a special place to observe—an anteroom opposite the altar. Since the service was in French, an interpreter helped us understand what was happening during the rather lengthy ceremony. The reception was held in the church courtyard, and we were amazed by the amount and variety of food and the pageantry of its presentation.

The pastor of the Fes church is Hans Lehmann, from Switzerland. He and his wife, Monique, are a delightful and energetic couple. Their love for the church was evident; they spoke fluent English, and so both could speak to the congregation in French and interpret for us. We were given the opportunity to participate in worship and, at the end of the service, we presented gifts to their congregation and received gifts to bring back to our congregation.

Since our visit to Morocco coincided with the waning days of Ramadan, Karen wanted us to experience *ftoor* (El Al-Fitr) in various settings. This is the feast that breaks the fast at the end of the day. Our *ftoors* included one with a wealthy family in their lovely and well-appointed apartment, and one where we sat on rugs on the floor of a hut, passing back and forth a sick, crying baby. We enjoyed variations of the same menu, and the hospitality was real. During these meals, as in every encounter with these new friends in Morocco, we recognized in them a passion to know us and to share a bit of themselves.

The participating Fellowship churches have been involved with their partner churches in Morocco in a variety of ways. KBF also sponsors activities to encourage interaction with all the congregations and the EEAM churches, and has intentionally tried to vary the ways in which we engage our relationship with the EEAM. One year, a group of KBF church choirs traveled to Morocco and met with members of the EEAM churches to perform concerts in the various partner churches. Another year, members of the EEAM churches came to Kentucky and joined with church choir members to present concerts to KBF churches, as well as to travel around the state to see the sights and enjoy a Labor Day picnic hosted by Living Faith. Another time, a group from Kentucky visited Al Akhawayn University in Ifrane to study Moroccan history, culture and customs. Many other groups have gone to build, teach and learn.

For me, for Living Faith and for KBF, Morocco is a laboratory where we can learn ways for Christians and Muslims to live side-by-side and enjoy participating with one another. As we watch our partner churches interact with their Muslim neighbors, we see ways in which we can interact with people of different faiths right here at home.

When departure day arrived, we had an assortment of memories to accompany us home: sheep nibbling at sparse grass along a rocky roadside; crowding onto a train for our return to Casablanca (and almost having to leave luggage on the train!); dodging laden donkeys that ambled through the market in the Medina; swatting at flies that alighted on dates that we anticipated seeing on the next day's *ftoor*; meeting and learning from Franciscan monks in Meknes; deaf children playing a game with the colorful parachute we had brought for them; treating the blisters on our feet resulting from a walk across the city to visit Hans and Monique for tea; and so many more.

As our plane bound for home soared above the airport at Casablanca, we could only reflect on our time in a culture so different from our own. Somehow we knew that our lives had been changed, our attitudes modified, our resolve solidified. Morocco crept inside our very beings and took a firm hold.

Alice Wright Mull is a retired high school English teacher and member of Living Faith Baptist Fellowship in Elizabethtown, Kentucky. An active lay leader in the Kentucky Baptist Fellowship, she currently serves on the Cooperative Baptist Fellowship Missions Council.

A New Way to be Baptist in the Palmetto State

By Marion D. Aldridge

The transition years from the late 20th to the early 21st centuries were exhilarating years in which to be alive. The ether was bombarded with electronic messages: emails, Internet and Wi-Fi. Change charged the atmosphere, literally and spiritually.

The ecclesiastical world in which I was immersed was equally electrified. Some Christians were (and are) dismayed by the changes and have been unable or unwilling to keep up. Others embraced new realities—and thrived.

When I was a teenager, no one in my world considered global warming, universal health care or predatory lending. There was no conversation anywhere about same-sex couples getting married. Baptists in the South avoided and resisted cultural transformation at every turn. Our track record on racism and sexism was shameful. Prophetic voices were ignored or marginalized.

Thank God for a new way to be Baptist!

"*The times*," as Bob Dylan sang, "*they are a-changin'.*"

For the past 25 years, change has occurred everywhere in every endeavor. The printing industry was permanently altered as newspapers and magazines died and Internet communication flourished. Far more couples nowadays meet via online dating sites than in person.

As the Coordinator of the Cooperative Baptist Fellowship of South Carolina from 1998 to 2013, I spent enormous energy attempting to convince many older church members that next year was not 1954. Rather than buying additional Yellow Pages advertisements, their churches needed to develop an online presence. Pastors and laity needed to make use of Facebook, Pinterest and YouTube for the glory of God. Many Christians began to give their tithes through PayPal rather than in the offering plate. Some church members now bring a Bible app on their iPhone or iPad to worship rather than a leather-covered Bible.

The Cooperative Baptist Fellowship was birthed in 1991 in the midst of seismic cultural and religious shifts. Women, excluded from leadership in Baptist churches and denominational structures, took on increasingly significant roles within CBF, serving as pastors, chaplains and even as the chief executive of our national organization. My pastor is female, and two other CBF churches in Columbia, South Carolina, have female pastors. All five local CBF churches have ordained women on their ministerial staffs.

During these transitional decades, we learned to listen, and we heard new voices. We discovered that previously disregarded members of churches had much to contribute to the body of Christ. A typical denominational power structure in Baptist life once consisted primarily of white male pastor-preachers, with a modest sprinkling of pastors' wives, and a few wealthy laymen serving on boards. As the Fellowship formed, not only were women and laity empowered, but also chaplains and ministers of music, education and youth. Divorced people were allowed the opportunity to serve. Young adults who had not yet earned their ecclesiastical stripes moved into positions of responsibility. Service became more important than power.

We witnessed a quiet revolution. It was a new day. Creativity and energy flowed. We made false starts. The Spirit of God flowed mightily and haphazardly, as winds always do. Sometimes we caught the breeze and soared. Other times our organizational kite crashed. We were allowed to make mistakes because CBF owned nothing. Great institutions with millions of dollars of assets were not at stake. The era was a gift from God. It was new wine and new wineskins.

Fresh terms floated around. What exactly did post-denominational mean? Nobody could point to the words *denomination, convention, resolutions* or *boards* in the Bible. Partnership rather than ownership became the Fellowship's model.

Innovative Baptist seminaries sprang up. In South Carolina, we teamed with Lutheran Theological Southern Seminary, a venerable local institution, to create a Baptist House of Studies on its campus. The theological cross-fertilization between Baptists and Lutherans was good for both.

Mission work had always been a source of pride for Baptists, even when we did it wrong. For decades our emphasis was on telling, proclaiming, preaching, exhorting, training and educating. We were rich with the Spirit of God and biblical knowledge and assumed all others were deficient. I remember no lessons as a child, adolescent or young adult about listening to the world or humbly allowing ourselves to learn from others.

The conversation and information flowed in only one direction. We invited strangers into our facilities, but we weren't likely to venture too deeply into their unsanitized, messy and dangerous world. Debbie Dantzler, who served a term as Moderator of CBF of South Carolina, said, "When we were younger, we proved we were good Christians by going to Baptist meetings and inviting people to Baptist meetings."

Jesus told us to demonstrate our compassion not by attending meetings, but by being helpful to those in need—the hungry, the cold, the joyless and the friendless. The task, as CBF reframed its understanding of a faithful Christian journey, was to use fewer words and let our actions define our witness as the presence of Christ in the world.

Our research at CBF of South Carolina showed the largest concentration of child poverty in our state was in and around the Union Heights neighborhood of North Charleston. We assigned two ministers, Bill Stanfield and Evelyn Oliveira, to represent us in ministry there. We asked them to listen to their neighbors for a year—to stand on street corners, ride the buses, go to city council meetings, and listen to pastors and social workers already ministering there.

Out of that initiative, Metanoia was born. Metanoia is a Greek word that means "pushing forward for positive change." The Metanoia work began ministries that helped community members by offering after-school and summer educational opportunities for children. Metanoia quickly outgrew our ability to provide for all its needs. After a few years, we blessed their independence, while continuing to support them with a significant baseline contribution each year. That's a new model. Metanoia's budget is now several times larger than that of CBF of South Carolina.

Simultaneous to the birth of Metanoia, another gigantic shift in missions occurred. Individuals and churches wanted to do mission work themselves rather than merely send others to act on their behalf. This was a positive instinct. Bill Stanfield and the staff of Metanoia helped CBF of South Carolina congregations understand right and wrong ways to be involved in mission trips. There is such a thing as toxic charity. We learned that speaking and acting from a position of assumed superiority is counterproductive to being the presence of Christ.

Baptists in South Carolina had, for half a century, been part of the ecumenical movement through the work of the South Carolina Christian Action Council. What is known as ecumenism—working together for Christian unity and cooperating for the common good—morphed to include interfaith relationships with Muslims, Buddhists and Hindus. With a desire to learn about people who believe differently than we do, we began to understand and celebrate those distinctions. During an era in which many Christians are most concerned about who their enemies are, it has been rewarding to be part of a movement that values expanding our friendships. The Christian Action Council also shares CBF's emphasis on justice and advocacy. We are pleased that Brenda Kneece, a Cooperative Baptist, is this valuable statewide organization's executive minister, a post she has held for 15 years.

No change in Baptist life has been more important than our rediscovery of grace. The need for mercy has always been foundational in the Christian faith. Many Baptists had begun to emphasize law, doctrine or "fundamentals" over grace. You might hear someone say, "I believe in grace, but . . . " Whatever words that came after "but" created problems for grace-oriented and freedom-loving Baptists.

Those of us in CBF discovered the Bible is a bigger book than we had known previously. We discovered God is bigger than we had imagined or acknowledged. God's love and grace know no boundaries.

Marion D. Aldridge served as Coordinator for the Cooperative Baptist Fellowship of South Carolina from 1998 to 2013. He is a preacher, speaker, workshop leader and award-winning writer. He received his Doctor of Philosophy degree from Southern Baptist Theological Seminary in Louisville, Kentucky.

Forming the Fellowship in the Sunshine State

By Carolyn C. Anderson

My husband, Pat, and I worked together to help create the Cooperative Baptist Fellowship of Florida, first as volunteers and later as paid staff. Before the Fellowship, we both had served as vice presidents of the Florida Baptist Convention and on the Florida Baptist Convention's State Board of Missions. We joined the effort to elect Daniel Vestal as president of the Southern Baptist Convention in 1990, the last organized attempt to stop the fundamentalist takeover of the SBC, so we *knew* moderate Baptists in Florida. When that effort failed and the Cooperative Baptist Fellowship began to develop, Pat, Jack Snell and Peggy Pemble served on the founding CBF Coordinating Council as representatives from Florida.

CBF of Florida had a simple beginning: a typewriter, a copier, a fax machine and a phone line, all located in an extra bedroom in our home. Our early financial system consisted of three-by-five index cards on which I posted donations with the donor's name and contact information on the front and the contribution information on the back. Later, Phoebe Delamarter became our financial secretary and immediately put our financial information into a program on our first computer—a Commodore 20.

After Hurricane Andrew hit South Florida on August 24, 1992, our office managed the money contributed to help with the recovery. Then in 1993, when the first Passport Camp was held in Florida, Phoebe agreed to provide accounting help for them. We soon outgrew our spare bedroom and moved into an apartment in our backyard. This would be our office home until 2001, when at last the Florida Fellowship had a home of its own.

From the beginning, Cooperative Baptists in Florida have been passionate about missions and eager to reach out and be the presence of Christ in our local communities, our state, our nation and the world. Virtually everything thing we have done and every dollar we have spent has been for the cause of missions. Our first missions offering, called "Keeping the Promises," provided resources for the defunded seminary in Rüschlikon, Switzerland. Our offering total was $110,000.

In 1992, Hurricane Andrew devastated the entire southern tip of Florida, hitting the migrant communities in Homestead especially hard. We realized that many poor persons, especially in the migrant farm labor communities, were in fact an "unreached people group." The response to our appeal for help from our partner churches and individuals was overwhelming and resulted in many truckloads of goods collected and delivered to these residents. For two years, we coordinated an extensive effort by volunteers to rebuild homes and lives. In Atlanta, the Global Missions office of the Cooperative Baptist Fellowship appointed David and Tracy Bengtson to serve as directors of the work. After surveying the situation, they concluded that this needed to be a permanent, long-term ministry, which would require a building space. CBF of Florida developed a partnership with CBF whereby Florida would build a building for the ministry, and CBF Global Missions would provide the professional personnel. CBF of Florida purchased a five-acre parcel of land for a building which CBF field personnel had requested.

We raised the $75,000 purchase price that year. Together, we issued a call for volunteers to help build the center in West Homestead. John and Christine Smith joined the effort full time after spending weeks as volunteers to provide extra hands in the ministry and so that John, a retired construction boss, could provide oversight to the hundreds of volunteers building the center. After some years, the Bengtsons were reassigned and other field personnel came, bringing the unique gifts needed at the time. When the building was completed and dedicated, a partnership was created with Open House Health Center, a nonprofit organization, to provide free medical care to uninsured low-income persons. Several other ministries comprised what became known as Open House Ministries, which continues to be a vital ministry.

This multi-year project was simply a warm-up for the next one. Keith Blakely, pastor of Miami's Central Baptist Church, approached CBF Global Missions about appointing personnel to work with his church in its ministries to the homeless community in downtown Miami. CBF field personnel Butch and Nell Green were named to serve alongside the church congregation. CBF of Florida was part of this partnership, with Pat serving on the board. The Greens expanded the scope of the ministry greatly and approached CBF of Florida with the need to provide new facilities to house these growing ministries. Again, CBF of Florida responded by purchasing a building at a cost of $550,000. Pat helped lead the fundraising effort to purchase the building, along with a large team of volunteers.

When the Greens were reassigned, Larry and Laquita Wynn became the new directors. Steven Porter, who now serves as Coordinator of Global Missions, joined the team, and Touching Miami with Love became a flagship missions program in the inner city.

When the Wynns resigned in 2002, Steven agreed to serve as director. He refined the ministry to include a stronger focus on children, youth and families. Eventually, a new site was found in the nearby neighborhood of Overtown. A former post office facility was renovated with volunteer labor, and Steven and the growing staff settled in to build stronger ties to the families in the neighborhood.

When Steven resigned to return to graduate school in 2005, new missions personnel were once again appointed, with Angel and Jason Pittman selected to serve as leaders of the Touching Miami with Love ministry. Open House Ministries and Touching Miami with Love have been premier examples of CBF's vision of creating partnerships to do missions. Today, these two ministries serve under a new umbrella structure, with Jason as the Executive Director overseeing the work of both sites.

"T" and Kathy Thomas joined the Florida staff in 2001 after having served as field personnel among the Roma in Europe, where T had started churches. T's focus was to continue the work of engaging Florida in missions locally and around the world, to facilitate church starting, and to represent the Fellowship in local congregations. In the fall of 2003, T and Kathy left Florida to serve with the Cooperating Baptist Fellowship of Oklahoma.

After 12 years as Florida's coordinator, Pat was asked to become the Missions Advocate for CBF Global Missions beginning in January 2003. After a period as the acting CBF of Florida Coordinator, in March 2003 I was asked to become the second Coordinator for the Florida Fellowship.

Throughout our history, missions has been the heartbeat of the Florida Fellowship. We became a thriving group of individuals and churches partnering together to offer opportunities for missions, education and fellowship, and to provide a place at the table for all members—male and female, clergy and laity. As we saw the mission fields in our own state, especially in Miami-Dade County, we began to plan and prepare for the day when we could begin to do work in Cuba.

One of my first tasks as acting coordinator in 2003 was to enlist Lucile and Richard Smith, who had worked as volunteers through the years, to serve as the Interim Directors of Open House Ministries. Wanda Ashworth was invited to be the new Director in 2004, with Leah Crowley joining her as the Assistant Director. One of my final acts as Coordinator was to request CBF Global Missions to commission Wanda as field personnel and to assume the support and supervision of her ministry.

In 2004, with our staff reduced due to relocations and resignations, the past moderators and other key leaders gathered to evaluate our priorities and to focus on the future of the Florida Fellowship. Their vision and commitment set the tone for the task of identifying goals and restructuring the organization.

By the end of 2004, we had sold the old Touching Miami with Love property, paid off the mortgage on the new facility, provided funds to renovate the new property, paid off the state office property in Lakeland, and replenished our reserve accounts. The amazing news is that all properties owned by the Florida Fellowship are debt-free, and the ministries are flourishing. Thanks be to God!

During that same year, a group of youth ministers led by John Uldrich and Brett Foster planned and held the first state youth missions conference at College Park Baptist Church in Orlando. This initial event was funded by a grant from the Lilly Foundation. Our state missions offering—"Creating Places of Grace"—focused on funding church starts, supporting scholarships for theological students, and providing the operational costs for Open House Ministries and Touching Miami with Love.

This year of 2004 was a time of transition and challenge, not the least of which was having four hurricanes hit during the season. With help from across the Fellowship, we provided responses to these disasters, which struck from Fort Myers to Daytona Beach to Pensacola and Lakeland.

Tommy Deal became the Associate Coordinator in January 2005, and George Borders agreed to serve as the part-time administrator of the Cooperative Baptist Fellowship Foundation of Florida. They were welcome help, and both hit the ground ready to work on their first days. Tommy prepared himself as a disaster response person, organizing the Disaster Assistance Response Team and recruiting volunteers to prepare, purchase and stock response trailers.

That summer, the state was visited by three hurricanes. Once again, volunteers from across CBF poured in to help us. When Katrina hit in Alabama, Mississippi and Louisiana, we responded there as well.

A new ministry was created to provide pulpit supplies for our churches in the initial weeks following the resignation of a senior pastor. We also trained clergy to serve as intentional interims and provided resources for pastor search committees. Doran McCarty, a highly respected former professor at Golden Gate Seminary in San Francisco, stepped up to assist in the work by serving as a resource to local congregations in training and mentoring church start pastors.

Indigo Baptist Church contacted us in 2006 to let us know of its decision to disband. This congregation of faithful Baptists voted to share the proceeds from the sale of its facilities with several nonprofits, including the Florida Fellowship. Indigo Baptist's gifts to the CBF Foundation allowed us to create a Church Start Endowment that generates funds for the budget needed for new churches—a gift that truly keeps on giving.

At the time of my resignation as Coordinator, we had achieved several key objectives. We were debt-free, with fully funded reserves for maintaining properties. We had created a church start endowment and had approved a new strategic plan and goals. We had restructured the Representative Assembly and updated the constitution and by-laws, and we had fulfilled our commitments to church starts with France, Portugal and Spain.

Thanks be to God! What a Fellowship!

Carolyn C. Anderson co-founded the Cooperative Baptist Fellowship of Florida alongside her husband, Pat. She served as Volunteer Office Manager (1990-1992), Associate Coordinator (1992-2002) and Coordinator (2003-2006). She graduated from Florida Southern College and attended Southwestern Baptist Theological Seminary, and has served on the Board of Directors of Open House Ministries (2003-2009), Touching Miami with Love (2003-2006) and Passport Camps (1993-present).

Beloved Partnerships: CBF Arkansas and Arkansas Baptist College

By Ray Higgins

In January 2006, Arkansas Baptist College, in its 122nd year, was in crisis. Enrollment was under 175 students. Accreditation was tenuous. By one count, there were 26 boarded-up homes and 87 reported crimes in the area surrounding the school.

Then, the Board of Trustees hired a former college football coach with a doctorate in education to perform a miracle. Dr. O. Fitzgerald Hill believes that God performs miracles when there's a crisis.

Now, in 2015, the college's annual budget has grown from $1.5 million to more than $20 million. Student enrollment peaked at 1,100 students and has settled around 950 students. Condemned homes have been renovated. Abandoned properties have been purchased. Seven new buildings have been constructed. Historic Old Main is the new Old Main. A car wash was purchased for the business students to run under the name "AutoBaptism." A GED Center has been estab- lished, and a charter high school for underserved students has opened on campus. At the May 2015 commencement, 143 students—the largest graduating class in the school's history (and slightly fewer than the total number of students enrolled when Hill became president)— received associate and bachelor's degrees.

Since February 2008, the Cooperative Baptist Fellowship of Arkan- sas, Hill's first faith-based partner, has been witness to the amazing combination of his unique leadership and God's miracles.

Arkansas Baptist College is a historically black, four-year liberal arts college (HBCU) in Little Rock. It was founded in August 1884 by the Colored Baptists of the State of Arkansas at their annual conven- tion in Hot Springs. From its beginning, it was supported by black and white religious leaders. It opened as a ministers' institute in November 1884 at Mt. Zion Baptist Church in Little Rock. In 1885, the school was named Arkansas Baptist College. The same year a block of land was purchased where the first building, Old Main, now stands..

As the only black Baptist college west of the Mississippi River, it offers associate and bachelor's degrees in business administration, human services, criminal justice and religious studies. The college focuses on reaching students who are underserved. It is affiliated with the Consolidated Missionary Baptist State Convention of Arkansas and is accredited by the North Central Association of Colleges and Schools.

Dr. Fitz Hill became the 13th president in February 2006. Hill grew up in Arkadelphia, where he was elected class president at Arkadelphia High School. He graduated from Ouachita Baptist University with a double major in communications and physical education and was an All-American receiver on the Tigers football team. He earned his master's degree and began his football coaching career as a graduate assistant at Northwestern State University in Natchitoches, Louisiana.

For 12 years, he served on the University of Arkansas football coaching staff. With his wife, Cynthia, he also earned his doctorate in education. In his dissertation, he examined how race influences employment opportunities for African American football coaches at Division I-A colleges and universities. With the help of sports journalist Mark Purdy, he published his dissertation under the title *Crackback! How College Football Blindsides the Hopes of Black Coaches.* Along the way, he served in Operation Desert Storm and Desert Shield and was awarded the Bronze Star and Commendation Medal.

From 2001-2004, he was the head football coach for the San Jose State University Spartans, compiling a 14-33 record in spite of challenging obstacles. He later became a Director of Fundraising at Ouachita Baptist University, was co-founder of Life Champ Sports (a youth sports program), and served as a visiting scholar and research associate at the University of Central Florida.

CBF Arkansas' partnership with President Hill and Arkansas Baptist College began in March 2007 at a catfish lunch in the school's aging cafeteria. I was invited by the Rev. Geroy Osborne, pastor of the Mt. Zion Baptist Church in Little Rock (the church where the college began), to join a group of pastors to hear Hill's vision for the college.

From 1970 to 1988, Dr. Robert U. Ferguson, Sr., served as Director of Cooperative Ministries with National Baptists. He built warm and genuine relationships with black Baptist pastors and churches throughout the state, including the leadership at Arkansas Baptist College. Dr. Ferguson and his wife, Mary, were active members of Second Baptist Church in Little Rock, where I served as pastor for 10 years. In the early 1970s, Second Baptist began worshiping annually with Mt. Pleasant Missionary Baptist Church, an African American congregation with close ties to Arkansas Baptist College. Eventually, this event was expanded to include another African American church, Mt. Zion, where Arkansas Baptist College was started and whose pastor, Rev. Osborne, invited me to the catfish lunch.

Our family moved to Little Rock during the summer of 1994, when I began serving as pastor of Second Baptist. We decided to put our sons in the Dr. Martin Luther King Elementary School, which is located only four blocks north of the college. Our sons then attended Dunbar Middle School and Little Rock Central High School. For 14 years, our family was actively involved in the public schools that encircled the Arkansas Baptist College campus and neighborhood.

In August 2005, in response to Hurricane Katrina, I brought a retired friend from Second Baptist onto our CBF of Arkansas staff as Disaster Response Coordinator. Charles Ray not only led our disaster response efforts but became the United States Disaster Response Coordinator for the Cooperative Baptist Fellowship. As a young boy in the 1940s, he grew up three blocks from the campus. Over a 30-year period as a business entrepreneur, he had created and worked with a crew that renovated 13 historic homes in downtown Little Rock.

At the time, our office was located in an office building in affluent west Little Rock. Hearing Fitz Hill's vision for the college inspired me to organize a luncheon with our CBF partner pastors and lay leaders in Little Rock.

On one particular April day in 2007, Hill and Ray crawled through an abandoned, boarded up and condemned house one block north of the campus and six blocks south of the State Capitol. Ray told Hill that the house, a historic 1890s Queen Anne cottage with five different ornate tin ceilings, could and should be preserved. Hill went about raising the funds to purchase the house (and an adjoining vacant lot) and funding the renovation.

In August 2007, I invited our CBF Arkansas Coordinating Council to meet on the steps of the Queen Anne cottage, which was to be torn down soon. Hill met us there and shared his vision for the college and the neighborhood. We prayed for God's direction and went to a downtown church to discuss the decision. On a marker board, I wrote three reasons to move our office to Arkansas Baptist College, and four reasons not to move it. I began with the three reasons for the move, ending each point with the phrase: "This gives us the opportunity to walk the talk. We Baptists are good at talking the talk, but not as good at walking the talk. God is giving us a great opportunity to walk the talk." When I presented each of the four reasons not to move—reasons I had heard people express—one of the council members would say, "That's not a reason not to move."

The board voted enthusiastically to move our office onto the campus of Arkansas Baptist College. Renovation work began in October 2007, and we moved into our new office in February 2008. It was a decision that Hill continued to describe as "in flight" as opposed to "white flight" as he brought community leaders through our office to share his vision for the college and the neighborhood.

Our partnership was born out of a common identity, "Baptist," and the fact that Hill's vision matched CBF Arkansas' mission "to serve Christians and churches as they discover and fulfill their God-given mission."

Our first public event was the screening of the newly released documentary from the Baptist Center for Ethics titled "Beneath the Skin: Baptists and Racism." We sponsored a screening and forum at Second Baptist Church with a panel of community and ministry leaders, including Dr. Hill. At the end of that meeting, two individuals gave Dr. Hill and the college property that they owned. Another pastor, Dr. Randy Hyde, went back to his church, which voted to give the college $11,000 to buy a piece of property.

Because of this success, the CBF pastors and churches in Little Rock began hosting an annual People Relations Service. In February 2009, more than 300 people attended the first service hosted by Pulaski Heights Baptist Church and its pastor, Randy Hyde. An offering of $7,000 was given to the college. Each year since, a combination of white Baptist churches and black Baptist churches have hosted the service, which has brought Baptists in the city together to promote and support President Hill and Arkansas Baptist College. To date, more than $30,000, along with a lot of attention and goodwill, has been raised for the college.

In November 2008, CBF Arkansas was the catalyst for starting Sharefest, an annual effort to bring 100 churches in the city together on a Saturday in the fall to do works of service in neighborhoods. More than 300 volunteers showed up at Arkansas Baptist College on a Saturday morning in November to work on the campus and in the neighborhood. This now annual event has created hundreds of new ambassadors for Dr. Hill and the college.

From our almost eight-year partnership with the college, here are some of the fruits:

• Four condemned houses were renovated and put to use by the college, and 20 other properties were fixed up or demolished.

• Dr. Hill has served as the keynote speaker for CBF Arkansas' Annual Gathering, hosted CBF's national, state and regional coordinators on campus, spoken in CBF churches around the state and, during the All Church Challenge sponsored by Together for Hope Arkansas, served as a panelist at the New Baptist Covenant meeting in Oklahoma City. He also has led a CBF pastors retreat in Florida.

• Arkansas Baptist College's Director of Fine Arts, Rev. Henry Parker, and the college's choir have performed at CBF Arkansas Annual Gatherings and in partner churches.

• "Coach" Hill has led two football clinics in partnership with Together for Hope Louisiana, bringing the primarily black public high school and the primarily white private high school together for the first time in their histories.

• CBF Arkansas brought Millard Fuller, founder of Habitat for Humanity, to Little Rock to be the keynote speaker for our Annual Gathering and to discuss urban housing philosophy with Dr. Hill.

• Dr. Stan Wilson, pastor of CBF partner Providence Baptist Church in Little Rock and director of the pastoral care department at Baptist Health, teaches the senior seminar for religious studies majors and created a chaplain intern program for these students.

• For the past three years, CBF Arkansas has awarded a scholarship annually to a student at Arkansas Baptist College.

• CBF Arkansas has contributed $2,000 to the Delta Classic 4 Literacy, an event Hill created when he coached at San Jose State.

• CBF Arkansas has brought Hannah McMahan, Coordinator of the New Baptist Covenant, to Little Rock for our Annual Gathering and to discuss the NBC with Dr. Hill.

On a Thursday evening in late September 2012, Derek Olivier, 19, a freshman from New Iberia, Louisiana, and a cornerback on the college's football team, was fatally shot by an unknown assailant while helping a friend change a flat tire across the street from the campus— and one block behind our office. Hill responded by announcing the establishment of the Derek Olivier Research Institute for the Prevention of Black on Black Violence.

During the summer of 2015, Hill announced that the new director of the center would be a retired assistant police chief with more than 30 years of service with the Little Rock Police Department. While the office for the center is being finished, Eric Higgins has moved into the CBF Arkansas office to begin his promising work.

Every day for nearly eight years, we have been witnesses to a college, a president and students, with the odds stacked against them, who are "growing hope," which is the title of an Emmy Award-winning documentary on Hill's leadership. That phrase, along with "It's a GOoD Thing," defines his mission.

Ray Higgins serves as Coordinator for the Cooperative Baptist Fellowship of Arkansas. He has previously served as a senior pastor, seminary ethics professor, special projects coordinator and youth minister. A graduate of Southwestern Baptist Theological Seminary (Master of Divinity) and Baylor University (Doctor of Philosophy in Religion and Christian Ethics), he teaches undergraduate and graduate courses in ethics and ministry. Ray and his wife, Judy, have two adult sons and a daughter-in-law.

Enduring Disaster in Alabama

By Terri Byrd

"It's gone. It's all gone."

Those were the words that Wendell McGinnis spoke to his wife, Carol, on the phone during the evening of April 28, 2011, after surviving one of the deadly tornados that ripped through Alabama.

He had somehow survived after being picked up by the tornado and set back down in a field on his property, with the pieces of his home lying all around him. With clothing torn from the force of the tornado, Wendell walked half a mile to a neighbor's home to call Carol.

Wendell looked out across the empty lot where their home once stood. "We knew it was close but didn't realize it was headed our way," he said. "We are so blessed to be alive."

The tornadoes of April 2011 worked their way across Alabama, devastating multiple towns and cities and leaving cars upturned, homes flattened, and many people killed or injured. In response, First Baptist Church of Williams, Alabama, immediately opened its doors and became the center of calm and assistance in the midst of the storm in the community. Within the first few weeks, the church served more than 1,000 meals, helped people find temporary housing, handed out supplies to hundreds of families, and connected victims of the storms to services and resources.

At that time, I was serving as the Associate Coordinator for the Alabama Cooperative Baptist Fellowship. Part of my job was helping to coordinate the efforts for disaster response in our state. I was still sheltered in my own basement on April 28 when I received my first phone call from Charles Ray, the Disaster Response Coordinator for the Cooperative Baptist Fellowship. From that moment on, I knew that CBF would journey alongside us throughout the months to come. However, I didn't comprehend that the long-term recovery from the tornadoes would become my primary job for the next two years.

Our disaster response efforts grew to encompass multiple sites. Several churches and denominations joined together to work in McDonald's Chapel, an area in west Birmingham that lost more than 35 homes, many of them rental properties or homes that had little or no insurance. That coalition of churches and individuals built homes and worked out of the local community center for more than a year.

A small CBF church in Tuscaloosa, Woodland Forest Church, pastored by a feisty 60-year-old pastor, Mary An Wilson, became a source of meals, clothing, furniture and supplies for months after the storm. Years later, the clothing ministry continues as the church partners with county social services.

Over the next two years, First Baptist Church of Williams and the community transitioned from emergency relief and debris removal to long-term recovery, building more than a dozen homes for people with limited or no insurance. The focus of their mission transformed the church, and FBC Williams continues to work with the most neglected in the community and beyond.

Thankfully, the state of Alabama has not endured such widespread damage in the years since 2011. But those years taught us a lot about the tenacious and compassionate spirit of the people in our Alabama CBF churches. There is an enduring bond that now connects us as a group of people partnering together in the renewal of God's world.

I became the Coordinator of Alabama CBF in 2013 and have experienced the ongoing joy of working hand-in-hand with CBF and the people of our churches. But it was those days in 2011 that cemented my connection with the people and the work of Alabama CBF. In the midst of darkness and sorrow, we formed together to become a family grounded in the love of Christ, resilient and strong.

Although the McGinnis family lost most of their earthly possessions in the tornado, they found hope and comfort in their faith and the outpouring of love they received from their church family and their extended Alabama CBF family.

"You learn real fast what's important," said Wendell McGinnis. "Faith in God, family and our church sustained us."

Terri Byrd has served as the Coordinator for the Alabama Cooperative Baptist Fellowship since 2013. An ordained minister, she is a graduate of Beeson Divinity School at Samford University (Master of Theological Studies) and served as a minister on the staff of three different churches before joining Alabama CBF. She is married to Paul Byrd, a pediatric chaplain, and they are parents to two young adults, Turner and Evann.

Emily Holladay embraces the Baptist Women in Ministry tagline, "This is What a Preacher Looks Like," on her graduation day from CBF-partner school McAfee School of Theology at Mercer University in Atlanta.

Our stories of journey are unique. Each is different from the other. My story of journey is not your story, and your story is not my story. But our stories share one critical point of commonality and connection: CBF. It is at the Fellowship that our stories begin to come together.

I find parts of my own journey in the stories of my friends and colleagues on the pages that follow. In Julie Long's story, I find our shared commitment to a Baptist identity rooted in freedom, handed down from the saints among us as well as those no longer with us. In Emily Holladay's story, I'm reminded of the "L word"—liberal—and how it was used against my family, friends and the churches of my childhood. But I'm also reminded of how the *bad* gave way to *good*. The experience of *labels* led to an experience of *liberation*. And in the stories of Rachel Gunter Shapard and Joshua Hearne, I find our shared gospel commitment as Cooperative Baptists to cultivating beloved community and serving those on the margins.

Our stories of journey are the stories of the Cooperative Baptist Fellowship. —**Editor**

Claiming My Baptistness Through CBF

By Julie Whidden Long

When I was eight years old, I informed my parents that I was ready to join our Baptist church and be baptized. My mother encouraged me to go and talk to our pastor about my decision, to which I replied, "I don't need to go talk to the pastor. I know what I'm doing!"

My family has laughed about this story through the years. I'm sure it was not my parents' first clue that I would continue in the line of strong, independent women in my family, and I think my parents were embarrassed to tell the pastor that I planned to walk the aisle but refused to talk to him about it. But perhaps my first declaration of my desire to be a Baptist Christian was indeed appropriate.

While I doubt anyone had ever told me of the doctrine of the priesthood of all believers, or of the Baptist ideals of freedom of conscience, or of our history of rugged individualism, I evidently had absorbed that spirit somewhere along the way. Tucked into that independent decision about my own faith journey was a desire to embody those ideals in the church in which I was being raised. I like to think that my earliest Christian confession was deeply Baptist, for Baptists have always held these two things in tension—a strong conviction of individual freedom and a deep calling to work together, despite our differences.

I picked up by osmosis a few other convictions in my Baptist church. Even though I found myself bored by church conferences as a youth, I absorbed a preference for making decisions in a way that allows everyone to have a voice. As I wrestled with the place of prayer in public schools for a high school term paper, my pastor led me to understand that religious freedom for all persons was not in conflict with my Baptist Christian heritage. I picked up enough openness from my Sunday school teachers and youth leaders that my faith was not crushed when I went to college and was exposed to new methods of biblical interpretation. This was the kind of Baptist spirit that surrounded me in my upbringing—the kind of Baptistness that I have come to associate with Cooperative Baptists.

When I began college at Mercer University in the fall of 1998, I had never heard of the Cooperative Baptist Fellowship. I probably should have, because in 1991 my church split over the fundamentalist controversy in the Southern Baptist Convention, and a new CBF church began in my community as a result. As a middle-schooler at the time, however, I had not been allowed to attend the heated church conferences and, while I observed the fallout of the church split, I did not really know why it happened.

My first real introduction to CBF came during my sophomore year at Mercer University, in Walter Shurden's Baptist Traditions class. In that class, Dr. Shurden put language and story behind the concepts that I had absorbed growing up in my Baptist church—principles like soul competency, religious liberty, autonomy of the local church and the priesthood of all believers. He introduced me to the names of our Baptist forebears, such as John Smyth and Thomas Helwys and Roger Williams and Walter Rauschenbusch and Carlyle Marney. I also learned the story of his involvement with the beginnings of the Fellowship. Somewhere along the way over the next three years, Dr. Shurden became a trusted mentor for me and deeply shaped my theology and my personal and vocational formation. I learned more about what it meant to be Baptist historically, and I was learning more about the kind of Baptist that I wanted to be.

I grew more passionate as a student of Baptist history and heritage, and I became involved in a congregation uniquely aligned with the Fellowship, even teaching preschool Mission Friends with the CBF missions education curriculum. My personal identification as a Cooperative Baptist was not a remarkable point of transition for me. Instead, I gradually found myself following people whom I loved and trusted to a community that allowed me to live out my calling.

After graduating, I attended seminary at Mercer's McAfee School of Theology in Atlanta, a decision made in large part because I wanted to stay connected to the Baptist communities I had grown to love. At McAfee, I became engaged not just with the idea of Cooperative Baptists, but with the organization of CBF itself. I was named a CBF Leadership Scholar, receiving scholarships and stipends to attend General Assembly and other CBF events.

Since the CBF offices were then located upstairs in the McAfee building on campus, I worked part-time in the CBF office between classes, doing administrative work that introduced me to the life of CBF churches. I got to know staff and others involved in the Fellowship. I served as a student representative on the Coordinating Council of the Cooperative Baptist Fellowship of Georgia. Ideas became relationships, and CBF became my spiritual and ecclesial home.

For me, being a part of the Fellowship means a commitment on my part to "show up." I think my presence is important, both as a practical offering of my gifts for the movement and as a symbolic show of my support. I have tried to say "yes" to as much CBF-related service as I feel I am able to manage—attending CBF General Assemblies and other gatherings, serving on committees and task forces, and serving with other CBF partners, such as Baptist Women in Ministry and Passport, Inc.

Sometimes, even when it felt like I was the token young woman asked to be on a committee, I embraced the invitation because I appreciated the genuine effort to have younger and female voices represented. While I have at times grown frustrated or impatient or discouraged, or have disagreed with others in the movement, I am committed to the Fellowship, and I am sticking with it. CBF has become family for me.

I have never seriously considered not being a Baptist. Those core values of intellectual and personal freedom, cooperation and respect for the beliefs of others became as much a part of my formation as the ethics and manners and practices instilled in me by my family. Being Baptist is a part of who I am.

In my story, my awareness of CBF came along at just the right time in my personal formation so that I could wholeheartedly continue to claim my "Baptistness." Cooperative Baptists uphold my core values and make space for me to live out my calling as a woman in ministry. I am a Baptist because I was born a Baptist and was formed a Baptist. I am a Cooperative Baptist because, in this time and place, this is the Baptist family that embraces and continues to form the convictions that are a part of my core identity.

Julie Whidden Long serves as Associate Pastor and Minister of Children and Families at First Baptist Church of Christ in Macon, Georgia. She and her husband, Jody, are graduates of Mercer University and Mercer's McAfee School of Theology. They have two children, Merrill and John Thomas.

From Oblivious to Community

By Rachel Gunter Shapard

CBF Oblivious

I was 15 years old when the Cooperative Baptist Fellowship came into existence. I must admit that in the spring of 1991, I was not paying close attention to the condition of my denomination. I was more concerned with friends, schoolwork, getting accepted into a popular social club, and wondering whether or not I would get a car for my 16th birthday (#firstworldproblems). As trivial as some of my preoccupations were, I was heavily involved in the life of my church—First Baptist Church in Tallahassee, Florida.

Outside of what I received at home, the beginnings of my personal spiritual development took place in the safe environment of my church. Though I was not attuned to the occurrence, it was during my upbringing at First Baptist that the congregation became identified with CBF. The people of this CBF church loved and nurtured me in faith. They told me the stories of scripture, making them come alive and giving me the opportunity to claim the sacred story as my own. It was there, among them, that I was initiated in the waters of baptism, publicly claiming my status as a follower of Christ.

When I first began considering a calling into full-time ministry, I spoke at length with Clint Purvis, the minister to college students at First Baptist. He encouraged me to jump head-first into leadership roles at church to help me discern whether ministry was the right career path. My church family welcomed me into various leadership positions, eventually granting me paid positions in the youth, college and music ministries. Alongside my family of origin, the ministers and lay leaders at my CBF church gave me the courage to consider gospel ministry as a viable vocational choice.

CBF Anxious

I will never forget the words of Doug Dortch, the senior pastor at FBC Tallahassee, on the day I made an appointment to speak with him about theological education. He had come to First Baptist when I was 18 years old and quickly gained my respect as I watched him minister with integrity through my four years of college. Because I was experiencing a barrage of advice on where to attend seminary (and had been relatively sheltered from occurrences in denominational life), I sought Doug's advice, knowing that he was connected and informed.

To my surprise, he did not point me in the direction of one of the well-established Baptist seminaries with which I was familiar. Instead, he encouraged me to consider one of CBF's newly formed partner institutions—Mercer University's McAfee School of Theology. "Those are the people I would entrust with my own theological education if I were in your shoes," he said.

What?! These fledging seminaries were still too young to have received accreditation by the Association for Theological Schools. McAfee had not even graduated its first class of students. But choosing a CBF partner school was not a gamble in Doug's mind. He knew the professors personally, believed in their philosophies of theological education, and trusted their abilities to instruct the next generation of ministers.

Doug Dortch's advice gave a confused 22-year-old the freedom to explore what had seemed a risky yet intriguing option. After visiting several seminaries, to my own surprise I took a chance and chose innovation over establishment. FBC Tallahassee, the Cooperative Baptist Fellowship of Florida and CBF came alongside me in this decision and provided scholarship monies towards my theological education. Knowing that my church, state and national organizations were venturing with me on an uncharted course settled all anxiety.

CBF Affiliated

My years at McAfee were good ones, filled with the hard work of taking apart my own theology and carefully considering what beliefs would be kept, what would be set aside and what new understandings would take root. I discovered that the foundation built with the influence of church and family could withstand in-depth examination. Thankfully, I was in the good company of peers and professors as I undertook such a challenging task.

I cannot express how grateful I am to have attended a CBF partner theological institution. The professors, students, ministers and lay people I met in connection to my graduate studies became a new set of encouragers, challengers and inspirers. To this day, they are a part of my personal cloud of witnesses.

At this point in my ministerial calling, I feel as if I have come full circle. Serving as the Associate Coordinator for CBF of Florida allows me to give back to the churches that are kin to the one that nurtured me in my faith beginnings throughout my home state. What a gift it is to walk alongside and serve as a resource to the very people that believed in me and supported me personally and financially throughout my formative years.

One of the things I love about my role with CBF of Florida is working with such an ethnically diverse group of people. Close to 40 churches within the Sunshine State comprise CBF of Florida and the Caribbean Islands, including a number of multiethnic congregations as well as six churches in the Bahamas and one in Puerto Rico. When our Administrative Council gathers, I have the privilege of sitting beside Rubén Ortiz, who in 2014 became the Moderator of CBF of Florida, the first Hispanic moderator of a CBF state or regional organization. Rubén is a strong leader and graces us with wisdom from his multicultural perspective.

The seven Caribbean churches that are included in our number relate to us not as mission communities, but as co-laborers. Representatives from the Bahamas and Puerto Rico attend our leadership meetings, weighing in on key decisions and voicing their viewpoints on the trajectory of the organization. The broader outlook that is afforded to us through diversity enhances our Fellowship immeasurably. We are fully aware that multicultural leadership and participation are essential for the health and growth of CBF of Florida.

One of the results of our relationships in the Caribbean is the cross-cultural exchange that occurs. Through the support of CBF of Florida and Passport, Inc., a Bahamian college student, Jacoby Thomas, was able to serve as a summer staff intern for PASSPORT*kids!* in 2014. This exchange allowed Jacoby to use and enhance his leadership abilities, reminded Passport attendees to approach the world with wonder as they watched him discover new aspects of American culture, and expanded the worldview of those who listened to his stories about Bahamian life.

In the summer of 2015, Jaime Fitzgerald, a seminary student and CBF Vestal Scholar, served with the Fellowship's congregational internship program, Student.Church, in Carolina, Puerto Rico, at Iglesia Bautista de Metrópolis. Jaime's stint within this United States territory, where the predominant language is Spanish, gave her a new appreciation for the practices observed and the people encountered. Jaime developed a love for a different expression of worship, one that is "vibrant, loud and full of energy." She came to a deeper appreciation of simplicity, making a commitment to declutter her life, both internally and externally. And she grew to love the people, including her mentor, Jesús Garcia, the members of her spiritual formation group, and many others who became her family in nine short weeks.

I am truly blessed to serve in our Fellowship that values diversity and is committed to expanding its multicultural participation and opportunities for cross-cultural engagement.

CBF Identity

Not long ago, our nine-year-old son came home from school with a project from his art class. The assignment was to fill a piece of paper with individual images that, when combined, would represent him as a person. As Drew sat at our kitchen table, adding color to the pictures he had drawn during class, I looked over his shoulder at the many images that filled the page. I found the five members of our family represented. His favorite subject in school was included, and music and baseball both were mentioned on his "All About Me" page. And, of course, he did not neglect a few of his favorite TV programs and foods!

There was one thing that I did not expect to see on his representation of himself. He had drawn a picture of a church. This by itself was no great shock, since his parents are both ministers and he practically lives at the church. It was what I found on top of the church that surprised me. Atop the steeple, Drew had sketched in a flagpole. The flag affixed there was emblazoned with the letters "CBF."

I was a bit taken aback that these three letters came to the forefront of our third grader's mind when he was tasked with describing himself. It was a blessing as a parent to see that faith made his list. As a professional, I could not shake the notion of responsibility. Playing a role in the shaping of a child's religious identity is no small task.

I am truly thankful that Drew identifies himself with CBF. What a blessing it is to know that this group of people that have become my fellow travelers on life's journey will contribute to shaping our child's worldview, walking with him as he develops the basic principles upon which to order his life. It is both a blessing and a responsibility.

CBF Community

What is CBF to me now? It is home.

CBF is the realm where I am most comfortable living out my calling in gospel ministry; the group I lean on for support, amusement and inspiration; the first network I turn to for resources and assets; the gathering of Christ-followers with whom I do not hesitate to partner in mission; the assembly of churches and individuals I go to when contemplating a response to global crisis; the community that teaches me to engage the world with integrity and authenticity.

Is CBF perfect? Of course not! But for better or worse, these are my people. I am a part of the Cooperative Baptist Fellowship, and CBF is a part of me.

Is CBF the only assemblage in Christendom that has formulated a response to Christ's invitation to follow with principles to which I adhere? Certainly not! But I cannot imagine walking the path of Christian discipleship without the company of this beloved community.

Rachel Gunter Shapard is the Associate Coordinator of the Cooperative Baptist Fellowship of Florida, where she has served since 2012. She is married to Tommy Shapard and they have three children: Drew, Kate and Mac.

A Place to Stay

By Joshua Hearne

To be honest, I'm not entirely sure how I ended up going to college where I did, but that hazily remembered decision changed everything for me. One day, my father brought home an application to Georgetown College and insisted that I add it to my list of prospective schools. When I heard it was a Baptist college in Kentucky, I knew immediately that I didn't want to go there. I had given up on church a couple of years earlier and had blithely assumed that if church people were those with whom Jesus associated, then I must not be interested in him either. But my dad insisted and the application wasn't too long, so I filled it out and sent it off, confident that there was no way I would end up there.

Fast forward several months to a campus visit. As I added items to my list of reasons not to attend the school, I was interrupted by an older gentleman who didn't look much like my mental image of a college professor. He wasn't wearing a single stitch of tweed! The professor introduced himself as "Doc" Birdwhistell and said that he taught some classes in the religion department. Before I even had time to dismiss this big man's overtures, he said that he had read something about me and had a few questions. Instantly, I was certain that he knew how I had secretly lost my faith and that he was going to harangue me for it while never releasing his grip on me with his surprisingly huge, yet somehow still slightly bony, hand.

"Mr. Hearne," he began, "I heard that you played John the Baptist in a production of *Godspell* back in Ashland."

I told him that I had, even while I was wondering how he might have heard that. "I love that show," he said, before asking, "Was it as much fun to kick in the doors singing as I always thought it would be?"

We spent the next hour talking about a number of things that didn't really matter all that much. Eventually he excused himself and, although I'm sure he had not come down from his office in the chapel just to talk to me about high school musicals and nothing in particular, it certainly felt that way in the moment. I ended up going to Georgetown because I figured I could get along with Christians like Doc, who did not make shared faith a requirement for shared love and did not name agreement as a prerequisite to welcome.

While I had a lot of doubt, I needed a place to call home for a while, and Doc seemed to be okay with that. Doc knew that folks need a place to stay.

While I did not know it at the time, Doc Birdwhistell was my first exposure to the Cooperative Baptist Fellowship. Doc became the standard by which I would try to figure out who could be trusted when it came to matters of faith. I took his classes even as I quizzically and quietly considered the tiny ember of faith still somehow hidden in my heart. For someone who still could not believe, I took a lot of religion classes. When I couldn't take one of Doc's classes, I would take classes with professors of whom he spoke highly, one of whom challenged me to read one of the Gospels (for a paper) to see what Christians might have to say about love. When I scoffed, he said I should read it as if it were a "philosophy assignment."

"You don't have to believe," he assured my fearful heart. "But Christians have said for almost 2,000 years that their religion is about love. You can't ignore that."

Noting my hesitation, he added, "You don't have to agree with them. If they're wrong, say so. But don't ignore them." He suggested I read Luke because it was particularly relevant. Instead, I read Mark, because it's the shortest.

Surprising things happen when you read scripture looking for love. It turns out that the Jesus in Mark boldly believed that love is not just as strong as death, but stronger! And the Kingdom of God is already in the midst of the world, changing it powerfully and subtly, like yeast in dough. Jesus seemed so convinced that faith was about more than just theology and understanding. With mystery as our nourishment, Jesus taught us to trust God first and understand in light of that trust. The ember of faith in my heart was flamed to life by the words of scripture, the movement of the Spirit, and the guidance of trustworthy mentors.

These were the kinds of Christians I wanted to be. They happened to be members of the Fellowship, so I thought maybe I could be too. With my still wobbly-kneed faith, I began to pray alongside Cooperative Baptists. On the days when it took all of me just to show up, it was Cooperative Baptists who prayed with me and for me. Even though I didn't have it all figured out—perhaps especially because I didn't have it all figured out—they were glad to call me brother. They knew that folks need a place to stay.

All these years later, my wife, Jessica, and I serve as CBF field personnel in Danville, Virginia, ministering with and among those struggling with homelessness, housing insecurity, hunger, poverty and addiction. We do this as two of the leaders of an intentional Christian community called Grace and Main Fellowship. This is a community that shares life and resources, opens its homes to those without a place to stay, develops leaders on the margins and prays together, joining the well-being of its members to the well-being of those on the margins. We do so for many reasons, but among them is the commitment we learned from Cooperative Baptists to make room for people in our lives as the foundation for God's work in their lives and in ours. Love grows in community.

God has called God's people to cultivate places where the disenchanted, the faithless, the downtrodden and the marginalized are welcomed. In our case, this looks like Grace and Main Fellowship. Whether it's through a conversation on the corner, a meal on a curb or at a dining room table, lifting a sign at a protest for tenants' rights, or welcoming a brother or a sister to join our household for a little while, we've discovered the tremendous power of community to change lives and transform our world. The communities we build become the stages upon which the grand play of God's love is seen by our world. We've learned this from folks like Doc, and we're still learning it from people like Roland.

Roland had been homeless for 18 years when we met him. He ate with us and began to walk with us in the neighborhoods downtown, where we had moved. After a few months of praying, eating and walking with Roland, we had become friends. When your friend is homeless, homelessness is no longer a "social injustice," it's a personal problem. So we helped him secure a fair lease and some furniture—a bed, a chair, a couch and a dining room table procured from the homes of beloved friends and supporters. He was thrilled to have a place of his own, not only in his new apartment but also in our fledgling community.

When we came to check on him the next day, we were shocked to see somebody we didn't know sleeping on his couch. Fearing that somebody had bullied or extorted their way into his new home, we took Roland aside to ask what was going on. He looked one of us in the eye and said, with a gentle, loving rebuke in his voice, "Folks need a place to stay." On his first night with shelter in almost two decades, he couldn't imagine having an empty couch when he knew there were people sleeping outside.

Without ever meeting him, Roland seemed to know exactly what Doc had known: God's love makes room for the unexpected people in the most splendid ways. Making room for those who can't find a place to stay is more than just about finding shelter for those without it. Often, it means making room in our lives, in our congregations and in our Fellowship for people who can't seem to find a place in this world, among those who will call them sister or brother, without preconditions or expectations of who they will be, what they will say or what they believe in that one particular moment.

There are lots of folks out there who haven't yet found a place like the one we've found in Grace and Main Fellowship and in the Cooperative Baptist Fellowship. There's work to do, and we're glad to be a part of it, because folks need a place to stay.

Joshua Hearne and his wife, Jessica, have served as Cooperative Baptist Fellowship field personnel since 2012. They are founding members of the intentional Christian community of Grace and Main Fellowship in Danville, Virginia, where they are learning the way of Jesus alongside those struggling with homelessness, poverty, hunger and addiction.

Removing Obstacles as a Fourth Culture Kid

By Alyssa Aldape

During the Hindu festival of Ganpati, a marching band of drummers invades the streets of Pune, India. Women and children laugh as the men dance, swaying in the streets to the beat of Indian drums. As a child watching this festival unfold, I remember hearing parents and their sons and daughters who had come home for the holiday singing holy songs together during the 10-day celebration of the birth of Ganesh.

If you're not up to date on your Hindu trivia, Ganesh is the god with the elephant head. More importantly, Ganesh is the "remover of obstacles." And, as one might imagine, there are obstacles when one is learning to live in a country different from that of one's birth. As an "MK" (missionary kid) in India, I had to learn how to live in two cultures. This is why many MKs are also called Third Culture Kids (TCKs)—kids raised in a culture outside that of their parents. TCKs must learn to live in the "foreign" culture, their passport country culture, while still being influenced by their country of origin. This combination of cultures basically creates a third culture—a blend of the two.

In my own case, as the child of Mexican-American parents who were serving in India as Cooperative Baptist Fellowship field personnel, I had the dimensions of a fourth culture to add to the mix!

I am convinced a TCK never actually stops living in the third culture—even when she leaves it. The experience has helped me to be more aware of the cultural differences I encounter in my own ministry and has enabled me to be more mindful of the spaces and the people whom I may not understand. I am thankful for my time in India because I learned so much about my own faith and how to respect others. As a minister, I feel it has taught me to better understand those who hold different views and has given me the ability to bridge the gaps that often exist when we encounter and minister to those who may look, sound or think differently than ourselves.

The Festival of Ganpati helps me to be mindful of the obstacles we face when trying to understand others and, with the help of the Holy Spirit, enables me to cross the barriers that often separate us and recognize the image of God in those who are different. In a world where the foreigner is often seen as "other," I am reminded of Jesus, who embraced those at the margins—people who were considered "different." That's what the gospel is all about—including all in God's kingdom and looking beyond any obstacles created by our differences. And that is reason for dancing in the streets!

Alyssa Aldape serves as the Minister of Missions at First Baptist Church of Dalton, Georgia. She previously served on the Cooperative Baptist Fellowship staff as a student assistant with Global Missions. Alyssa grew up in India as the child of CBF field personnel Eddie and Macarena Aldape.

Finding a Home in CBF

By Rubén Ortiz

"Your people will rebuild the ancient ruins and will rise up the age-old foundations; you will be called Repairer of Broken Walls, Restorer of Streets with Dwellings." Isaiah 58:12 (NIV)

It was 2006 when I decided to make a call that I had postponed. I connected to the Internet, searched for that group of Baptists who were said to respect the fundamental Baptist freedoms, and left a message with Bernie Moraga who, at that time, was the Hispanic Initiative National Consultant with the Cooperative Baptist Fellowship.

I called because I was tired of many things. The local church consumed all my energies, and clergy within my network did not answer my calls, let alone support my goals for mission engagement. My spiritual life had begun to change, and I needed a dependable space to help me develop in a healthy manner.

Bernie responded almost immediately and we had a great conversation, one that in just a few minutes made me feel as though we had known each other all our lives. Two days later, Tommy Deal, the Assistant Coordinator of the Cooperative Baptist Fellowship of Florida, was in my office. His kind manner, friendliness and transparency during our conversation left me wanting to know more about CBF.

The word *fellowship* was what intrigued me the most. Camaraderie, friendship, community, brotherhood, fraternity—that was exactly what I was looking for. I could not believe there was a family of faith that met my needs. A few months later, I was ordained in the First Hispanic Baptist Church in Deltona. To my surprise, Bernie and Tommy were there by my side, making agreements and sealing pacts. It was more than a distinctive ministerial title; it was the beginning of a commitment to a family of faith who wanted to create spaces for my greatest mission adventure through building bridges of brotherhood, communicating with each other, making friends and sharing dreams. This was amazing.

CBF of Florida was in transition. Carolyn Anderson had announced her retirement as Coordinator, and the organization was in the process of finding a new candidate. Although I didn't know the organization that well, I could see the potential of CBF through its steadfast commitment to Baptist principles, the flexibility of its organizational structure, the quality of its leaders, and its commitment to care for the needy and be the presence of Christ.

Tommy introduced me to CBF national leaders, with whom we started working in the Caribbean. The first trip was coordinated by the Eastern Baptist Convention of Cuba (Convención Bautista de Cuba Oriental). This experience proved meaningful for Bo Prosser, CBF's Coordinator of Strategic Partnerships, as he enjoyed the frank and open dialogue of the Cuban people. It began to shape a covenant of cooperation with Eastern Cuba for missionary exchange and integrated projects.

Shortly thereafter, we visited the Dominican Republic and met up with pastor Jesús Garcia, who was on a mission assignment with members of his Baptist church in Metrópolis Carolina, Puerto Rico. Jesús felt the same sense of family that had encouraged me to be part of the Fellowship. The Baptist Church of Metrópolis is now connected with CBF of Florida and is a great example of a missional church to the Caribbean.

In 2007, the committee to elect the new coordinator for CBF of Florida was spot-on in choosing Ray Johnson. He had all the necessary qualities. He came from a ministry background in Miami, and he had experience working with people of various ethnic cultures, a compassionate heart for others and a visionary mind.

It was not difficult for Ray to realize the potential of CBF in the state of Florida. He also proposed to include the Caribbean Islands and change the organization name to "CBF of Florida and the Caribbean Islands." From his arrival, he began to create spaces for newcomers who brought fresh voices to the organization, and we immediately began to participate in the Representative Assembly of CBF of Florida. It was Ray who proposed me as the first Hispanic state/regional moderator in the short life of CBF.

Ray has traveled several times to Cuba and led in the Caribbean Bahamas missionary projects. Through this work, these projects were strengthened. Today, CBF of Florida has six affiliated churches that, since 2011, comprise the Cooperative Baptist Fellowship of the Bahamas. These churches have already forged ties through theological education, local missions and immediate disaster response. In each of these places, Ray has been an ambassador for those who are Cooperative Baptists.

Because there is still so much work to be done to break stereotypes, heal wounds and promote the Kingdom, we have engaged in all of these areas since that time. We have been accompanied by many, especially by Carlos Dario Peralta, Director of Encuentro Ministries, who has been a friend and collaborator in this journey.

Over the past 10 years, CBF of Florida and the Caribbean Islands has become the most compassionate and welcoming space for those tired from their local ministries and exhausted by the rigid structure of denominations, jaded misgivings, inert spirituality, vain doctrinal discussions and lack of ministerial confidence. For us, to welcome someone is to create spaces for those eager to rebuild the foundations of yesteryear through spiritual formation, repair the crumbling walls of ministerial confidence and restore avenues of social justice.

I have been pastor of First Baptist Church of Deltona, Florida, since March 2002. We are not a large church—not more than 250 members—but we have a giant heart for God and God's redemptive work in the world. We have learned to dream together that a different world is possible, that the church has a prophetic voice proclaiming justice to the world in need, and that the local church must be the first center of transformative action in society.

CBF has been with us through thick and thin. When we didn't have a way to send our mission funds to Cuba, CBF quickly intervened and was granted a legal way to do it. When we wanted to celebrate the first spiritual formation experience in the Dominican Republic and Cuba, CBF provided a spiritual disciplines curriculum. In October 2009, when my father was arrested in Cuba while doing mission work, CBF quickly made all arrangements and advocated through the necessary channels for his release, while helping me through my sadness and concern. When I experienced personal crises, my CBF colleagues wept beside me and embraced me with their care.

When a natural disaster affected the Caribbean populations, CBF responded to our call with prayers and visible actions of love and care. When I dreamed of creating new spaces for missions and reconciliation with other organizations such as Encuentro Ministries, the Baptist Churches of Puerto Rico, the Association of Hispanic Baptist Churches of Florida, the Baptist Convention of Cuba Oriental, the Fraternity of Baptist Churches of Cuba, The Upper Room and the Evangelical Seminary of Nicaragua, among many others, CBF supported me every step of the way. Alongside CBF we have rebuilt houses, fed families affected by hurricanes and floods, planted more than 35 churches and ministries, learned to create community gardens, delivered food monthly to more than 200 families, purchased bicycles for missionaries, built cisterns for drinking water, laid floors for families living in thatched-roof houses, and shared a holistic gospel of transformation.

We had already tried to do it alone, but we have done it all with CBF. Through serving together, we have made new friends, lifted up hurting leaders, strengthened sad churches, received foreigners and helped the widow. This is the gospel. Cooperative Baptists are my family, because they think like me and because "the Fellowship" beats alongside my heart.

In his book *The Ragamuffin Gospel*, Brennan Manning says that more than 100 years ago in the Deep South, the now common phrase "born again" was almost unknown. Instead, the phrase used to describe the time to begin a personal relationship with Jesus Christ was: "I was trapped by the great affection."

I am personally dedicated to build bridges and eternal friends with this family called CBF, and yes, "I am trapped by the great affection."

Thank you CBF. Happy 25th Anniversary . . . and many more!

Rev. Rubén Ortiz is a native of Santiago de Cuba, Cuba. Since 2002, he has served as senior pastor of the First Hispanic Baptist Church of Deltona, Florida. He has served as a member of the Representative Assembly since 2009 and as Moderator of the Cooperative Baptist Fellowship of Florida and the Caribbean Islands from 2013-2015. He is also a member of the CBF Missions Council and the Advisory Board of the Academy of Spiritual Formation. He and his wife, Xiomara Reboyras, are the parents of two teenagers, Natalia Sofia and Daniel Andrés.

CBF: Mi Nueva Casa

Escrito por Rubén Ortiz

"Tu pueblo reconstruirá las ruinas antiguas y levantará los cimientos de antaño; serás llamado 'reparador de muros derruidos,' 'restaurador de calles transitables.'" Isaías 58.12 (NVI)

Fue en el año 2006 cuando decidí hacer una llamada que había estado postergando. Me conecté al Internet, busqué por ese grupo de bautistas que decían respetar las libertades fundamentales y dejé un mensaje a quien entonces era el consultante nacional de la Iniciativa Hispana con Coperative Baptist Fellowship, Bernie Moraga. Llamaba porque estaba cansado de muchas cosas: la iglesia local consumía todas mis energías, la denominación no respondía a mis llamadas, y menos a mis expectativas misionales. Además, mi vida espiritual había comenzado a cambiar y necesitaba de un lugar de confianza para desarrollarse sanamente.

Aquella llamada fue respondida casi de inmediato, tuvimos una gran charla, una de esas que a los pocos minutos parece como que nos conocíamos de toda una vida. Dos días después, me encontraba recibiendo en mi oficina al Coordinador Asistente de CBF de Florida, Tommy Deal. Hablé tanto con Tommy que en algún momento pensé que el cubano era él. Su trato amable y la transparencia de su conversación me dejó más deseoso de saber qué era CBF, la palabra *Fellowship* era la que más me intrigaba. Camaradería, compañerismo, comunidad, comunión, hermandad, fraternidad, eso era exactamente lo que estaba buscando. No podía creer que había una familia de fe creada a mi medida. Unos meses después sería mi ordenación en la Primera Iglesia Bautista Hispana de Deltona, para mi sorpresa, Bernie y Tommy estaban ahí, a mi lado, haciendo acuerdos, sellando pactos. Nacía algo más que un distintivo título ministerial, nacía también el compromiso con una familia de fe que quería crear espacios para mis más necesitadas aventuras misionales: construyendo puentes de hermandad, comunicándonos mutuamente, haciendo amigos, compartiendo sueños. Y eso era algo muy bueno.

En ese tiempo, CBF de Florida estaba en transición, luego que Carolyn Anderson anunciara su jubilación como coordinadora estatal se inició el proceso para buscar un nuevo candidato. Aunque no conocía bien la organización podía ver el potencial que tenía CBF por su firme compromiso con los principios bautistas, la flexibilidad de su estructura organizacional y la calidad de sus líderes, gente comprometida a la enseñanza de Dios de cuidar al necesitado y ser la presencia de Dios en todo momento y en todo lugar.

Tommy Deal me había presentado a otros líderes nacionales con quienes comenzamos a trabajar en el Caribe. El primer viaje fue coordinado por la Convención Bautista Oriental de Cuba, esta experiencia enamoró a Bo Prosser, CBF Coordinador, por su gente franca y abierta. Se comenzaba a gestar un pacto de colaboración con Cuba Oriental para intercambio misionero y proyectos integrales. Luego fue la República Dominicana donde se nos encontramos con el pastor Jesús García, quien estaba de misiones con miembros de su iglesia Bautista de Metrópolis en Puerto Rico. Jesús sintió la misma sensación de familia que me había animado a ingresar a CBF. La Iglesia Bautista de Metrópolis es hoy parte de CBF de Florida y un ejemplo de iglesia misional para todo el Caribe.

En el 2007 el comité para elegir el nuevo coordinador de CBF de Florida no se equivocó al escoger a Ray Johnson. El reunía todas las cualidades necesarias para ser su líder en esa época. Venia de hacer ministerio en Miami, tenía la experiencia para trabajar con gente de varias culturas étnicas, un corazón compasivo por el extranjero y una mente visionaria. No fue difícil para Ray darse cuenta del potencial de CBF de Florida en lo estatal, sino que propuso incluir a las Islas del Caribe y cambiar su nombre a CBF de Florida y el Caribe. Desde su llegada comenzó a crear espacios para los recién llegados quienes traían voces frescas a la organización y enseguida comenzamos a participar en la Asamblea Representativa de CBF de Florida. Luego Ray, me propuso ser nombrado como el primer Moderador Estatal Hispano en la corta vida de CBF.

Ray ha viajado varias veces a Cuba y con su liderazgo en el Caribe se fortalecieron los proyectos misionales de Bahamas hasta el punto que hoy cuenta con 6 iglesias afiliadas y reconocidas desde el 2011 como Cooperative Baptist Fellowship of the Bahamas. Con estas iglesias ya se han forzado lazos a través de la educación teológica, misiones locales y respuesta inmediata a catástrofes. En cada uno de estos lugares Ray ha sido un embajador para quienes somos bautistas moderados. Porque hay mucho trabajo que hacer para romper estereotipos, sanar heridas y promover el Reino. Y en eso nos hemos enfocado desde entonces. Hemos sido acompañados por muchos, sobre todo por Carlos Darío Peralta, Director de Ministerios Encuentro, quien ha sido un amigo y colaborador en la jornada.

Con el pasar de estos 10 años, CBF de Florida y el Caribe ha llegado a ser el lugar más compasivo y acogedor para aquellos cansados con sus ministerios locales, agotados por la estructura de denominaciones rígidas, hastiados de los recelos, de la espiritualidad inerte, de las vanas discusiones doctrinales y la falta de confianza ministerial. Dar la bienvenida para nosotros es crear espacios para aquellos deseosos de reconstruir los cimientos de antaño a través de la formación espiritual, de reparar los muros derruidos de la confianza ministerial y de restaurar las avenidas de la justicia social.

He sido pastor de la Primera Iglesia Bautista de Deltona desde marzo del año 2002. No somos una iglesia grande, no pasamos los 250 miembros, pero tenemos un corazón gigante para Dios y su obra redentora en el mundo. Con esta iglesia hemos aprendido a soñar juntos que un mundo diferente es posible, que la iglesia tiene una voz profética que proclama justicia al mundo en necesidad, que la iglesia local tiene que ser el primer centro de acción transformadora en la sociedad.

Y CBF ha estado con nosotros, en las buenas y las malas. Cuando no teníamos manera de enviar nuestros fondos de misiones a Cuba, CBF intervino y rápidamente se le fue concedida una manera legal de hacerlo. Cuando quisimos celebrar la primera experiencia de formación espiritual en República Dominicana y en Cuba, CBF se hizo presente con su equipaje cargado de disciplinas para el alma. Cuando en Octubre del 2009 mi padre fue detenido en Cuba mientras misionaba, CBF enseguida hizo todas las gestiones necesarias para su liberación y mientras me acompañaba en mi tristeza y preocupación abogó y utilizo toda su influencia para su posterior liberación. Cuando atravesé crisis personales fueron mis colegas de CBF quienes lloraron junto a mí y me abrazaron con su cuidado. Cuando algún desastre natural ha afectado a las poblaciones del Caribe, CBF ha respondido a nuestro llamado con oraciones y acciones visibles de amor y cuidado. Cuando he soñado con crear espacios nuevos de misiones y reconciliación junto a otras organizaciones como Ministerios Encuentro, Las Iglesias Bautistas de Puerto Rico, la Asociación de Iglesias Bautistas Hispanas de la Florida, La Convención Bautista de Cuba Oriental, La Fraternidad de Iglesias Bautistas de Cuba, El Aposento Alto y el Seminario Evangélico de Nicaragua, entre otras tantas, CBF ha apoyado en cada paso del camino.

Junto a CBF hemos reconstruido casas, alimentado familias afectadas por huracanes e inundaciones, plantado más de 35 iglesias y ministerios, aprendido a hacer huertos comunitarios, entregado alimentos para más de 200 familias mensuales, comprado bicicletas para misioneros, construido cisternas para agua potable, pisos para familias con casas de techo de palmas; hemos compartido el evangelio de la transformación integral.

Ya habíamos intentado hacerlo solos, pero lo hemos hecho junto a CBF, y ha sido la mejor decisión. Porque así, sirviendo juntos hemos encontrado a nuevos amigos, hemos levantado a líderes caídos, reforzado iglesias en crisis, recibido al extranjero y ayudado a la viuda. Esto es el Evangelio y por eso, toda CBF es mi familia, no solo comprende igual la misión del Reino, sino que palpita junto a mi corazón.

Dice Brennan Manning en su libro El Evangelio de los Andrajosos que *"hace más de cien años, en el Sur, una frase tan común en nuestra cultura cristiana de hoy—nacido de nuevo—era casi desconocida. En lugar de ello, la frase utilizada para describir el momento de iniciar la relación personal con Jesucristo era: 'Me atrapó el poder del gran afecto.'"*

Eso fue hace 100 años en el sur de los Estados Unidos, espero que ahora no suene anticuado decirlo, pero personalmente me dedico a construir puentes y amistades eternas en esta familia llamada CBF y sí, yo también estoy atrapado por el poder del gran afecto.

¡Gracias CBF, deseándote un feliz aniversario 25 y muchos más!

El Rev. Rubén Ortiz es natural de la ciudad de Santiago de Cuba, Cuba. Ha servido como Pastor titular de la Primera Iglesia Bautista Hispana de Deltona, FL desde el año 2002. Ortiz ha servido como miembro de la Asamblea Representativa (desde el 2009) y como moderador electo-en funciones-moderador anterior (2013-2015) para CFB Florida y el Caribe. Es también miembro del Concilio de Misiones y de la Junta Consultiva de la Academia de Formación Espiritual, un ministerio del Aposento Alto. Ortiz está casado con Xiomara Reboyras, ministra ordenada. Son los padres de dos magníficos adolescentes: Natalia Sofía y Daniel Andrés.

That "L" Word

By Emily Holladay

While attending my first Cooperative Baptist Fellowship General Assembly, I stood in line to meet the one and only James Dunn. Shaking with anticipation, I could barely put two words together when I finally arrived face-to-face with Dr. Dunn. This man was not only a Baptist icon, but one of my heroes for the many ways he fought to create and maintain a space where I could grow up true to historic Baptist principles.

Approaching the desk where he sat signing books, I stood speechless. I didn't know how to appropriately thank the man who stood on Capitol Hill to share a faith that believes in freedom of religion, creating a space where all people can worship freely and all voices are heard.

When I finally got up the nerve to speak, I introduced myself. "Dr. Dunn, my name is Emily Holladay. I'm so honored to meet you."

"Oh, Emily!" His familiar response rattled me a little. "I remember staying at your house in Louisville when you were in diapers."

If I had a dollar for the number of times I've heard someone speak those exact words to me . . .

You see, I am a "Baptist Baby." I was born in Louisville, Kentucky, the daughter of a Baptist minister. I grew up in a little white house on Grinstead Drive, directly across the street from Southern Baptist Theological Seminary. Before I even celebrated a birthday, I was enrolled in my first "class" at the seminary, where I spent four years in daycare and preschool before starting public school. And once I started elementary school, I became a member of the SBTS Saints swim team. To say I was born to go to seminary is not a bit ironic.

My parents hosted many Baptist heroes in our home, and many people for whom I have such great admiration today knew me when I was in diapers. In fact, I think I was a Baptist first and a child second.

When I was four years old, Daniel Vestal, Cecil Sherman, Jimmy Allen and others invited their moderate Baptist friends to a meeting in Atlanta, Georgia, to discuss their future together. My dad and grandparents journeyed to Atlanta as participants in what would be the creation of the Cooperative Baptist Fellowship. My dad would become the first Moderator of the Kentucky Baptist Fellowship, with my grandpa not too far behind as one of the moderators of the Cooperative Baptist Fellowship of Georgia.

Admittedly, I was too young to understand what was happening to my Baptist home. Years would pass before my family truly experienced the aftershock of the controversy shaping Baptist life in the 1980s and 1990s.

I remember the day that I began to realize what was going on as the day I had to quit swim team. I had secured my spot on the team because my dad taught Supervised Ministry Experience classes at Southern Seminary, but when the seminary "didn't need him anymore," my days as an SBTS Saint were over.

I told my coach that the seminary didn't like us anymore because my dad was "some word that starts with an L." Though I was too young to recall the word "liberal," I understood that something had changed and that I was not welcome in my home across the street anymore.

It was not long before many of my friends left school and moved away because their parents lost jobs at the seminary. I never moved, but it felt like my life had been uprooted. I felt a profound sense of loss. Truly, my *home* had been stripped from me.

All of this happened before I even finished elementary school! By middle school, I had added a new phrase to my vocabulary: dually aligned. As a youth, I spent one week of every summer at the SBC-sponsored GA camp and one week at CBF-sponsored Passport camp. During the year, I learned about tithing, so I gave a little bit to every fund on offering envelopes—CBF, SBC, Lottie Moon, Annie Armstrong and the CBF Offering for Global Missions.

In high school, I had three different youth ministers: One taught me I could probably be anything I wanted to be. One taught me I could even be a minister if I wanted. The other taught me that I shouldn't aspire to any higher position in a church than president of the youth council. This left me confused and frustrated, with a deep longing for a place where I belonged—a place that I could call *home*.

In the fall of 2005, I moved to Alabama to attend Samford University. I was most excited about my first Sunday in Birmingham as a college student. That Sunday would be the first time I ever got to choose for myself where I went to church.

I attended Vestavia Hills Baptist Church for two years before accepting an internship at Southside Baptist Church. These places became my sanctuaries in college. During my time at Samford, I learned that I could do whatever I wanted to do, but that not everyone would support me. It was no longer just my dad and his friends who were too "liberal." I was too.

I needed Vestavia Hills and Southside to remind me that God had not left me alone or without a home. The people I met at church taught me that I was called to serve a God who is greater than our differences, and that I was a part of something much bigger than myself.

In 2008, I graduated from Samford and started working for Passport Camps at its national office in Birmingham. The two years I spent at Passport were the most formative in shaping how I understood myself as a Cooperative Baptist and as a person called to ministry. I became aware of how much these people did so that I could grow up thinking that female pastors were normal, that ecumenical cooperation was a necessity, and that we are all called to minister to a global community.

And after two years of watching, listening and learning, I decided that it was my turn. God was calling me to give my life to the ministry in the freedom they had helped to create.

I entered Mercer University's McAfee School of Theology and studied Christian Social Ethics, hoping to minister in the local church so I could create space for people like me to find their *home.*

Within my first month at McAfee, I started a temporary job at the CBF Resource Center, calling churches to promote the Offering for Global Missions. In the course of a year, I called at least 1,000 churches to tell them about the myriad of resources CBF offered to help promote the Offering.

As I talked to people from all over the country, I heard encouraging stories of how CBF impacted their lives. I also listened as people shared discouraging stories of how lonely it was to be the only CBF church for miles. The experience opened my eyes to the many ways our Fellowship is still needed, and to the hundreds and thousands of voices still searching for a place to call home.

During this time, I was impressed that CBF Executive Coordinator Daniel Vestal was deeply interested in the impressions of a young contract employee. He wanted to know the stories that I and others were hearing from the people with whom we spoke. Dr. Vestal listened to my words with a sense of compassion I have yet to experience from another person. He truly desired to find a place for those individuals and earnestly took on the role of inspiring the CBF staff to do just that. I worked with Dr. Vestal for nearly three years, and his fervor for the least of these—even among our own Fellowship—never dwindled. During my time at CBF, he stopped by my cubicle often and spoke to me with such sincerity that I thought I might be the only person he had time to speak to in that way. Sometimes we talked about family, other times about CBF. But his compassion was a constant companion throughout all our conversations.

In 2011, when Dr. Vestal was looking for a young voice to participate in his Coordinator's Report at the 20th Anniversary CBF General Assembly, he asked me to represent my generation on stage. He sat beside me and listened as I challenged CBF to create a place where other 20-somethings could feel like they belonged.

Over the next year, Dr. Vestal's last at CBF, we had many conversations about how to give younger people a place to feel at home in the Fellowship. He was keenly aware of the many people in CBF life who didn't have a voice, and he sought to give them one. At his staff retirement lunch, many colleagues spoke of their experience with Dr. Vestal. The common theme running through all the remarks was, "Daniel was not just my boss. He was my pastor."

If we could retroactively change Dr. Vestal's title, I think many would agree that CBF Pastor would be more fitting. He truly epitomized what it means to serve others, and he constantly reminded those of us who worked with him that we are to be servants of the people we minister to and not masters. We are to listen to their needs and create resources based on what we hear, not what we want to force people to need.

Today, I am honored to carry Dr. Vestal's name as one of the first Vestal Scholars. I pray often that my ministry will be a reflection of the love and compassion he continues to demonstrate with so many. If I have even a fraction of the empathy he shares with "the least of these," I will feel that I have accomplished much.

I may have been born into Baptist life and come into contact with many Baptist heroes over the course of my childhood, but it's the relationships with people like Daniel Vestal that help me to call CBF home. I continue to be inspired by the passion, dedication and commitment of past and present leadership. There is room for me in CBF, and I truly believe that the work we do together is life-changing, transformative and a faithful testament to the God who created and loves this world.

Emily Holladay is Associate Pastor for Children and Families at Broadway Baptist Church in Louisville, Kentucky. She received her Master of Divinity degree from Mercer University's McAfee School of Theology, where she was named one of the first CBF Vestal Scholars. Prior to her service at Broadway Baptist, she served on the staff of the Cooperative Baptist Fellowship in communications and development.

Reflection & Remembrance

Molly T. Marshall (left), President of Central Baptist Theological Seminary, lays hands on Pam Durso (right), Executive Director of Baptist Women in Ministry, and offers her a blessing during Durso's ordination service on February 28, 2015 at Smoke Rise Baptist Church in Stone Mountain, Georgia.

"Each generation offers a foundation for those to come," said Ruth Perkins Lee, Director of Ministries for the Cooperative Baptist Fellowship. "Molly and Pam significantly contributed to the foundation of my ministry long before I ever heard my calling. Our stories are deeply connected in ways that I may never be able to articulate and for which I am eternally grateful."

The stories of Molly Marshall and Pam Durso as well as the stories of reflection and remembrance of other CBF leaders—from Bill Leonard to Julie Pennington-Russell to George Mason to Kasey Jones and many more—are shared in the following pages. —**Editor**

The Maturing of a Movement

By Molly T. Marshall

I am grateful for the opportunity to reflect on our movement's 25th Anniversary. We have experienced God's resurrecting power, and the Spirit has beckoned us into a new future story.

CBF as Sanctuary for Healing

Some of us came to the Cooperative Baptist Fellowship rather beaten up. We were tired of being called heretics, skunks, infidels, theologically bankrupt, godless feminists, *ad nauseam*. We needed a new spiritual home place. I do remember the Convocation in 1991 and how grateful I was to connect with people of like mind. The ministry of dissent—a great Baptist spiritual practice—was illumined as we found one another.

We recognized one another as persons of reflective faith. We recognized the creeping creedalism for what it was—a dangerous threat to Baptist identity. We recognized that God would tend our battered hearts and set us to new horizons. We recognized a future, with hope. We could forge a new way of being Baptist.

The challenge for the CBF movement has been that the founding membership arrived with such a profound sense of institutional and personal loss that we revisited our narrative at the expense of some really fresh ideas. A sanctuary for healing is important; however, it can become reactive or insular—or both. Trusting new leadership who generationally were not a part of "the controversy" has taken longer than perhaps it should. But it is the CBF reality now.

CBF as New Baptist Narrative

For many, the term "Baptist" equates with being a Southern Baptist. This ignores years of American Baptist identity, historic Black Baptist traditions and global Baptists. Perhaps you have been in the position to offer the following disclaimer: "But I am not that kind of Baptist"—meaning other than a Southern Baptist. CBF has preserved the goodness of the name "Baptist" for those no longer willing to be identified with the Southern Baptist Convention.

During the spring of 1995 (after I had been thrown from the Southern Baptist train, which had decided to travel on a narrow gauge into the past), I spent a great deal of my time speaking at state

CBF meetings. I guess everybody knew I needed a job and might be available to come and speak.

I believe my engagement with those fledgling groups kept my sense of vocation alive. There were stirrings of the Spirit and vibrant hope as the varied expressions of CBF took flight. Those were heady days, indeed.

Twenty-five years of freedom and innovation have allowed us to tell a new story of grace and promise. No longer part of a denominational behemoth, Cooperative Baptists have learned that "small" and "excellent" can be used in the same sentence. We have learned that vulnerability and even financial fragility are media preferred by God, who became small and dependent, too. Entering the world, sustained only by a slender umbilical cord, Jesus cried: "Take care of me."

Cooperative Baptists have a unique identity that our world needs. The kinds of freedom and gospel accountability that define our story are good news, truly.

CBF as Movement of the Spirit

The greatest need of CBF persons today, in my judgment, is to trust that God's Spirit continues to guide and empower for ministry. Understanding our common life as a movement of the Spirit allows us to risk and to welcome the unexpected.

The Spirit works in freedom, calling the church and society to new forms of service in the world. In a day when participation in congregational life is in rapid decline, freedom-loving Baptists must make a compelling case for the role that the gathered community plays as a transformative agent of the Spirit.

Discerning the movement of the Spirit remains a demanding spiritual practice now, as it did in early Christianity. I believe we have been attentive to God's holy nudge.

It was a bold vision that prompted CBF to become a new movement. Not only did the Fellowship want to find ways to do mission with greater humility (when you don't own a lot of stuff, it requires more faith), CBF also knew that our future required new forms of theological education. And so new seminaries were birthed—and an old one (Central) was strengthened—through the vibrant new movement. CBF has yet to birth an *ovarium*, but it will come, I am sure!

It is a profoundly hopeful task to start new things and trust that God will prosper our work. It also calls us to love deeply. St. John of the

Cross wrote: "In the evening of life, we will be judged on love alone." Yet hope and faith undergird love, all gifts of the Spirit.

The Spirit usually nudges us toward what will require radical dependence upon divine assistance. At our best, Cooperative Baptists discern that unaccompanied ministry will founder; the Spirit opens the presence of God to us and makes us present to God and one another. CBF draws from the wells of its heritage, but it is a living, dynamic way of faith. I trust we will continue to be an instrument of grace.

Molly Marshall is President and Professor of Theology and Spiritual Formation at Central Baptist Theological Seminary in Shawnee, Kansas. Her passion in life is preparing women and men for ministry experience. For more than 30 years, she has been in theological education. A graduate of Oklahoma Baptist University and Southern Baptist Theological Seminary (Master of Divinity; Doctor of Philosophy), she previously served as youth minister, campus minister and pastor in churches across several states.

By Water and the Word

By Bill J. Leonard

"The Church's one foundation is Jesus Christ her Lord. She is his new creation by water and the word." So Samuel Wesley's powerful hymn begins. The phrase, "new creation by water and the word," overwhelms me every time we sing that song; the simple idiom captures the internal and external essence of the Church as Body of Christ. Applicable to Christian communions in general, the words enhance my own celebration and struggle with Baptist ways of articulating and living the gospel.

To reflect on the first 25 years of Cooperative Baptist Fellowship history is to revisit the image of a "new creation by water and the word." Like many "new creations" within Christianity, CBF began out of deep divisions in the larger Baptist family. A decade of turmoil between factions in the Southern Baptist Convention finally took its toll, convincing some people that it was time to stop fighting over doctrine and denomination and move on, leaving the SBC to itself. CBF was born of that decision—not easily, and not without varying degrees of hesitation. Divorces, familial or ecclesial, are always painful.

I really don't think much about the mayhem of those divisive years, except perhaps when friends remind me of specific "crisis events" we shared together. And then the old memories descend. Riding the SBC rapids bonded some of us for life. Thankfully, 25 years of participation in CBF, and membership in two predominantly African American Baptist congregations, still instruct and enliven me with grace recovered in the "water and the word" of Christ's church. Gratitude for such grace influences the following observations on CBF as a "new creation" of Christian community.

First, from its earliest days, CBF has sought to be a place where individuals and congregations have found healing from the "Baptist wars" and other continuing ecclesiastical divisions. This is a gift, not simply to so-called "ex-SBCers" but also to those who still experience struggles in and with the Church and the world. May such gospel triage continue, even increase.

Second, also from the beginning, CBF has facilitated exploration of Baptist identity—past, present and future—in multiple approaches and ministry possibilities. Whatever else we may be or become,

Baptists are a people who affirm the "water and the word" of a believers' church, in which the "glad river" of believer's baptism becomes an outward sign of inward experience with Christ. That identity "centers" us as a people, emboldening our engagement with the broader church and beyond. CBF helps us own our "Baptistness," confessing our sins and reaffirming that the Kingdom of God (God's New Day) really has come near.

Third, across these 25 years, CBF has worked diligently to nurture and facilitate theological education for new generations of Baptist ministers, an essential blueprint for the future. In fact, one of the most hopeful signs of CBF—indeed the Baptist—future is present in these young women and men who are taking their place in congregational and community leadership. Likewise, the Fellowship has developed programs for "Young Leaders," assisting new networks of recent seminary graduates that enhance friendship, connectedness and strategies for the future. And these young people are rising to the challenge in congregations nationally and internationally. Through these emphases, CBF extends its "new creation" substantially.

Fourth, what about the future? Questions abound:

- What about the "water?" How will CBF and its related churches retell the Jesus Story in ways that draw persons to transformation through faith in Christ and baptism into Christ's body, the Church? As old methods for describing "new life in Christ" wane or disappear altogether, where will we find Jesus?
- What about the "Word?" Have years of debate over theories of biblical inspiration kept us from the biblical text itself and the challenge of biblical interpretation? Can CBF encourage participant churches and individuals to rediscover biblical study not simply as an end to itself, but as a way of enlivening personal and communal faith beyond crass or selective literalism?
- And what of CBF itself? Might it continue, even extend, its partnerships with like-hearted communions such as the American Baptist Churches USA, the Progressive National Baptist Convention, the Alliance of Baptists and the New Baptist Covenant, not only because we need their fellowship, but because none of us can make it alone?

"The church of CHRIST is a company of faithful people," the Baptist confession of 1611 declares, "knit unto the Lord, & one unto another, by Baptism, upon their own confession of the faith and sins." The water, the word, and "a company of faithful people" knitted together, by grace. Let's keep at it. Amen.

Bill J. Leonard is the James and Marilyn Dunn Professor of Baptist Studies and Professor of Church History at Wake Forest University School of Divinity in Winston-Salem, North Carolina. He is a graduate of Texas Wesleyan University (Bachelor of Arts), Southwestern Baptist Theological Seminary (Master of Divinity) and Boston University (Doctor of Philosophy). An ordained Baptist minister, Leonard is the author or editor of more than 24 books.

Freedom Is Our Watchword

By George Mason

When the Cooperative Baptist Fellowship began, we were fired and inspired by a passion for freedom. We had felt the crushing force of fundamentalism that had robbed our Baptist way of life of its signature virtue.

So many revolutions echo the cry for freedom. Whether Moses telling the pharaoh to "Let my people go," or the brave-hearted William Wallace shouting "Freedom!" with his last breath, or Patrick Henry defiantly declaring "Give me liberty or give me death," or Martin Luther King, Jr., imploring every dreamer to "Let freedom ring," the Spirit of God stirs in the human soul until it bursts forth in a new birth of freedom. CBF was just such a new birth.

In all movements, there are factions that join together against a common foe at first, then show their differences from each other in the years following. CBF is no exception. All came together under the banner of freedom from fundamentalism, but increasingly there came a call among others for something more—freedom for faithfulness. We began to call ourselves free and faithful Baptists.

Freedom has these two sides: freedom *from* and freedom *for*. And Cooperative Baptists have, since the early days, fostered both in a fellowship that allowed each to flourish.

A segment of our Fellowship has continued to watch the rear flank, so to speak, maintaining that freedom from tyranny of any kind is a gift of God. They have guarded the wall of separation of church and state. They have monitored the freedom of individual conscience. They have reminded us that dissent is rightly exercised in service to the unity of the church and not in service of schism. They have resisted denominational conformity and held up voluntary cooperation as a higher value.

The voices of freedom for mostly began with those whose passion was holistic mission work. Southern Baptists had narrowed the scope of mission to evangelism and church planting, depriving many missionaries of the freedom to meet human need even as they shared the liberating Gospel of Christ. They saw CBF as a means of renewing the Baptist mission to the world, and they worked and prayed and gave and went in order to see it happen. They considered our mission efforts frontline work—we were a vanguard of the kingdom. And to that end, we chose to boldly go where no one had gone before. We started work with unreached people groups and the poorest of the poor.

Others have added to this freedom for dimension by giving more content to our faith rather than merely affirming the right to believe without compulsion. Our partner theological schools give the next generation the tools to extend the franchise. They teach both deeds and creeds (small "c") so that the Baptist way of following Jesus has heart and head and hands. Increasingly, they are nurturing an ecumenical spirit that both honors our separatist origins and acknowledges our unity with the larger Church.

In recent times, we have added social justice and Christian advocacy to our freedom for causes. We understand that we must stand with the oppressed and the marginalized in society. We are willing to use our influence for God and for good to see justice emerge as a visible witness to the coming peace of Christ.

Our leaders across these years—Cecil Sherman, Daniel Vestal and Suzii Paynter—have all played their parts in their time. They have kept us moving forward together, when at any time we might have split or splintered. We owe them, and the countless staff, clergy and lay leaders who have served with them, an enormous debt of gratitude.

From the beginning, I have been an eyewitness to this remarkable spiritual movement of freedom. And to the extent that I have participated in it, I am the more because of it and the more blessed by it.

The Apostle Paul was right: For freedom Christ has set us free. Free to be faithful.

Freedom is still our watchword, faithfully understood.

George Mason has served as senior pastor of Wilshire Baptist Church in Dallas, Texas, since 1989. He holds degrees from the University of Miami (Bachelor of Business Administration) and Southwestern Baptist Theological Seminary (Master of Divinity and Doctor of Philosophy). At Wilshire, he birthed and directs the unique pastoral residency program that has become a model for other congregations nationwide. A native of New York City, George and his wife, Kim, have three adult children.

Finding Possibility, Finding Hope

By Pamela R. Durso

Because I teach Baptist history, I know dates. I know the date of our Baptist tradition's origin. I know the dates for convention foundings and seminary beginnings, the dates of missionary sendings and church plantings, and the dates of controversy brewings and resolution passings. But some of those dates are not just markers on the calendar for me. Some of those dates are intertwined with my personal story.

In addition to my work with Baptist Women in Ministry, I am blessed to teach regularly as an adjunct professor at Mercer University's McAfee School of Theology. In those semesters in which I teach Baptist Heritage, I am always reminded that, as I talk to students about the recent years of our history, my personal story has been forever shaped by the story of the Cooperative Baptist Fellowship.

In 1980, I entered Baylor University as a freshman. During that first year of college, as I sought to understand a sense of calling that had long been with me, I discerned that the Spirit was nudging me toward ministry, perhaps the ministry of teaching. So I changed my major to religion. I was in the midst of opening the doors of my imagination at the same time that the larger Baptist community of my childhood began to close its doors to me. In 1979, the year before I enrolled at Baylor, Southern Baptist fundamentalists inaugurated their plan to take over the denomination, and the Southern Baptist Convention that I had known and loved became embroiled in a controversy that became a constant shadow in my life.

I graduated with a bachelor's degree from Baylor in May of 1984. One month later, the SBC adopted a resolution titled "On Ordination and the Role of Women in Ministry." It is a long resolution with many "whereas" clauses, including these two:

> WHEREAS, The Scriptures teach that women are not in public worship to assume a role of authority over men lest confusion reign in the local church; and

> WHEREAS, While Paul commends women and men alike in other roles of ministry and service, he excludes women from pastoral leadership to preserve a submission God requires

because man was first in creation and woman was first in the Edenic fall;

The resolution ended with these words:

Therefore, be it RESOLVED, That we not decide concerns of Christian doctrine and practice by modern culture, sociological and ecclesiastical trends or by emotional factors; that we remind ourselves of the dearly bought Baptist principle of the final authority of Scripture in matters of faith and conduct; and that we encourage the service of women in all aspects of church life and work other than pastoral functions and leadership roles entailing ordination.

To say that the resolution was unsettling for me is an understatement. Although ordination was not even on my radar, ministry and leadership were. This resolution seemed to be condemning the teaching of men by women, which was where I sensed my career path was heading. So I began to question my own sense of calling. I wondered if I had misinterpreted God's calling. Maybe God did not want women in positions of leadership. Maybe God wanted me to stay quiet and find other avenues of doing ministry.

Yet I could not give up my calling, nor was I willing to give up my understanding of a grace-filled God who invites us all, regardless of gender, to use the gifts we have been given. So off to seminary I went, committed to preparing fully for what God had called me to be and confident that the God who had called me would find a ministry for me—a place where I could serve.

I finished a Master of Divinity degree at Southwestern Seminary in 1987. During my three years there, the controversy heated up. Southwestern's president, Russell Dilday, and some of my professors spoke out against the fundamentalists, and soon there was great tension on our campus. The faculty, staff and students were all anxious. Much of the hallway conversation was about the controversy. A gray cloud hung over us all.

In 1987, I began doctoral work at Baylor, still convinced of God's calling to a teaching ministry. For five years I studied hard, read an endless number of books, and finished my dissertation—all the while wondering if I would ever have a teaching position in a Baptist school. I now had serious doubts that a Baptist university or seminary would ever hire me, and I greatly feared that my education would never be used. My calling would go unfulfilled.

Despite my fears, I pushed forward, finishing my doctorate in church history in May 1992, one year after the Cooperative Baptist Fellowship was birthed. I soon discovered that I was not alone. So many other Baptists had been living with the shadows and gray clouds. Finally, there was a Baptist body that was saying "Yes" to me and "Yes" to my calling. This new Baptist group was opening doors, letting in the sunlight, affirming women as ministers, and offering me a new place to call home.

But my ministry story and CBF's story were just beginning in 1992. I wish that I could say that the founding of CBF calmed all my fears and that, through CBF, I immediately had opportunities to use all my gifts. But this was not the reality. In 1992, CBF was just getting on its feet, setting up an office and figuring out how to support missionaries and connect like-minded Baptists. In those first few years, while CBF leaders and churches proclaimed their openness to women in leadership and women ministers, the reality is that this new movement and its affiliating churches did not yet reflect much openness. CBF churches were often willing to ordain women, but only a handful of those churches called women to serve as pastor, using the painful words, "Our church is not ready yet." The truth, too, is that CBF in those early years was still male-dominated when it came to leadership and decision-making.

So in the mid-1990s, when my connection with the Fellowship began, what I found was not paradise or perfection. What I did find was possibility. This new organization gave me hope. Because of CBF, I sensed that full gender inclusion was possible. I began to believe that I might find opportunities for service. With CBF, I finally had hope. I settled myself into the Fellowship, put down roots and pledged to stay.

Then, slowly but steadily, CBF helped create new seminaries and divinity schools. It built an organizational structure, and changes came. In 1999, seven years after I completed my doctorate, I was hired by one of the new CBF-affiliated schools to teach. I moved my family across the country and began living into a 20-year-old calling at Campbell University Divinity School.

After four years, I joined the staff of a CBF-partner organization, the Baptist History and Heritage Society; and in 2009, I was called by the leadership team of another CBF-partner, Baptist Women in Ministry, to be the organization's Executive Director.

When I look back and review the dates of my own life, I see clearly how the unfolding of my ministry is tied so closely to the growth and development of the people who call themselves Cooperative Baptists. Today, my love for CBF is strong, not because I have found paradise or perfection, but because this body of Baptists has, like me, committed to the continuing journey of discovering and embracing God's call. What was true 25 years ago is true still today. What I have found and keep finding among Cooperative Baptists is possibility. CBF gives me hope.

Pam Durso is Executive Director of Baptist Women in Ministry, where she is an advocate and resource for women serving in all areas of Christian ministry. She is also an adjunct faculty member at Mercer University's McAfee School of Theology in Atlanta.

Baptist Messiness

By Joy Yee

Finger painting all over the paper and the desks in kindergarten, decorating cookies with tiny ricocheting candy sprinkles in children's fellowship, figuring out what to do with closets filled with items that no one wants to keep or throw away—these are not peaceful activities for those of us who like life to unfold in an orderly fashion.

What I have always loved about the Cooperative Baptist Fellowship is our willingness to engage things that are messy—soul freedom, Bible freedom, church freedom, religious freedom. You know—Baptist things. All the stuff that makes us want to say "Amen!" but becomes puzzling and frustrating when we find ourselves swimming around what it means to be the people of God. The meanings are as numerous as the participants at any given General Assembly when we're talking about matters such as women in ministry, the restructuring of governance, executive coordinator searches, LGBT concerns, the best ways to do missions and ministry, and more.

Mess is hard to control. Mess is, by definition, not always orderly. Mess cannot be defined accurately in a sound bite. But the "Baptist kind of mess" is great because it invites us to live right between trust in God's guiding presence and humility to see the perspectives and contributions of others as needed and valuable. In the words of the hymn "Sing a New Church," mess makes us "rich in our diversity." Baptists at their best have always affirmed the messiness that honors space for God to be God, and for God to do God's work.

One of my vivid memories is of a General Assembly business session when we were discussing hiring policies. One person in particular came to the microphone, stated his opinion and then said, "These are my convictions. But whether or not the Assembly votes in alignment with my convictions, my wife and I will still be strong supporters and a part of CBF."

These words were like oxygen for my soul because, at the time, I lived in a church context where lines were always being drawn at the expense of fellowship. I needed to know that a common confession of Christ as Lord did not always have to be threatened by differences in faith practice or theology. You know—Baptist things.

The year that I served as CBF Moderator was a profound gift. I had been barred somewhat from ministry and was in a difficult season of needing to prove that women could be pastors. It was life-giving to offer my gifts and to experience people's grace-filled and genuine reception of them. This "flesh and blood" affirmation was the solid ground underneath that announcement that CBF had elected a female senior pastor for the first time to serve as its moderator.

My term began with a business session concern that the Fellowship's commitment to Jesus was not stated blatantly enough in our constitution. I was never anxious about Jesus' importance in our lives as the God we love and follow to the best of our ability. But it was disquieting to think that perhaps we were headed for painful struggles similar to the ones we had left behind when CBF was formed. New habits are often hard to establish, and we were not that far from difficult experiences we knew firsthand.

Would we be able to be truly Baptist in our life together—a diverse and free people, united by our confession of faith and sense of mission alone? Thankfully, we were. By the time the newly composed Preamble to the CBF Constitution was presented and affirmed at our General Assembly, and the people who had originally voiced the concern expressed their respect and appreciation for the outcome, we knew once again that it was possible to come out of dysfunctional patterns and find new ways of being the people of God together.

Along with that experience, we began to practice more spiritual discernment in our discussions and decision-making as a body. To do this was a daunting prospect because it invited us to fully trust the movement, revelation and care of God's Spirit in the complex task of doing the work of the kingdom. To pray, to listen to varied perspectives and opinions, to offer our thoughts and to hold others' thoughts with honor, and to move forward with consensus that did not necessarily demand complete agreement were all actions that we began to engage on different levels at the Coordinating Council and in our General Assembly. The task of discernment was always challenging and sometimes ethereal, but it led us to keep acknowledging the mysterious, frustrating, humbling, awesome truth that our God is larger than we can imagine. And perhaps that is the greatest gain we can ever hope to achieve as we continue to be the presence of Christ in our beautiful world.

For those of us who like life to unfold in an orderly fashion, the tension of painting with fingers, decorating cookies, cleaning closets and being the people of God together as CBF is always going to be there. I will gladly be a part of it because of our potential to do what God envisions for us.

I am so thankful for who we are together. I love that we are willing to engage the often complex and messy business of people of God. It is always my prayer and hope that, in the coming years, we will keep a sense of humility and dependence on our God, and continue to love each other and walk together so that all the world might be healed and whole.

Joy Yee served as Moderator of the Cooperative Baptist Fellowship from 2005-2006 and has served as senior pastor of Nineteenth Avenue Baptist Church in San Francisco, California, since it merged with New Covenant Baptist Church in 2005. A graduate of Golden Gate Baptist Theological Seminary, she received her Master of Divinity degree in 1992 and was ordained in 2000.

Enlarging the Baptist Family

By Emmanuel L. McCall

The first 17 years of my life were spent in Pennsylvania. But in 1953, I left my family, kinfolk and church community to become a student at the University of Louisville in Louisville, Kentucky. It was there that God began fashioning a new and larger Baptist family for me when I joined the Baptist Student Union. The group involved in BSU took me in and made me feel at home. Through the BSU, I was led to do theological preparation at Southern Baptist Theological Seminary in Louisville, where the seminary students, faculty and staff became my larger Baptist family. Friendships were formed there that are lasting even until this day.

As a pastor in Louisville for eight years, my "family" expanded as I became a fellow laborer with other Baptist pastors. In the 1960s, our nation was in turmoil with racial strife. In Louisville, Baptist pastors and other ministers formed an Interracial Baptist Ministers Conference designed to help us cross barriers and become a witness for Christ. As a result of the work of this conference, Louisville was not paralyzed by racial turmoil as were many other cities across the nation.

In 1968, my Baptist family expanded yet again. I was invited to become a staff member of the Home Mission Board of the Southern Baptist Convention. Even though the issue of racial reconciliation was heated in the 1960s through the 1980s, I remained in contact with my Baptist family members who were determined to make reconciliation a reality. Some paid a dear price and were terminated from church staffs and positions at colleges and seminaries.

I stayed in contact with my Baptist family in the SBC. We informed, encouraged, prayed for and inspired each other to "good works." As we ministered together under the guidance of the Holy Spirit, our sense of family kept expanding. We had wonderful times when we gathered at various conferences, both state and national. We studied God's Word, renewed our commitment to mission endeavors, and worshipped Christ in the "beauty of holiness." Whenever the family gathered, we renewed our faith and loyalty in Jesus Christ.

Then came the "family feud"—to borrow the name of the popular television show. Our Baptist "family feud" was more serious because worldwide eternal values were at stake. My Baptist family became smaller because of the feud. However, God allowed us through the Holy Spirit to regroup. We were determined that the principles and values of our Baptist heritage would be kept alive.

The Cooperative Baptist Fellowship has been the vehicle of God's grace that has enabled the "family" to continue to flourish. I rejoice over the many ways that God is keeping us together. Some from my Baptist family are now rejoicing in God's eternity. They wait for us to join them. Others of us are still trying to enlarge the family, even in retirement.

God is doing a glorious thing with one of my Baptist family members. Former CBF Executive Coordinator Daniel Vestal and I, while in retirement, have been interim pastors. He is at the oldest predominantly Anglo church in Atlanta—Peachtree Baptist Church. I served at the oldest African American church in Atlanta—Friendship Baptist Church. One day over lunch, we decided that these two churches ought to form a partnership. This we have done. In doing so, we have enlarged the Baptist family.

Daniel and I are also co-teaching a course at Mercer University's McAfee School of Theology in Atlanta titled "Leadership in Black and White." We continue to enlarge the Baptist family. The real Baptist family belongs together.

So may it ever be.

Emmanuel McCall served as Moderator of the Cooperative Baptist Fellowship from 2006-2007. He is currently an adjunct faculty member at Mercer University's McAfee School of Theology and served as interim pastor of Friendship Baptist Church in Atlanta from 2013-2015.

Baptist to the Core

By Tony Campolo

I have been involved with the Cooperative Baptist Fellowship from its earliest days, and I have come to believe that this is a movement committed to asserting basic Baptist principles—particularly the principle of the autonomy of the local church. This principle has come under attack in many ways, especially when it comes to the ordination of women and the right of local churches to appoint women as pastors.

For years, women had been trained to serve Baptist churches throughout the Southern Baptist Convention (SBC), and these women had done so with faithfulness and effectiveness. Most had graduated from Southern Baptist seminaries and gained distinction with some of the highest grades in their preaching classes. Decisions were made, however, on the denominational level and by the ruling boards of SBC seminaries that ended the opportunity for women to serve as pastors in most Southern Baptist circles.

This, of course, was not the only issue that gave rise to CBF, but it was symptomatic of the changes that were being wrought as a group of dedicated fundamentalists took over the denomination. Little by little, the institutions related to the SBC applied litmus tests as to who, and which churches, could be bona fide members of this denomination in good standing. CBF, on the other hand, adhered to a belief that, with Baptists, there should be no official creedal statements. Instead, in accord with a tradition that goes back to the founding of the Baptist movement, there has been a belief among Cooperative Baptists that the Bible was the basis for Christian truth.

CBF has also expressed a willingness to grant to individual believers the freedom to interpret the scriptures as the Holy Spirit guides them. These convictions set CBF on a course that placed them in opposition to many in the SBC who increasingly spelled out what could and could not be believed if membership in the SBC were to be allowed. Ironically, a great proportion of the members of CBF actually agree with the evangelical doctrines held by most Southern Baptists, but resist the right of a denomination to dictate what can and cannot be the practices of local congregations.

Over the recent past, many Cooperative Baptists have had trouble with some of the social policies voted in as resolutions and affirmed by the SBC during its annual meetings. For instance, the refusal of the SBC to acknowledge the existence of global warming troubled many Cooperative Baptists. The support which the SBC gave to the United States president in his pursuit of the war in the Middle East was seriously questioned by some as well. These are only two of the variety of issues that seemed to many Cooperative Baptists to be marrying the SBC to the right wing of the Republican Party. CBF chooses to steer clear of any hint of partisan politics.

As I have come to know the leaders of the Fellowship, I have found them to be evangelical to the core. At the annual General Assembly, you will hear the old-time gospel being preached and sung. It is their emphasis on religious freedom—both for individuals and for local churches—that makes them distinct and in line with the historical Baptist tradition.

Being an ordained minister with the American Baptist Churches USA, I have found that my own denomination seems to be in perfect harmony with CBF—that mission involves preaching a holistic gospel that unifies in a single message calling people into a personal saving relationship with Christ, as well as into a commitment to social justice on behalf of those whom Jesus called "the least of these."

Tony Campolo is Professor Emeritus of Sociology at Eastern University and the founder of the Evangelical Association for the Promotion of Education. A popular speaker and author of more than 35 books, he is one of the founders of the Red Letter Christian movement.

Serving Alongside Cecil Sherman

By Justin Joplin

On Sunday morning, July 29, 2007, the people of Westover Baptist Church in Richmond, Virginia, voted to call not one, but two pastors. I was one of those pastors. A brand new graduate of the Baptist Theological Seminary at Richmond, I was eager to jump into my first full-time ministry placement. Plus, I had been hoping and praying for an opportunity that would keep me in the Richmond area, where my wife, Kristy, was doing fulfilling work with the local chapter of the Multiple Sclerosis Society. The other pastor Westover called on that day was Cecil Sherman, the retired founding Coordinator of the Cooperative Baptist Fellowship.

I should point out that I'm using the word "retired" in the loosest sense. To tell the truth, I'm not sure Cecil ever fully retired. His energy and productivity during that phase of his life surpassed many of us at the heights of our careers. When he wasn't teaching at the seminary, he was writing commentary for the Smyth & Helwys Sunday school curriculum. When he wasn't doing that, he was working on his memoirs. He made time to meet with area ministers, usually encouraging them to support CBF and BTSR.

Cecil was serious about physical fitness, making time to exercise nearly every day. Often, when we met, he was wearing his gray Baylor University sweatshirt, having recently finished a spell in the workout room. He dedicated much of his time to caring for his wife, Dot, who stayed on the Alzheimer's hall in the same complex as his apartment.

On top of all this activity, Cecil also devoted his time to local churches. He may not have believed in retirement, but he certainly believed in congregations. Cecil took on numerous interim pastorates during his final years. Large or small, vital or struggling, when a congregation needed Cecil's help, he answered the call.

As it happens, my first encounter with Cecil came during his season as interim pastor at Richmond's River Road Church. After visiting River Road one Sunday morning, I shook Cecil's hand on the way out the front door, saying something like, "Dr. Sherman, you teach at my seminary, and I'm planning to take your class next term." I had no idea at the time that our connection would extend beyond the classroom.

In calling both Cecil and me to join the pastoral team, Westover was plotting a creative strategy for its future. The church could continue to benefit from Cecil's decades of outstanding congregational leadership while he mentored me as his soon-to-be successor. Over time, Cecil would take on less and less responsibility and I would take on more. In a year or two, he would step away, and I, with valuable experience under my belt, would become the senior pastor. It was an innovative plan, and Westover was excited to see it come together. As for me, I was excited to be sharing an office with Cecil Sherman.

Many people knew Cecil as a prophetic voice speaking out against the racism of the 1960s Jim Crow South and fundamentalism in the 1980s. Many knew Cecil as a denominational pioneer, a leader who helped write a new and inspiring chapter in the Baptist story. I didn't get to know *that* Cecil—not personally, that is. I heard about *that* Cecil in the stories he recounted in his seminary course on the life and work of a pastor. I read about *that* Cecil in his 2008 memoir *By My Own Reckoning* and, when he passed away in 2010, in an impressive write-up in the *New York Times*.

I got to know Cecil as a fellow pastor in the service of a small church in a changing urban neighborhood. I listened to him deliver sermons in such a plainspoken, matter-of-fact style that he would conclude by declaring, "That's the end of the sermon." I watched him conduct funerals; he would say, "I'm not here today because I knew Mrs. Smith well in life. I am here as the teller of an old, old story." Then he would speak of the resurrection.

I marveled as he improved the church by reviving common-sense practices like asking longtime attendees to become church members and encouraging people to pledge to the budget. I once overheard him teaching a classroom full of little children how to sing "Little Bunny Foo Foo." Cecil believed we could better connect with children and families by starting a children's choir, and when nobody was available to direct it, he did it himself.

Serving a local church with Cecil Sherman showed me just how passionate he was about churches. He had experienced some of the worst congregational conflict and denominational politics, yet still maintained an enduring love and respect for church people. He believed that laypeople were a gift—that they showed up at church because they sincerely wanted to help make the world a brighter place in Jesus' name.

For these kinds of lessons, modeled in the local congregation and in the forming of a new kind of denomination, I believe Cecil was a gift. Working beside him was a blessing I'll never forget.

A native of North Carolina, Justin R. Joplin relocated to the Toronto area in 2014 to serve as pastor of Lorne Park Baptist Church. He earned his Master of Divinity degree from Baptist Theological Seminary at Richmond and served on the CBF Coordinating Council from 2009 to 2012. He and his wife, Kristy, have two sons, J.R. and Reuben.

Seeking Freedom and Peace

By Winnie V. Williams

Several years ago, my husband and I spent our vacation at Waikiki Beach in Hawaii, relaxing in a hotel that housed a three-story-high salt-water aquarium containing more than 70 varieties of fish. They ranged in size from just a few inches long to four feet, and their tinges of colors reminded me of a brilliant sunset. The most amazing thing about this amalgamation of fish was that they did not aggressively invade each other's space, nor did they attempt to devour each other, but dwelled in peace, respecting each other.

For 400 years, Baptists at their best relished peace and tolerance of the variability in Baptist life. Twenty-five or so years ago, freedom and diversity were considered strengths, but somehow this way of life began to unravel. Thus began the skirmish to maintain the right to express our freedoms. It was a long, hard and painful struggle for free and faithful Baptists. However, those of us who chose to be free and autonomous discovered how much we needed each other. Renewed hope occurred when courageous individuals led us to form the Cooperative Baptist Fellowship. We nudged onward in God's ministry, continuing to be as diverse as the fish in the tank. Yet we are whole, authentic and faithful Baptists.

I cannot begin to quantify my spiritual journey, which has been protected, strengthened and endowed since the early 1990s because of CBF. Having attended most of the 25 CBF General Assemblies as well as numerous retreats and seminars, and having had the privilege of sitting at the feet of theological giants, these years are a celebrated journey. In May 1991, I was selected to serve on the first CBF Coordinating Council along with three other South Carolinians. This began a new and exciting chapter of my life.

Being placed on the Constitution Committee provided me minor input regarding gender equality, which was one of the controversial issues in Baptist life. It was necessary to address the issue because of the resistance by some male council members regarding the status of women in leadership positions. I recall the proceedings to select subcommittee members to study the path of a proposed mission ministry. A male council member who had been designated to bring recommendations for membership for the Missions Committee submitted to the council a list of 20 men, primarily ministers. Due to a few emphatic women whose ire bounced off the ceiling, a new "suggested list" was submitted at the next council meeting that better represented gender equality.

Some of the highlights from the General Assemblies that warmed my heart include: the occasion when Dr. Keith Parks announced joining CBF to coordinate our global missions, President Jimmy Carter's declaring his support of CBF, and Dr. Daniel Vestal's agreeing to serve as CBF's Executive Coordinator. Another exalted moment for me was the gender breakthrough when Suzii Paynter became Executive Coordinator in 2013.

The Cooperative Baptist Fellowship of South Carolina could not have existed without the committed, dedicated volunteers who nurtured our Baptist entity over the past 25 years. We have had numerous, first-rate paid employees. However, the nuts and bolts of the mission programs and a significant portion of the administration of CBF of South Carolina has come from volunteers who served on state and national councils and committees, implemented dozens of mission projects, led emergency efforts, and planned our state meetings.

When we were in the early stages of seeking our bearings, I became the fifth Moderator of CBF of South Carolina. Our focus was continuing the development of the organization, searching for our next target and spurring people onward. Forward movement included increasing the number of participants on our state council, establishing an office and laying the groundwork to hire a coordinator. We desperately needed at least a part-time staffer in those early days, but it was problematic due to a lack of funds.

As Moderator, I sensed the dilemma pondering our next move when Beverly Greer agreed to become a part-time office manager. A Christian gentleman, Jonny Faris, offered CBF of South Carolina a small house for office space in Laurens. We were set to go.

While serving in the Laurens office, Beverly also served as chair of our Missions Committee. Several years later, she was selected to serve on the CBF Missions Council. Due to her undying love for the Fellowship's mission, she was awarded the inaugural national Coordinating Council Alumni Award at the 2010 General Assembly. She is an example of the countless volunteers who have contributed significantly to the mission of the Fellowship in South Carolina. There have been many others who have donated hours and resources to make CBF of South Carolina a viable body of ministry in the state.

It has been through the Fellowship and the nurturing of my faith that I renewed the exploration of God's word that has impacted my life and provided me with a better understanding of ministry. I have become more alert to global interconnections and more attentive to our obligations to treat everyone, regardless of ethnicity, with dignity and respect rather than being judgmental and/or critical. I now embrace a vision of loving and ministering to individuals whether they are poor, needy or underserved. I am convinced that all people are God's children.

In his book, *A New Call to Missions*, Daniel Vestal wrote: "The greatest joys in life come from being loved and being able to love." The freedom of loving and being loved by individuals that I have encountered through CBF over these past years is an indefinable blessing. Some of the dearest people in God's earthly Kingdom are those I have encountered who are doers, not just proclaimers. These dear friends have supported and loved me during some difficult periods of my life and have lifted me beyond periods of grief. Many of them I encounter only at CBF General Assemblies, but they are faithful, trustworthy and authentic disciples who have provided me with a little piece of God's Kingdom.

"It is for freedom that Christ has set us free." (Galatians 5:1)

Winnie V. Williams is a retired Associate Professor from Southern Wesleyan University in Central, South Carolina. A graduate of Mississippi College, New Orleans Baptist Theological Seminary and Clemson University, she served on the first Coordinating Council of the Cooperative Baptist Fellowship. She and her husband, Woodie, reside in Clemson, South Carolina.

Calling

By Grace Powell Freeman

Some of my favorite times in my early days serving with the Cooperative Baptist Fellowship were those when field personnel candidates would spend several days in the CBF office in Atlanta, going through a discernment process we call exploratory conference. To be honest, it was a holy time, but also a time when I did not completely understand how these decisions were made. How did someone decide to give up the life they had been living and move to some faraway place to start over in a ministry that would be difficult?

There was one moment I will never forget. A dear young couple—the wife being far along in her pregnancy—was going through the discernment process. Each candidate had a staff person assigned to walk through the process with them, and it was my privilege to work with this particular couple. The exploratory conference went well for them, and after all the test results were in, the interviews completed and the paperwork reviewed, it was determined by CBF Global Missions staff that it would be a match to ask this couple to join with us in ministry in a faraway country.

I drove to the hotel where the couple was staying to share the news with them. I continued to wonder: How does a young couple, especially one expecting a new baby, do this? How does this work? What makes them feel so compelled to take this step?

I walked into their hotel room and explained that the Global Missions staff wanted to walk alongside them in the next steps of appointment. I sat and wondered what their response would be, again pondering how this "call" thing works.

The husband and wife looked at each other with tears welling up in their eyes. I asked what the tears meant, and they began to talk more about their calling and how they could not imagine being happy doing anything other than what they were being asked to do. God was fulfilling a call in their lives that they had both felt for years.

Suddenly, the "call" thing became a bit clearer to me. It is a powerful moment to be able to experience someone following the direction God has in his or her life—even when it is something you cannot understand, something so different from your own calling. Calling looks different to each person. When we can be respectful and honor that call, we realize that we are on holy ground. Letting God be who God is and watching God work in lives is truly amazing to witness.

I am grateful for all the field personnel with whom I have been able to walk alongside during my time with CBF Global Missions. They are some of the most inspiring people I know. It has truly been a blessing and an honor to watch them live out their lives of calling.

Grace Powell Freeman served with the Global Missions staff of the Cooperative Baptist Fellowship for more than 21 years. Previously, she served with the American Bible Society in New York City and the Kentucky Baptist Convention. An ordained minister and graduate of Shorter College, West Georgia College and the Southern Baptist Theological Seminary, Grace and her husband, Bob, are proud parents to two young adults.

The Future Is Bright

By Jimmy Allen

The adage that hindsight is 20/20 is dramatically demonstrated as we celebrate the 25th Anniversary of the Cooperative Baptist Fellowship.

When I presided at the sessions in June 1979 as President of the Southern Baptist Convention, I thought that launching a missions-focused worship service—a service in which more than 1,000 persons dedicated two years of their lives to service—would fuse us together to accomplish Kingdom tasks. Instead, it became the beginning of the invasion of secular political methods in our process.

I agreed to serve as convener of the 1990 Consultation of Concerned Baptists in Atlanta, which would lead to the formation of CBF. Looking back over these 25 years, I view with joy the restoration of the place of laity in leadership that the Fellowship has demonstrated. I see the affirmation of the place of women in ministry. The place of women in preserving and magnifying mission service has been a significant part of Baptist life over the years, but their gifts and talents have often been treated as second-class service in the Kingdom. It is significant that our Executive Coordinator, Suzii Paynter, is an extremely talented woman.

The reaching out in partnership across racial lines also allows a new energy to the impact of our witness. We make a place for individuals to join us, rather than messengers of congregations. There was a period of time when I joined President Carter in communication with key pastors in the effort to find ways to avoid the separations that were evolving. It was frustrating to find no way to reach common ground. In retrospect, I realize that the parting of ways between fundamentalist Baptists and Cooperative Baptists is in our gene pool.

The future is bright for this fellowship of believers. I remember the moment in the discussion at the 1991 Convocation in Atlanta as we talked about what we would call ourselves. The key word became "cooperative" because we wanted to emphasize that we chose to work willingly with each other. We wanted to be careful to affirm our heritage as the "baptizers" of believers that our predecessors had been called.

We did not want a new convention. We wanted a Fellowship that recognized our freedom of choice and would allow individuals as well as groups to join us. We wanted to stimulate creativity.

The future is as bright as the promises of God. New generations of young believers who live and think in a world without borders are emerging.

Jimmy Allen is Coordinator Emeritus of the New Baptist Covenant, a diverse movement of Baptist organizations from throughout North America that he helped launch alongside former President Jimmy Carter. A graduate of Howard Payne University (Bachelor of Arts) and Southwestern Baptist Theological Seminary (Doctor of Theology). Allen is a respected pastor, author, ethicist, denominational leader, Emmy-winning television producer and pioneer Baptist advocate for racial equality and human rights. He served as President of the Southern Baptist Convention from 1978-1979.

Keep the Journey Going

By Jack Glasgow

I remember well the motion placed before our congregation by the Denomination Relations Committee during the fall quarter conference in 1990:

"When the group in Atlanta is ready to receive our funds for missions, we move that Zebulon Baptist Church direct all but $500 of its missions budget currently supporting the Southern Baptist Convention be sent to the new organization."

The motion passed with only one dissenting vote. We were fully engaged with a group of people in a mission endeavor that was truly in its infancy. We were not yet certain of its name, but we were certain we wanted to be identified with these Christians and Baptist congregations ready to embark on a new pilgrimage of faith.

Twenty-five years later, the partnership with the Cooperative Baptist Fellowship has blessed our congregation in so many ways. It has been helpful for Zebulon Baptist Church in Zebulon, North Carolina, to have clarified its identity as a "new kind of Baptist" church. The congregation has generously allowed me to serve in numerous positions in Baptist life, including as Moderator of CBF. Laypersons from Zebulon have served at the state and national levels. Youth and adults from Zebulon have partnered in mission in Homestead and Miami, Atlanta, New York City, northeastern North Carolina and Helena, Arkansas, as well as internationally in Belize and Romania.

The resources, themes and emphases of CBF energize us. The leaders of CBF inspire us. The mission of CBF to be the presence of Christ among the most marginalized motivates us. And the relationships within CBF continually bless us.

In its early days and with its past history, CBF made sure that it would be difficult to politicize and control the Fellowship. Business practices for General Assemblies were carefully crafted to avoid any meetings that resembled the turmoil of the past. As a result, the attendees at the annual Assembly could sometimes feel stifled in getting motions to the floor and passed. Two instances come to mind that portray the real desire of CBF throughout its history to include the ideas of its constituents, even when the business protocol at first made it seem otherwise.

In 2005, at the CBF General Assembly in Grapevine, Texas, the Fellowship adopted a revision of the CBF Constitution and Bylaws. In the discussion, it was pointed out that the revision had removed a direct reference to Jesus Christ. The discussion was heated, but the rules for discussion were followed and the revision passed without modification, to the consternation of more than a few in the room. Critics were quick to accuse the Fellowship of wanting to distance itself from Jesus Christ.

Over the course of the next year, the Coordinating Council developed a beautiful Preamble to the CBF Constitution and Bylaws. The new preamble clearly identified the Fellowship as followers of Jesus, believers in the Triune God, and passionate about following the Great Commandment and Great Commission of Jesus. The process surely ruffled a few feathers and exposed us vulnerably to critics. But in the end, we arrived at a good conclusion. Jesus was rightly positioned and affirmed as Lord of the Fellowship!

In 2007, in the nation's capital, the General Assembly was presented a motion to affirm the Millennium Development Goals of the United Nations, which were to "eradicate poverty and hunger, achieve universal primary education, promote gender equality, reduce child mortality, improve maternal health, combat HIV/AIDS, malaria and other diseases, to ensure environmental sustainability and develop a global partnership for development."

Again, the procedures in place called for a business breakout session. This seemed cumbersome, especially to the many young adults in CBF who were unimpressed with a procedural process that kept us from simply endorsing these goals so important to the human family the world over. Yet we stayed the course of our process.

Over the next year, we worked diligently in the Coordinating Council to become completely familiar with these goals. We looked at how we could encourage congregations and Cooperative Baptists to embrace these goals in tangible ways. By the next General Assembly in 2008, the Millennium Development Goals (MDGs) were highlighted. Resources were available for congregational use. Once again, CBF had stayed the course with its adopted procedures, but over the course of the next year, had proven more than willing to incorporate the spirit and ideas of its constituents.

These two stories illustrate important truths about CBF. Yes, CBF was birthed with no small amount of painful labor. From the beginning, there was a desire to make sure that our life together in the Fellowship would not be dominated by power politics. The processes put in place may at times seem too protective and reactive. But my experience is that the desire to take seriously the concerns and ideas of the constituents in the Fellowship has been genuine.

Staff and elected leaders have labored to be responsive to congregations and individuals. The Preamble adopted in 2006 and the Millennium Development Goals presentation in 2008 are the direct result of CBF wanting to do the right thing, the right way.

Out of the conversations with Colleen Burroughs, who presented the MDG motion in 2007, a friendship developed that led to my asking her to chair the Finance Committee of the CBF Coordinating Council. She would later become Moderator. I have enjoyed the relationships shared with other moderators. I am pleased at the number of women we have asked to lead our Fellowship. I am pleased that, as a pastor of a mid-size church, I was given the opportunity to serve in leadership.

I know we have been blessed by remarkable laypersons who have served well in leading the Fellowship. And as a member of the search committee for the Executive Coordinator following the retirement of Daniel Vestal, I am proud that we presented the name of our current leader, Suzii Paynter. Inclusion is most visibly practiced when leadership decisions are exercised, and I believe CBF has lived out its values when it has named its leaders.

In the middle of his leadership of CBF, Executive Coordinator Daniel Vestal encouraged a three-year emphasis on building community, spiritual formation and missional engagement. The next three General Assemblies focused on one of these three themes. To me, these three things have been the "big ideas" of the Fellowship in our first 25 years of existence.

We are a Fellowship—both in name and in practice. We need our connections and enjoy our times together. We are not all alike, but I do believe we make every effort to like one another. There is an acceptance and warmth we have found together that has healed our early wounds and strengthened us for a bright future together.

We take spirituality seriously—a spirituality rooted in the disciplines that have blessed the church and its people through the centuries. While committed to our Baptist heritage and core values, we have reached out to the broader Christian community for fellowship and partnership. We have learned from other traditions and have become more comfortable with silence, liturgy, the use of all the senses in corporate and personal worship, and with new and different forms for celebrating the Lord's Supper.

This spirituality has not been marketed or trumpeted. It is just a part of the early, emerging DNA of CBF to which I am indebted and for which I am thankful. When I receive the bread and cup at General Assembly each year with my brothers and sisters in Christ and in the Fellowship, I am always made aware of the spirituality of the CBF movement.

Missional engagement is what happens when the people of God get together and start taking their faith seriously. The signs of the Kingdom are at hand. Amazing work is done. Marvelous field personnel are called and become figures of inspiration to the churches. The individual Christian and congregation are energized by connection to a mission endeavor so large and wonderful. A pastor like me can tell stories of transformation at Vacation Bible School or when promoting the Offering for Global Missions. CBF has strengthened our connection to the mission of God in the world and made us more aware of how to be an effective outpost of God's mission in our local community.

I am glad our congregation sent those first mission funds to those folks in Atlanta. It has been a joyful quarter century of journeying with an amazing group known as the Cooperative Baptist Fellowship. Our community, spirit and mission have been enhanced by this relationship. Let's keep this journey going!

L. Jack Glasgow, Jr., has served as senior pastor of Zebulon Baptist Church in Zebulon, North Carolina, since 1981. A graduate of the Georgia Institute of Technology and Southeastern Baptist Theological Seminary, he served as CBF Moderator from 2008-2009.

Leading in the Midst of Change

By Kasey Jones

Implementing change isn't easy. Change is usually met with an array of mixed emotions. Excitement, fear, anticipation, anxiety, expectation and anxiousness are a few of the emotions associated with change. The Cooperative Baptist Fellowship over the past five years has endured a great deal of change.

Leading up to the 20th anniversary of CBF, Moderator Hal Bass appointed a 2012 Task Force to examine CBF structures to determine the best way to help CBF fulfill its mission. A major part of the work was to listen to the Fellowship. As a member of the 2012 Task Force, it was wonderful to hear the hope from listening sessions that took place across the Fellowship. While the discourse regarding denominations focused on decline, conversations with Cooperative Baptists focused on hope—hope for its future and impact in the world.

The 2012 Task Force members consistently heard that CBF was a place to call home for so many Baptist believers to live out their faith. Concerns expressed about CBF were met with meaningful and thoughtful dialogue on how to improve efficiency for greater ministry impact. Following the two years of listening and preparing recommendations, the Task Force recommendations were unanimously approved at the 2012 CBF General Assembly in Fort Worth. The vote was a testament to the significance of the hope in the future of CBF.

As the Executive Coordinator position transitioned from Daniel Vestal to Suzii Paynter, the 2012 Task Force Report became the road map to move forward. Suzii used the report to inform and guide the beginning of her tenure as Executive Coordinator. With road map in hand, and with Suzii's wisdom and incredible capacity to connect with people, CBF has not skipped a beat.

In the midst of a great deal of change, CBF staff, churches and individual members have formed together to face change, with all its mixed emotions. The transitions have revealed the Fellowship's ability to be innovative and seekers of excellence. The trust, patience and hope displayed convey a Christ-like character that is an awesome testimony. In an era when the future of denominations is in question, our testimony demonstrates a fundamental understanding that we are better together than apart.

Kasey Jones is senior pastor of National Baptist Memorial Church in Washington, D.C. She earned her Master of Divinity degree from Wesley Theological Seminary after working for more than 15 years as a community organizer and advocate. A member of the Fellowship's 2012 Task Force, she served as Moderator of CBF from 2014-2015.

Breathe!

By Reba Cobb

During the takeover of the Southern Baptist Convention in the 1980s and 1990s, moderate Baptists watched with astonishment as our seminaries were plundered, our mission efforts undermined around the world, and our denominational fabric shredded. As painful and devastating as that time was, however, it can now be viewed as an enormous gift to us.

Without that catalytic event in our history, many of us would still be experiencing life in a 19th-century denomination that excludes women, elevates pastors as the supreme heads of churches, and diminishes ecumenical and interfaith efforts. And that, my friends, would suffocate the life out of most of us, and out of our churches.

Now, 25 years later, we can be grateful to God for catapulting us into a new age with a new movement, the Cooperative Baptist Fellowship, offering us a place where we can breathe and flourish and live out our spiritual lives with integrity; a place where we can question, explore and evolve in our faith; a place that tries to be nimble, flexible, inspiring, authentic; a place that practices Baptist principles; and a place where we can do justice, love mercy and walk humbly with our God.

As we ponder and explore the reformation of the church in our time, it is a joy to be part of a movement that is emerging as an intimate partner with the once and future church. While we may not have it all just right, CBF is moving in a visionary direction.

So let us take a deep breath and be joyful. Inhale . . . because our environment offers us life-giving oxygen that fills our spiritual lungs, flows in our blood streams and invigorates our hearts. And if that isn't enough, the Beloved has provided us with a host of wild and wonderful companions with whom to share this journey.

Thanks be to God.

Reba Sloan Cobb is a lifelong Baptist who served on the founding committees of both the Cooperative Baptist Fellowship and Baptist Women in Ministry. A graduate of Samford University and Southern Baptist Theological Seminary, she is an ordained minister. She lives in Louisville, Kentucky, near her two sons and two grandsons.

Such Abundance!

By Julie Pennington-Russell

As Parker Palmer said so insightfully in *Let Your Life Speak:* "Vocation does not come from willfulness. It comes from listening. . . . Before I can tell my life what I want to do with it, I must listen to my life telling me who I am."

Early in 2000, while in my second year as pastor of Calvary Baptist Church in Waco, Texas, I received an email from a Southern Baptist layperson, copied to several presidents of Southern Baptist seminaries, which began with these words:

"First, allow me to address the subordinated marriage partner of that would-be leader of a Baptist Church in Waco, Texas, i.e., the depressingly-hyphenated Ms. Julie Pennington-Russell—whose last name says all there is to say about her subscription to yet another passage of scripture—(i.e., that one found in Colossians 3:18 which goes something like this: 'Wives, submit to your husbands . . . '): I shall pray for you this day, Mister Pennington-Russell, because you are obviously in dire need of it."

(Had the gentleman asked, I could have supplied any number of reasons why my dear, long-suffering marriage partner should be prayed for, regularly!)

In the lifelong process of self-discovery, there will always be voices pressing in to tell us who we are—and who we should and shouldn't be. I am ever so grateful to have had, since early adulthood, voices from the Cooperative Baptist Fellowship family speaking bright, hopeful, graceful words into my life. A few particular moments rise up in my memory:

- Sitting with my classmates in the large, airy chapel of Golden Gate Baptist Theological Seminary in Mill Valley, California, on a crystal clear morning in 1984—before CBF even existed—as I watched a bright-eyed, energetic young pastor-professor walk confidently to the pulpit, open her Bible and begin to speak. From the moment Molly Marshall began her sermon—the first I'd ever heard from the lips of a woman—something like an electric current ran through me. The plates shifted under my feet, and I knew that what my life was experiencing was nothing short of a sea change.

- Standing in a kitchen in Waco, Texas in 1998, a cup of coffee in my hand, as the chair of the pastor search committee from Calvary Baptist Church told me, "Daniel Vestal recommended your name to us."
- Attending a CBF gathering organized by Terry Hamrick in June of 2001 and hearing these words, maybe for the first time: *"Being church is not about maintaining an institution. It's about following Jesus into life and transformation."*

In short, I'm so lucky to have been surrounded for 25 years by this beautiful cloud of witnesses whose voices continue to help me understand who I am and what I'm meant for. Folks like Bill Leonard, Suzii Paynter, Pam Durso, Brent Walker, Bill Wilson, James Dunn, Carolyn Weatherford Crumpler, the men and women from two pastors' peer groups, and more prophetic, compassionate young CBF ministers than I can possibly name here. And of course, the thousands of Baptist women and men I've come to know and love along the way who, every day, are worshiping, serving, tithing, teaching, building, blessing, caring and planting seeds of faith and hope in the church and in the world. Such abundance!

I thank God for you, Cooperative Baptist Fellowship. Happy 25th.

Julie Pennington-Russell serves as senior pastor of First Baptist Church of the City of Washington, D.C. A graduate of Golden Gate Theological Seminary (Master of Divinity), she served on the CBF Coordinating Council from 1993-1996. A popular speaker and writer, she and her husband, Tim, are parents to two adult children, Lucy and Taylor.

AFTERWORD

Christ's Love Compels Us Toward the Future

By Suzii Paynter

Christ's love has compelled us—each one of us—on a journey of faithful and adventurous obedience. These essays speak of the incomplete but elegant connection that is the work of God's creative hand among our very lives and the churches gathered in the Cooperative Baptist Fellowship. They ask us to attend to and visualize ourselves as a constellation of witnesses. We are many voices and many hearts being called and drawn toward the center of our common life in Jesus Christ.

In the foreword, Daniel Vestal recounts the story of the 1990 Consultation of Concerned Baptists that would birth the Fellowship. My late colleague and dear friend Phil Strickland was there and said of the beginning, "We are going to a meeting in Atlanta that has to do with the renewal of the Christian Church in America." The emerging Fellowship would indeed become a community formed by narratives of authentic faithfulness and hopes for renewal of individual Christian disciples and renewal of the church. It will continue on the same God-given journey.

Seeds of the future

The CBF story is relevant and full of surprising gifts because it is grounded in the greater Gospel story. We are not the creators of spiritual gifts nor the blessing of Christ-like loving, but we acknowledge the bounty given to us and seek stewardship into our future. The strength of a fellowship is in its aspirations and the authenticity of mentors, pastoral inspiration, friendship and common purpose in mission across miles and times. The blessing of community is also a signpost of hope in the valley of our shadows. During both the light and dark, CBF has been a community of imperfect but strong spiritual connection.

Outwardly, CBF connections have been characterized by sincere ecumenical friendship across the larger Christian community and with positive collegiality in interfaith endeavors. In a context of increasing religious pluralism here in the United States alongside the expanding outreach of the Global Church and world religions, CBF will invest toward diversity in our leadership and deeper, productive ecumenical and interfaith connections. The near future calls for a public witness of common purpose for biblical justice, an amplified voice for religious liberty, and the healing of racial divides.

Christ and the Church are the center; CBF is the support

CBF pioneered the structure for a global organization of churches and individuals to provide identity and collective missions based upon a network that serves Baptist Christians and churches. In 1990-1991, I served on the Interim Steering Committee that would give rise to the CBF Coordinating Council. Our discussions were deliberately exhaustive because everyone was keenly aware that we were building the enabling structures from the ground up and that (for better and worse) structure begets potentials. This is true of our past, and it will be true of our future.

Now, sitting in the Executive Coordinator chair and navigating the 21st century religious landscape, I believe it is clear that the flexible expressions of connectional life expressed in our Fellowship are firm enough to provide organizational structure. Yet these flexible expressions are also nimble enough to allow for adaptation and restructuring. Rather than aspire to be something else, CBF is a denomi-network and is defining its identity as such. Central to this identity is the practice of friendship among individuals and partnership with other, mostly autonomous organizations. This is a genuine web of diverse organizations that are both autonomous and interdependent and charting a course into a changing future.

Loose affiliations and independent funding of partners allow for partnerships to come and go. The evolving nature of the collection of CBF partners is not accidental but intended to change and to add vitality to CBF as new and varied partners are explored for scale, strength, and common Christian aspiration and impact. There are always tensions for funding when so many organizations coexist, but the priority of *freedom*, referenced so often throughout these essays, is reflected in this partnership paradigm. CBF will extend this sustainable model by exercising the art and practice of faithful friendship and collaborative partnership.

The future as unapologetically global

CBF has reaffirmed a primary commitment to cooperative global missions, continuing the tradition of Baptists that have been forming together for more than 200 years to make disciples of all nations. The

CBF endeavor of cooperative missions is complex, substantial and long term. This is co-missioning. It is not cheap, nor is it the kind of venture that can be run for the coins in your car cup holder. This type of 21st-century Christian engagement is worth the lives of our partners and field personnel, and it is worth our serious investment. The Gospel task—bringing the word that God is with us, *Imago Dei*, and *Missio Dei*—is not "just another charity." It is a way of being, a way of living, and a way of sharing God's love and the witness of Christ. This is eternal.

CBF is embodying mission distinctives to offer Cooperative Baptists a common framework for local and global mission engagement based on the following commitments:

- Cultivating Beloved Community—*to love and empower people.* We cultivate communities of reconciliation and hospitality that serve as instruments, signs and foretastes of the Kingdom of God.
- Bearing Witness to Jesus Christ—*to speak of and show Christ.* We bear witness to the Gospel through words that invite faith in Jesus and actions that embody the way of Jesus.
- Seeking Transformational Development—*to use assets to make meaningful change.* We seek to transform systems that suppress the capacity of individuals and communities in order to recognize, claim and celebrate the God-given gifts of all people and places.

Field personnel serve in many places across the United States and around the world. Through their leadership and church engagement, our Global Missions enterprise puts its focus in three broad contexts:

- Global Poverty—Cooperative Baptists seek sustainable responses to systems of poverty that devalue life and diminish the image of God.
- Global Migration—Cooperative Baptists extend hope and hospitality to those who are driven by circumstance or drawn by opportunity away from their homes.
- Global Church—Cooperative Baptists befriend Christians from around the world to share and receive gifts and to engage in God's mission together through worship, fellowship, education and service.

Listening to, caring for and finding tomorrow's Church

At the core of our Fellowship is the journey of forming together. We are each moving within our time—we are on a pilgrimage that includes decline and hospice and renewal and movement toward our spiritual home. How do we find tomorrow's Church? The answer, of course, is to *be* tomorrow's Church.

One reason to join in fellowship with CBF is for the present journey. Describing her visit to the United States, a Hungarian journalist said, "I am a reporter here in Eastern Europe. When I got a chance to go to America, I said no to your Disneyland and your Universal Studios and left my travel group because I had to see the place where people stopped a war." She was speaking of the modest front steps of Sproull Hall at the University of California-Berkeley, where Mario Savio ignited the Free Speech Movement of the 1960s. The sacred pours forth from openings we never imagined possible until we hear about it in the voices of people who have made great journeys to witness it. It has been my practice to visit CBF churches widely and often. Every week I meet people who have made great journeys to find God.

The friendship, witness, wisdom, scriptural insight and care from the people and practice of their CBF church is repeated in stories of genuine inspiration, joy and healing. The sacred pours forth. The depth of an authentic faith narrative repeated by a simple witness of church members is stunning, and so hopeful. They are true followers of Christ. The congregation may be limping in another way, but undoubtedly the miraculous and beautiful manifestation of tomorrow's faithful Church resides in us. Chances are it will not be found at Disneyland or its ecclesiastical equivalent.

It is our mission to tune our ears to the work of the Holy Spirit and amplify the beautiful strength in the Church right where we are, with new and diverse fellow pilgrims. Nurturing this journey is not an institutional given but a process of honest sharing and a practice of blessing the important transformational moments of God at work, even if they are not the headline events.

There is no doubt that the need to manifest God's kind of love is urgent in our context of objectification, hate and despair. "For God so loved the world that he gave his son" is a radical message and a simple call to bring love, compassion and humaneness to bear everywhere. CBF churches are responding to their communities with life-changing—if not always headline-making—ministries. We need the help that comes from those also committed to Christ-like living to navigate our course.

I am certain that tomorrow's Church will grow from the seeds and good soil that are already here, but likewise not many new pilgrims will be drawn to Christ because a church is focused on celebrating its past. In comparing the American church to the Chinese church, a lay pastor in Chengdu said, "Perhaps the U.S. church has been more comfortable being the loaf, not the yeast." We are in for a yeasty future. God has called us into this time and is asking something creative, fragrant and dynamic of us. CBF is committed anew to supporting and equipping churches, pastoral leaders and young Baptists for tomorrow's Church.

As CBF, we have shared aspirations for lives of spiritual vitality and peace, for renewal of the Church in our time, and for discarding the encumbrances that would hinder us from God's great realm that is both at hand and yet to come. We all need a journey, and we all need a home.

Suzii Paynter is Executive Coordinator of the Cooperative Baptist Fellowship.

The Fellowship's elected officers and their spouses stand on stage and receive a round of applause for their work from attendees at the 1994 General Assembly in Greensboro, North Carolina. From left to right: CBF Recorder Cindy Johnson and her husband, Stan; incoming CBF Moderator-Elect Pat Anderson and his wife, Carolyn; outgoing CBF Moderator Hardy Clemons and his wife, Ardelle; and incoming CBF Moderator Carolyn Crumpler and her husband, Joe.

"Forming something as fragile as the Cooperative Baptist Fellowship is not a move we make lightly."

So begins the introduction to the Fellowship's founding document—"An Address to the Public"—presented as "information" on behalf of the Interim Steering Committee to attendees at the 1991 Convocation in Atlanta. Twenty-five years later, Cooperative Baptists are still forming together—compelled by Christ's love to support Global Missions, form healthy congregations and nurture young Baptists.

These concluding pages include this founding document along with other resources of historical significance and central to the stories of the Cooperative Baptist Fellowship.
—Editor

Editor's Note: The following is an edited version of a statement written by Dr. Walter B. Shurden the day following the Convocation of The Baptist Fellowship in Atlanta, May 9-11, 1991. At the time of this writing, Dr. Shurden was Callaway Professor and Chair of the Department of Christianity at Mercer University and a member of the Interim Steering Committee instrumental in forming the Cooperative Baptist Fellowship. Now retired, he serves as Minister at Large for Mercer. This document in its original form can be found in the CBF archives at the Tarver Library of Mercer in Macon, Georgia.

A Brief History of
"An Address to the Public"

By Walter B. Shurden, Sr.

I went with excitement to the first annual meeting of the CBF in Atlanta, GA, on Wednesday, May 8, 1991, and I had in my brief-case a document titled "The Preamble to the Constitution of the Baptist Fellowship." I had been commissioned by the Interim Steering Committee of "The Fellowship" to draft a "preamble" to the proposed constitution that was to be adopted at the General Assembly. Actually, a committee that I chaired was to come up with the document, but the committee had not had a chance to meet before the meeting of the Steering Committee on May 8. I carried the document to the Interim Steering Committee, fully expecting that after discussion of the document by the plenary session of the Interim Steering Commit-tee that it would be referred to the sub-committee which I chaired. To my surprise, the Steering Committee voted not to submit it to the sub-committee on "Purpose and Policy" and overwhelmingly endorsed the statement as I presented it.

Here is the history of that statement. I read it to the May 9, Thurs-day night session of "The Fellowship" and titled it "An Address to the Public from the Interim Steering Committee." The Interim Steering Committee had previously met in Atlanta, Georgia, on March 7-9, 1991, at the Airport Sheraton, two months before the first annual meeting of CBF. I was co-chair of the sub-committee on "Purpose and Policy," and on Friday, March 8, 1991, I submitted, on behalf of the committee, article two of the proposed constitution which was a statement of purpose and read as follows: "The purpose of the Baptist Fellowship is to enable the people of God to carry out the Great Commission under the Lordship of Jesus Christ (Matthew 28:18-20), in a fellowship where every member exercises God's gifts and calling."

After some very helpful and constructive debate, the Steering Committee adopted a statement of purpose which read as follows: "The purpose of the Baptist Fellowship is to enable the people of God to carry out the Great Commission under the Lordship of Jesus Christ, in a fellowship where every Christian exercises God's gifts and calling." As you can see, there were two alterations. One, the scripture reference was dropped. Two, "member" was changed to "Christian."

That statement of purpose was essentially proposed in the sub-committee by Dr. Duke K. McCall, former president of The Southern Baptist Theological Seminary in Louisville, Kentucky, and also the former president of The Baptist World Alliance. We debated many statements of purpose, some of them very long, before deciding to go with the brief but inclusive statement of Dr. McCall's.

Upon adoption of the statement of purpose by the Steering Committee, a very significant thing happened. Dr. Cecil Sherman, in my judgment the single most important member of the Interim Steering Committee, proposed that the sub-committee on "Purpose and Policy" submit at the next meeting of the Steering Committee a "preamble" to the Constitution which would state the historical context out of which the Fellowship had emerged. As chair of that committee, I was charged with that responsibility.

Before I left the Interim Committee meeting on March 8, I asked several members of the committee to send me some suggestions regarding the preamble. Among those specifically requested were: Charles Wade, pastor of the First Baptist Church in Arlington, TX and co-chair of the sub-committee; Dr. Cecil Sherman, pastor of the Broadway Baptist Church in Fort Worth, TX; Dr. Duke K. McCall; and Dr. Grady Cothen, former president of the Sunday School Board of the Southern Baptist Convention.

As time drew near for the next meeting of the Interim Steering Committee and the first annual meeting of The Baptist Fellowship, I called three people to ask for input into the document. Those three were: Dr. Duke K. McCall, Dr. Cecil Sherman, and Dr. Nancy Ammerman. Only Sherman sent a document, and it was a magnificent piece of work. The original document which Sherman sent me is in the CBF archives in the Tarver Library of Mercer University in Macon, GA. I did minor scribblings on it. I thought the Sherman document was too long for the purposes specified, so I set out to write one of my own. My document ended up being every bit as long and not nearly as good as the Cecil Sherman document. So, I set mine aside and began to work on editing his. I edited the document by calling on the phone several people and asking them to listen to me read the document and to make suggestions.

The first person I called was Dr. Kenneth Chafin, pastor of Walnut Street Baptist Church in Louisville, Kentucky. Chafin and Sherman were the most influential leaders within the Steering Committee. Chafin listened to several paragraphs of the document and asked, "Who wrote this, Cecil?" I responded, "Yes." I will never forget his words. Chafin said, "Walter, this could be Atlanta!" By which he meant that this could be the most historic occurrence at the meeting of the Fellowship May 9-11 in Atlanta. He was high in his praise of the document, saying that this is what people would remember about our meeting and that it would give the people something to take back to their churches. As I read through the document, Ken would interrupt, making suggestions. Sherman had described the origin of CBF as "breaking away" from the SBC. Chafin was particularly insistent that I delete the "breaking away" language in the document, encouraging me to use more positive "forming" language instead. This I did, and it was wise. This was Chafin's most important contribution to the document, though he made some other editorial suggestions.

I called Dr. Nancy Ammerman, planning to get her feedback on the document, but she was teaching a course for Candler School of Theology at Marietta, GA. I called Dr. Duke McCall and I missed him as well.

I then called my brother, Dr. Robert Shurden, chair of the religion department at Carson-Newman College and a New Testament scholar. He listened to the document, taking notes and not interrupting my reading. After I finished reading, he made several suggestions. His most important, however, was his recognition that there was no statement on the Bible in the Sherman document. He said, wisely I think, that we could not issue a statement without tackling the central issue in the entire controversy: the Bible. I agreed. I asked him what he would say. He talked and I took notes. In the final document I decided to place the article on the Bible in a prominent place. Under the second major heading that reads "Our Understandings Are Different," I placed the statement on the Bible first. The idea and language for the article came from my brother. I thought at the time it was a crucial addition to the document, vastly improving it but also making it more controversial. I thought, however, that if we were going to say anything, we had to tackle the fundamentalists on the nature of the Bible. This is where they were most wrong, but they had used the emotional appeal of the Bible to beat us to death. Moderates had been too afraid to confront them on this central issue.

I then called Dr. Hardy Clemons, pastor of the historic First Baptist Church in Greenville, SC. He quietly listened as I read through the entire document. He had nothing but high praise for it. I asked him what he thought about adding a statement on the Bible, and he said he thought it would be appropriate and relevant.

The last person I called before editing the document in its final form was Dr. Leon McBeth, Professor of Church History at the Southwestern Baptist Theological Seminary in Fort Worth, TX. I called Leon because he was a dear friend, a good historian who tended to be far more conservative than I in terms of our attitude toward the SBC, and because he had just finished publishing two books on Baptists, one of which was a book of documents. Because of the latter, I knew that he would sense the significance of what I was doing. As I expected, Leon was the least enthusiastic of the people I talked with about the document. He feared the separation in the SBC that the document foretold.

Also, as I expected, McBeth made some very helpful suggestions. He was particularly concerned about the statement on personal evangelism, thinking that it gave fundamentalists too much, as he said, "of the good stuff." He also advised on making the last paragraph before the Conclusion sound less like there was a total "giving up" on the SBC. Like too many in my estimation, he was still living with the myth that the SBC would change to reflect the historic and mainstream attitude of the Southern Baptist people. I disagreed. But I thought his language softened the last paragraph, so I inserted what became the first and second sentences of the last paragraph before the Conclusion. Those sentences begin and end with: "We can no longer . . . in overt political activity."

After taking these suggestions from wise and insightful people, I gave myself to the task of editing and rewriting. Three other people read the document in full before I took it to Atlanta. They were my wife, Kay Wilson Shurden, my secretary, Ruth Cheves, and one of my colleagues in the Christianity Department at Mercer University, Dr. Richard F. Wilson. All were helpful in suggesting editorial changes.

On Wednesday morning my secretary, with the assistance of Mrs. Jeannette Taylor of the President's office at Mercer University, duplicated copies so that I could have them for the Steering Committee on

Wednesday afternoon at our meeting at the Colony Square Hotel in Atlanta. Daniel Vestal, chair of the Interim Steering Committee, and I had agreed that I would first read the statement to the Committee before passing it among them to read. He said he wanted them to "hear" the statement without comment, though he had no idea what was contained in the statement.

As I recall, the room became deathly quiet as I read. Daniel Vestal later wrote that this was "a telling moment in the work of the [Interim Steering] Committee" ("The History of the Cooperative Baptist Fellowship," in Walter B. Shurden, editor, *The Struggle for the Soul of the SBC: Moderate Response to the Fundamentalist Movement* (Macon, GA: Mercer University Press, 1993), 263.). After we distributed the document, several committee members raised questions and made suggestions. I had mentioned that the statement was in many ways more like the "Address to the Public" adopted by the SBC in 1845 when it separated from American Baptists than it was a "Preamble" to a constitution. Rudy Zachary, one of the youngest and a very helpful member of the Steering Committee, suggested that it be received and titled as an "Address to the Public" rather than a "Preamble." This was agreed by the group. A number of positive comments were made about the document. I think it is not too much to say that the committee was "moved" by the document.

The only major content concerns came from Charles Wade of Arlington, TX. He made the point regarding the section on women that we ought as Christians stress the mutual submission of all Christians and not give the impression that Christians are not to be submissive people. Secondly, he wondered if it is enough to say "Being Baptist should ensure that no one is ever excluded who confesses 'Jesus is Lord.'" He wondered aloud if there should be some statement, for example, on believer's baptism. Those suggestions got no support from the group.

The discussion then focused on whether the document should be returned to committee or accepted as is. Dr. Kenneth Chafin and Dr. Jimmy Allen both encouraged the group to endorse the statement as it was and forego the committee work and wrangling over words. The vote was overwhelming in favor to do so. That night I gave Rudy Zachary, a computer whiz, my floppy disc and a hard copy with minor corrections, and he made me a copy which I read to The Fellowship on Thursday evening prior to the presentation of The Proposed Constitution. He also made a copy for distribution to the press.

On Thursday morning at the next Steering Committee meeting, I approached Kenneth Chafin and said, "Ken, I really think that Cecil Sherman should read the 'Address to the Public' tonight; what do you think?" "I think you should read it," he said. Kenneth Chafin and Cecil Sherman had been the two most important Moderate leaders in the twelve year resistance to the Fundamentalist takeover. In my judgment, Sherman had been the single most influential Moderate leader. In that leadership role he had to speak out; when he did he spoke clearly, with more reference to the truth of the situation than to the politics of the situation, and he, therefore, was often accused, falsely in my judgment, of being abrasive. Because Sherman was perceived by the Moderate public as more of a "firebrand" than I (though I never found myself in disagreement with Sherman in the twelve year conflict with fundamentalists), and because I had the advantage of being heard as a historian, Chafin thought I should read the statement. But it was precisely the historian in me that wanted Sherman to read the statement; I certainly did not want history to think that it was primarily my statement. And I knew it would be so perceived.

As a measure of the greatness of Cecil Sherman, he was far more interested in the statement being heard than he was in getting credit for the statement. As soon as I walked off the platform after reading the statement to the general assembly on Thursday evening, Cecil Sherman walked up to me, shook my hand, and said, "You did it right and you did it well." Actually, he had done most of it. It was an emotional moment. We sat down in two folding chairs near the platform and commiserated on the importance of the meeting and the importance of the statement. We had hope. We had hope that something new and significant in Baptist life was being born.

Editor's Note: "An Address to the Public" is regarded as the founding document of the Cooperative Baptist Fellowship. It was presented as "information" on behalf of the "Interim Steering Committee" at the Convocation of the Baptist Fellowship in Atlanta on May 9, 1991, and adopted by the assembly.

The original version of this document refers to the Interim Steering Committee's proposed name of "United Baptist Fellowship." That proposed name was rejected in favor of "Cooperative Baptist Fellowship" (which is used here) on May 10, the day following the adoption of "An Address to the Public." The document is the result of the work of two people, Mercer University professor Walter B. Shurden and Cecil E. Sherman, who would later become CBF's founding Coordinator. Sherman is considered the principal author.

"An Address to the Public" was written primarily to distinguish moderate Southern Baptists from fundamentalist Southern Baptists while offering insight into what moderates believed to be consistent with the Baptist tradition of freedom and responsibility. Reflecting on this historic document 25 years later, it can be said that "An Address to the Public" embodied the Fellowship's commitment to an egalitarian theology that champions women in ministry in all aspects of church leadership, as well as its firm and growing embrace of ecumenical relationships and an inclusive attitude. "An Address to the Public" also formally laid the foundation for a Baptist identity rooted in what Shurden popularly described as the "four fragile freedoms"—CBF's "core values" of soul freedom, Bible freedom, church freedom and religious freedom.

"An Address to the Public"

Introduction

Forming something as fragile as the Cooperative Baptist Fellowship is not a move we make lightly. We are obligated to give some explanation for why we are doing what we are doing. Our children will know what we have done; they may not know why we have done what we have done. We have reasons for our actions. They are:

I. Our Reasons Are Larger Than Losing.

For twelve years the Southern Baptist Convention in annual session has voted to sustain the people who lead the fundamentalist wing of the SBC. For twelve years the SBC in annual session has endorsed the arguments and the rationale of the fundamentalists. What has happened is not a quirk or a flash or an accident. It has been done again and again.

If inclined, one could conclude that the losers have tired of losing. But the formation of the Cooperative Baptist Fellowship does not spring from petty rivalry. If the old moderate wing of the SBC were represented in making policy and were treated as welcomed

292

representatives of competing ideas in the Baptist mission task, then we would co-exist, as we did for years, alongside fundamentalism and continue to argue our ideas before Southern Baptists.

But this is not the way things are. When fundamentalists won in 1979, they immediately began a policy of exclusion. Non-fundamentalists are not appointed to any denominational positions. Rarely are gentle fundamentalists appointed. Usually only doctrinaire fundamentalists, hostile to the purposes of the very institutions they control, are rewarded for service by appointment. Thus, the boards of SBC agencies are filled by only one kind of Baptists. And this is true whether the vote to elect was 60-40 or 52-48. It has been since 1979 a "winner take all." We have no voice.

In another day Pilgrims and Quakers and Baptists came to America for the same reason. As a minority, they had no way to get a hearing. They found a place where they would not be second-class citizens. All who attended the annual meeting of the SBC in New Orleans in June of 1990 will have an enlarged understanding of why our ancestors left their homes and dear ones and all that was familiar. So forming the Cooperative Baptist Fellowship is not something we do lightly. Being Baptist should ensure that no one is ever excluded who confesses, "Jesus is Lord (Philippians 2:11)."

II. Our Understandings Are Different.

Occasionally, someone accuses Baptists of being merely a contentious, controversial people. That may be. But the ideas that divide Baptists in the present "controversy" are the same ideas that have divided Presbyterians, Lutherans, and Episcopalians. These ideas are strong and central; these ideas will not be papered over. Here are some of these basic ideas:

1. Bible.

Many of our differences come from a different understanding and interpretation of Holy Scripture. But the difference is not at the point of the inspiration or authority of the Bible. We interpret the Bible differently, as will be seen below in our treatment of the biblical understanding of women and pastors. We also, however, have a different understanding of the nature of the Bible. We want to be biblical—especially in our view of the Bible. That means that we dare not claim less for the Bible than the Bible claims for itself. The Bible neither claims nor reveals inerrancy as a Christian teaching. Bible claims must be based on the Bible, not on human interpretations of the Bible.

2. Education.

What should happen in colleges and seminaries is a major bone of contention between fundamentalists and moderates. Fundamentalists educate by indoctrination. They have the truth and all the truth. As they see it, their job is to pass along the truth they have. They must not change it. They are certain that their understandings of the truth are correct, complete and to be adopted by others.

Moderates, too, are concerned with truth, but we do not claim a monopoly. We seek to enlarge and build upon such truth as we have. The task of education is to take the past and review it, even criticize it. We work to give our children a larger understanding of spiritual and physical reality. We know we will always live in faith; our understandings will not be complete until we get to heaven and are loosed from the limitations of our mortality and sin.

3. Mission.

What ought to be the task of the missionary is another difference between us. We think the mission task is to reach people for faith in Jesus Christ by preaching, teaching, healing and other ministries of mercy and justice. We believe this to be the model of Jesus in Galilee. That is the way he went about his mission task. Fundamentalists make the mission assignment narrower than Jesus did. They allow their emphasis on direct evangelism to undercut other biblical ministries of mercy and justice. This narrowed definition of what a missionary ought to be and do is a contention between us.

4. Pastor.

What is the task of the pastor? They argue the pastor should be the ruler of a congregation. This smacks of the bishops' task in the Middle Ages. It also sounds much like the kind of church leadership Baptists revolted against in the seventeenth century. Our understanding of the role of the pastor is to be a servant/shepherd. Respecting lay leadership is our assignment. Allowing the congregation to make real decisions is of the very nature of Baptist congregationalism. And using corporate business models to "get results" is building the Church by the rules of a secular world rather than witnessing to the secular world by way of a servant Church.

5. Women.

The New Testament gives two signals about the role of women. A literal interpretation of Paul can build a case for making women submissive to men in the Church. But another body of scripture points toward another place for women. In Gal. 3:27-28 Paul wrote, "As many of you as are baptized into Christ have clothed yourselves with Christ. There is no longer Jew or Greek, there is no longer slave or free, there is no longer male and female; for all of you are one in Christ Jesus (NSRV)."

We take Galatians as a clue to the way the Church should be ordered. We interpret the reference to women the same way we interpret the reference to slaves. If we have submissive roles for women, we must also have a place for the slaves in the Church.

In Galatians Paul follows the spirit of Jesus who courageously challenged the conventional wisdom of his day. It was a wisdom with rigid boundaries between men and women in religion and in public life. Jesus deliberately broke those barriers. He called women to follow him; he treated women as equally capable of dealing with sacred issues. Our model for the role of women in matters of faith is the Lord Jesus.

6. Church.

An ecumenical and inclusive attitude is basic to our fellowship. The great ideas of theology are the common property of all the church. Baptists are only a part of that great and inclusive Church. So, we are eager to have fellowship with our brothers and sisters in the faith and to recognize their work for our Savior. We do not try to make them conform to us; we try to include them in our design for mission. Mending the torn fabric of both Baptist and Christian fellowship is important to us. God willing, we will bind together the broken parts into a new company in preview of the great fellowship we shall have with each other in heaven.

It should be apparent that the points of difference are critical. They are the stuff around which a fellowship such as the Southern Baptist Convention is made. We are different. It is regrettable, but we are different. And perhaps we are most different at the point of spirit. At no place have we been able to negotiate about these differences. Were our fundamentalist brethren to negotiate, they would compromise. And that would be a sin by their understandings. So, we can either come to their position, or we can form a new fellowship.

III. We Are Called to Do More than Politic.

Some people would have us continue as we have over the last twelve years, and continue to work with the SBC with a point of view to change the SBC. On the face of it this argument sounds reasonable. Acting it out is more difficult.

To change the SBC requires a majority vote. To effect a majority in annual session requires massive, expensive, contentious activity. We have done this, and we have done it repeatedly.

But we have never enjoyed doing it. Something is wrong with a religious body that spends such energy in overt political activity. Our time is unwisely invested in beating people or trying to beat people. We have to define the other side as bad and we are good. There is division. The existence of the Cooperative Baptist Fellowship is a simple confession of that division; it is not the cause of that division.

We can no longer devote our major energies to SBC politics. We would rejoice, however, to see the SBC return to its historic Baptist convictions. Our primary call is to be true to our understanding of the gospel. We are to advance the gospel in our time. When we get to heaven, God is not going to ask us, "Did you win in Atlanta in June of 1991?" If we understand the orders we are under, we will be asked larger questions. And to spend our time trying to reclaim a human institution (people made the SBC; it is not a scriptural entity) is to make more of that institution than we ought to make. A denomination is a missions delivery system; it is not meant to be an idol. When we make more of the SBC than we ought, we risk falling into idolatry. Twelve years is too long to engage in political activity. We are called to higher purposes.

Conclusion
- That we may have a voice in our Baptist mission . . . for that is our Baptist birthright . . .
- That we may work by ideas consistent with our understanding of the gospel rather than fund ideas that are not our gospel . . .
- That we may give our energies to the advancement of the Kingdom of God rather than in divisive, destructive politics . . .

The Baptist Identity: Four Fragile Freedoms
For these reasons we form the Cooperative Baptist Fellowship. This does not require that we sever ties with the old Southern Baptist Convention. It does give us another mission delivery system, one more like our understanding of what it means to be Baptist and what it means to do gospel. Therefore, we create a new instrument to further the Kingdom and enlarge the Body of Christ.

Editor's Note: The following is a brief timeline of significant events from the history of the Cooperative Baptist Fellowship.

A Historical Timeline

By Aaron D. Weaver

1990

- Baptist Cooperative Missions Program (forerunner of the Cooperative Baptist Fellowship) chartered as a nonprofit corporation in Georgia on August 1 with Duke McCall as incorporator and a 17-member board of directors
- August 23-25 meeting of moderate Baptists in Atlanta (Consultation of Concerned Baptists) convened by Baptists Committed with Jimmy Allen as convener; 70-member Interim Steering Committee forms, chaired by Daniel Vestal, to receive and distribute funds through the BCMP and develop a detailed plan and distribution formula for the alternative mechanism for funding missions of Southern Baptist agencies and institutions, as well as non-SBC entities
- Cooperative Baptist Fellowship of Florida forms in November at Bayshore Baptist Church in Tampa (incorporated May 1991)

1991

- 70-member Interim Steering Committee meets in January, agrees on name "The Baptist Fellowship" for recommendation to a planned Convocation in Atlanta May 9-11
- Cooperative Baptist Fellowship of Arkansas forms March 21-22 at Lakeshore Drive Baptist Church in Little Rock; originally the Arkansas Fellowship of Concerned Baptists; incorporated as CBF of Arkansas on March 5, 1994
- Kentucky Baptist Fellowship forms March 19 at St. Matthews Baptist Church in Louisville
- Interim Steering Committee approves proposal in March to establish an ongoing relationship with *SBC Today* (now *Baptists Today*) for news coverage of "The Fellowship"
- First employee, Sandra Davey, hired on April 15
- Cooperative Baptist Fellowship born May 9-11 in Atlanta at "Convocation of The Baptist Fellowship;" adoption of

constitution, bylaws and organizational name "Cooperative Baptist Fellowship;" John Hewett elected as first Moderator as well as 79-member Coordinating Council; adoption of Fellowship's founding document "An Address to the Public" and a three-track funding mechanism with a proposed budget of $545,000; more than 5,000 in attendance

- Convocation attendees adopt giving plans for 1992 which include funding for new seminaries George W. Truett Theological Seminary at Baylor University (begins classes in Fall 1994) and Baptist Theological Seminary at Richmond (begins classes in Fall 1991)
- Baptist Fellowship of Missouri (now CBF Heartland) incorporates June 16 and a board of directors selected; September 15, 1990 meeting at Little Bonne Femme Baptist Church in Columbia, Missouri, instrumental in birthing BFM
- Cooperative Baptist Fellowship of South Carolina forms October 1 at St. Andrews Baptist Church in Columbia
- Midwest Region Cooperative Baptist Fellowship (formed/renamed as North Central Region in 2000) holds first meeting October 11-12 at New Christian Valley Baptist Church in South Holland, Illinois; bylaws adopted June 1992
- CBF provides financial support via designated contributions to Associated Baptist Press (founded July 17, 1990; now Baptist News Global) and the Baptist Joint Committee on Public Affairs (founded 1936; now Baptist Joint Committee for Religious Liberty)

1992

- CBF Coordinating Council votes to expand its missions program and hire specific missionaries in Europe who no longer want to work for the Foreign Mission Board of the Southern Baptist Convention
- CBF begins sending funds to the Baptist Theological Seminary in Rüschlikon, Switzerland, including scholarships to students, and sends funds to the new Baptist Center for Ethics (formed in July 1991 and led by Robert Parham)
- Cecil Sherman becomes first CBF Coordinator on April 1
- Baptist Cooperative Missions Program merges into CBF on April 1

- Southern Baptist Women in Ministry (renamed as Baptist Women in Ministry in 1993) holds its annual gathering in conjunction with the CBF General Assembly in Fort Worth, Texas
- 6,000 people attend the General Assembly in Fort Worth, April 30-May 2; attendees affirm guiding statement on global missions and welcome first four CBF "missioners" (called "missionaries" beginning in 1993): John David and JoAnn Hopper and Charles "T" and Kathy Thomas (all recently resigned Southern Baptist missionaries)
- General Assembly attendees pass statement on racial reconciliation, confessing their complicity in "sin of racism in our own heritage" and pledging to work to address the "critical needs of all people of color" (resolutions on human sexuality and ecology were referred to the Ethics and Public Policy Ministry Group)
- General Assembly revises giving plans to devote more money for Fellowship ministries and decrease funding for SBC entities; attendees receive greetings via telegram from Billy Graham
- Inaugural CBF Offering for Global Missions is received with the theme "Keeping the Promises" and raises nearly $2 million
- CBF state leaders organize network at September 9-10 meeting; 22 people representing 16 CBF state and regions participate
- Election of Patricia Ayres as CBF Moderator, the first female and layperson in this position
- Baptists in Texas form steering committee that meets informally (later known as Cooperative Baptist Fellowship of Texas and legally incorporated July 3, 2002); part-time coordinator hired in 1994 and full-time coordinator named in 2000
- CBF West forms at Nineteenth Avenue Baptist Church in San Francisco, California (incorporated in 1997)
- Cooperating Baptist Fellowship of Oklahoma forms February 29 at First Baptist Church of Norman, Oklahoma (officially incorporated March 26)
- Tennessee Cooperative Baptist Fellowship forms July 24 at Woodmont Baptist Church in Nashville
- Fellowship provides relief beginning August 27 to South Florida following Hurricane Andrew, marking its first disaster response effort

- Cooperative Baptist Fellowship of Mississippi forms October 16 at Edison-Walthall Hotel in Jackson
- Cooperative Baptist Fellowship of Virginia forms in November at First Baptist Church in Virginia Beach
- Cooperative Baptist Fellowship of Georgia forms November 9 at First Baptist Church of Christ in Macon
- Scholarships awarded to 19 Baptist students at eight theological schools, including students at Baptist Theological Seminary at Richmond for the 1992-1993 academic year as well as students at the Baptist Studies Program of Candler School of Theology (Emory University) and the Baptist House of Studies of Duke Divinity School (Duke University)
- CBF and the Alliance of Baptists hold dialogue session September 9 and issue a joint statement stating plans not to merge

1993

- Keith Parks hired as first CBF Global Missions Coordinator, begins January 18
- Baptist Fellowship of the Northeast forms January 30 at Greenwich Baptist Church in Greenwich, Connecticut
- Cooperative Baptist Fellowship of Louisiana forms in May
- Former United States President Jimmy Carter gives keynote address at General Assembly in Birmingham, Alabama, challenging attendees to embrace racial reconciliation, women in ministry and the world's poor; Assembly adopts new constitution due to sunset clause in 1991 constitution; new constitution limits membership to contributing Baptist individuals and churches (rather than anyone in attendance) and prohibits introduction of resolutions and similar motions from the floor of an Assembly business session
- CBF produces first missions resource titled "Doing Missions in a World Without Borders"
- Fellowship commissions at General Assembly first missionaries who were not former employees of the Foreign Mission Board: Bert and Debbie Ayers (Albania); six additional new missionaries commissioned in September: David and Tracy Bengtson (Miami), Allen and Verr Dean Williams (Czech Republic) and Stanley and Kay Parks (Indonesia)

- Fellowship continues to award scholarships to students pursuing theological education at numerous non-SBC schools for 1993-1994 academic year
- First CBF missions education study series created for children, youth and adults in December, adapted from *Formations* curriculum of Smyth & Helwys Publishing, Inc.
- CBF begins partnership with Seeds of Hope, Inc., a Waco, Texas-based ministry providing hunger publications and resources for churches and individuals

1994

- Cooperative Baptist Fellowship of North Carolina forms January 21 at First Baptist Church in Winston-Salem
- CBF Foundation created in February to provide investment and endowment services for CBF supporters and churches; Ruben Swint named as first president
- Alabama Cooperative Baptist Fellowship forms May 6
- SBC votes in June to refuse to channel contributions to its agencies and institutions through CBF (in 1993, CBF sent just over $2 million to support SBC missions); CBF officers vote July 6 to replace Fellowship's three giving plans with a single plan which supports only Fellowship causes and its partners
- Ethics and Public Policy Ministry Group of CBF partners with Bread for the World supporting its "Covenant Church" program, where congregations agree through worship and study to understand the causes and solutions to global hunger
- Mid-Atlantic Cooperative Baptist Fellowship incorporates August 16 and holds second annual General Assembly at Woodbrook Baptist Church in Baltimore, Maryland, on October 22
- Earl and Jane Martin become CBF's first emeritus missionaries after three decades of mission service in East Africa, Rwanda and Baptist Theological Seminary in Rüschlikon, Switzerland

1995

- CBF Coordinating Council adopts a formal mission statement in February, highlighting the Fellowship's goals to "network, empower and mobilize Baptist Christians and churches for effective missions and ministry in the name of Christ"

- CBF Coordinating Council votes to give $50,000 to support capital needs of Central Baptist Theological Seminary, a new partner with historic ties to American Baptist Churches USA
- CBF announces in March the move of its retirement and insurance plans for employees and missionaries from the Southern Baptist Annuity Board to the Minister and Missionaries Benefit Board of American Baptist Churches USA
- CBF Global Missions expands with the appointment of two-year missionaries to service alongside career missionaries (later renamed/formalized as Global Service Corps program)
- CBF's 100th missionary is appointed
- Woman's Missionary Union (WMU) announces July 12 it will produce missions education supplements for CBF to be sent to churches wishing to study the work of CBF missionaries
- CBF Global Missions gives $100,000 grant to First Baptist Church in Abilene, Texas, to help build a Hospitality House for the visiting families of inmates at two area prisons
- American Baptist Churches USA host CBF leaders at American Baptist Assembly at Green Lake, Wisconsin, for first joint gathering.
- CBF Coordinating Council approves agreement to purchase tract of Atlanta property from Mercer University and enters into a five-year rental agreement for its headquarters to be housed in what will become the building for Mercer's McAfee School of Theology on the Atlanta campus (giving Mercer $2 million to build its theology school)

1996

- CBF launches website: *www.cbfonline.org*
- CBF Global Missions initiates Envoy program to spread a network of secularly employed Christians around the globe
- Attendees to General Assembly in Richmond, Virginia, vote for CBF to remain a network of individuals and churches rather than become a convention/denomination
- Cecil Sherman retires, becomes visiting professor at Baptist Theological Seminary at Richmond; Tommy Boland selected to serve as Interim CBF Coordinator from June through December
- Daniel Vestal selected in December to succeed Cecil Sherman as CBF Executive Coordinator

1997

- CBF makes first venture into China in July-August, sending a volunteer team to help Chinese English teachers develop better conversational skills
- Student scholarships for theological education are renamed as "Leadership Scholarships" beginning with the 1997-1998 academic year to foster a stronger connection between student scholars and the Fellowship, including funds to participate in CBF events such as General Assembly
- CBF Albania missions team evacuated during Albanian Rebellion of 1997, a violent uprising marked by disorder and anarchy in which the government is overthrown and 2,000 people are killed; CBF missionary Debbie Ayers suffers a head wound from a stray bullet during the evacuation
- Upon the recommendation of a study committee, CBF declares itself a "religious endorsing body" for the purpose of endorsing chaplains and pastoral counselors
- New Global Missions initiative launches for local churches in June called "Adopt-A-People" to assist CBF-related churches to become directly involved in "World A" missions by identifying and "adopting" an unreached people group
- Passport Camps (formed in 1993) uses its summer mission offering collected from teen campers to fund the construction of 10 huts in Thailand to assist the work of CBF field personnel

1998

- Fellowship endorses first five chaplains and pastoral counselors and later in the year endorses its first military chaplains; CBF recognized in summer by Department of Defense as an endorsing body
- CBF recognized by the United Nations as a non-governmental organization (NGO), allowing the Fellowship to participate directly in U.N. processes
- Presidents and deans of CBF-related theological schools gather for third annual retreat and vote to become a consortium of schools partnering with CBF
- First student at Campbell University Divinity School (founded in 1996) to be awarded a CBF Leadership Scholarship

1999

- Keith Parks retires as Global Missions Coordinator; Barbara and Gary Baldridge appointed in October as Co-Coordinators of CBF Global Missions
- Fellowship begins ministry in November to plant new churches with matching grant from Georgia-based Venture Ministries and with support of Atlanta's Dunwoody Baptist Church
- CBF begins officially providing reference and referral services for churches and ministers

2000

- First CBF Young Leaders retreat, held in spring
- Donna Forrester becomes first ordained woman to serve as CBF Moderator
- CBF Coordinating Council adopts during its fall meeting an administrative policy on homosexual behavior related to personnel and funding, stating "we believe the foundation of a Christian sexual ethic is faithfulness in marriage between a man and a woman and celibacy in singleness"
- Church Benefits Board incorporates in September to provide benefits to Fellowship staff, field personnel, ministers and partner organizations; Gary Skeen, CBF's Coordinator of Finance and Administration, named as founding president

2001

- CBF holds inaugural True Survivor conference for Christian educators (now known as ChurchWorks)
- 10th anniversary celebration of the Fellowship at three-day General Assembly in June at the Georgia World Congress Center in Atlanta includes "Decade of Promise" banquet and keynote address from former United States President Jimmy Carter
- Together for Hope—CBF's rural poverty initiative and 20-year commitment to offer funding and resources to people in and around 20 of the poorest counties in the United States—is launched
- CBF responds to 9/11 terrorist attacks in Washington, D.C., and New York City, allocates emergency relief funds to field personnel and Metro Baptist Church in NYC
- CBF joins with World Vision to provide emergency relief ministries for Afghan refugees facing conflict and drought following

the U.S. invasion of Afghanistan in October; CBF contributes $100,000

- CBF becomes partner with Samaritan Ministry, a ministry of Central Baptist Church of Bearden in Knoxville, Tennessee, founded in 1996 by Wayne Smith to serve people affected by HIV/AIDS

2002

- "It's Time" is theme of General Assembly in Fort Worth, Texas, where CBF Executive Coordinator Daniel Vestal casts his vision for churches to represent Christ in the world; book published by Vestal titled *It's Time!: An Urgent Call to Christian Mission*
- CBF Global Missions begins commissioning "field personnel" rather than "missionaries," adopting new language due to the growing negative connotation of "missionary" in many parts of the world and to allow commissioned individuals to enter certain areas where they might not otherwise be welcomed
- CBF Coordinating Council adopts statement during its fall meeting defining the Fellowship as a "Baptist association of churches and individuals" separate from the SBC, but declines to call itself a convention or denomination; statement made in response to request by the Membership Committee of the Baptist World Alliance to demonstrate that CBF was not an "integral part" of any BWA member, specifically the SBC
- CBF launches Student.Go, a student missions initiative to send undergraduates and graduates to serve alongside CBF field personnel and partners around the world
- CBF begins partnership with Center for Family and Community Ministries of Baylor University School of Social Work (founded in 1998); Center tasked to provide congregational assessments using the church census for leadership planning, workshops on family and internship opportunities for social workers who are Cooperative Baptists

2003

- Fellowship forms partnership agreement with Hispanic Baptist Theological School (now known as Baptist University of the Americas)
- Lilly Endowment awards CBF $2 million to participate in a national program called "Sustaining Pastoral Excellence,"

part of an effort to maintain excellence in the nation's pastoral leaders; grant helps fund Fellowship's Initiative for Ministerial Excellence, which includes Peer Learning Groups, sabbatical study, and a residency program for prospective ministers studying at CBF-partner theological schools

- Baptist World Alliance votes to extend membership to CBF on July 11
- CBF continues relief efforts in war-torn Iraq, distributing food, clothes, shoes, hygiene kits to an estimated 20,000 Iraqi families

2004

- CBF and Passport Camps co-sponsor Antiphony, a retreat for college students and seminarians which was the Fellowship's first national event for young adults
- Formation at Clemson University of the first Cooperative Student Fellowship
- CBF participates in its first meeting of the North American Baptist Fellowship as a member of the Baptist World Alliance; sixteen member bodies of NABF represent 17 million Baptists
- CBF and Lutheran Theological Southern Seminary in Columbia, South Carolina, create partnership to develop Baptist studies program under leadership of Rev. Dr. Virginia Barfield (a Cooperative Baptist) to offer opportunities for Baptist students to take specialized courses in Baptist history and theology and also to provide continuing education for Baptist ministerial staff members and laity in the state
- CBF partners with Center for Congregational Health (formed 1992) for the Center to provide consultation to CBF churches in areas including strategic planning, interim ministry, conflict management, staff relationships and leadership

2005

- Jack Snell, CBF's Associate Missions Coordinator, named as Interim Global Missions Coordinator following the February resignation of Barbara Baldridge and December 2004 retirement of Gary Baldridge
- CBF launches response to Southeast Asia tsunami, contributing and raising more than $2.5 million for relief and development projects

- CBF responds to Hurricane Katrina, and over next five years donates more than $1.5 million to long-term recovery work
- Attendees at General Assembly in Grapevine, Texas, give $45,000 in support of first Jimmy and Rosalynn Carter Offering for Religious Liberty and Human Rights
- Joy Yee assumes CBF Moderator duties at conclusion of General Assembly, becoming Fellowship's first female senior pastor and first Asian American to hold the position

2006

- Rob Nash selected to serve as Global Missions Coordinator at June meeting of CBF Coordinating Council
- HIV/AIDS summit held on eve of General Assembly in Atlanta
- Emmanuel McCall assumes duties as CBF Moderator, first African American to hold this position
- CBF becomes founding participant in the ecumenical organization Christian Churches Together
- CBF receives second major Lilly Endowment grant to continue and expand its Initiative for Ministerial Excellence to offer sabbatical grants and support to Peer Learning Groups as well as a ministerial residency program
- Faith in 3D student conference is held at Walt Disney World Resort in Orlando, Florida—a partnership of CBF, Passport Camps, Presbyterian Church USA and the Episcopal Church
- CBF offers missional ministry grants to encourage Fellowship churches in their missional journeys; eligible churches complete *It's Time: A Journey Toward Missional Faithfulness*
- CBF Coordinating Council votes in October to approve four schools as "identity partners" to receive institutional funding, scholarships and initiative support (Mercer University's McAfee School of Theology, Baptist Theological Seminary at Richmond, Campbell University Divinity School and Baylor University's George W. Truett Theological Seminary), and nine schools as "leadership partners" whose students apply for CBF Leadership Scholarships: M. Christopher White School of Divinity at Gardner-Webb University, Central Baptist Theological Seminary, Logsdon School of Theology at Hardin-Simmons University, Baptist House of Studies at Duke Divinity School, Baptist Studies Program at Candler School of Theology, Wake Forest University School of Divinity,

the Baptist Studies Program at Brite Divinity School of Texas Christian University, Baptist Seminary of Kentucky, and the Baptist Studies Program at Lutheran Theological Seminary; Baptist University of the Americas and International Baptist Theological Seminary named as global partners
- CBF age-graded missions education resources *Form*, *Spark*, *Ignite* and *Affect* are introduced
- CBF partner Baptist History & Heritage Society publishes "Beginnings of the Cooperative Baptist Fellowship" booklet by Pam Durso

2007
- Historic joint gathering of CBF with American Baptist Churches USA in Washington, D.C., in conjunction with the CBF General Assembly and ABC-USA Biennial Summit
- General Assembly adopts United Nations Millennium Development Goals, which aim to eradicate extreme poverty and hunger, achieve universal primary education, promote gender equality and empower women, reduce child mortality, improve maternal health, combat HIV/AIDS, malaria and other diseases, ensure environmental sustainability, and promote global partnerships for development
- CBF and ABC-USA jointly commission Marcia and Duane Binkley and Nancy and Steve James to serve as co-appointed field personnel in the United States (with Karen refugees and Haiti, respectively)
- Leaders of 30 Baptist organizations, including CBF, announce plans for a "Celebration of a New Baptist Covenant"

2008
- "Celebration of a New Baptist Covenant" meeting held in Atlanta, where more than 15,000 Baptists gather as part of an effort to unite Baptists in North America around the Luke 4 mandate to "bring good news to the poor, proclaim release to the captives and recovery of sight to the blind, to let the oppressed go free, and to proclaim the year of the Lord's favor"
- Eight historic Baptist colleges and universities announce they will offer undergraduate tuition scholarships for the children of CBF field personnel (Mercer University made a similar commitment in 2007)

- On the seventh anniversary of the 9/11 attacks, CBF co-sponsors national summit on torture on the Atlanta campus of Mercer University

2009

- Rob Sellers, a professor at Logsdon School of Theology of Hardin-Simmons University, represents CBF at a historic Baptist-Muslim dialogue comprised of a diverse group of Baptist and Muslim leaders at Andover Newton Theological School near Boston, Massachusetts, on January 9-11
- CBF develops partnership with Japan Baptist Convention to send field personnel to the country; Carson and Laura Foushee appointed in 2013 as first CBF field personnel to Japan

2010

- CBF creates Collegiate Congregational Internship program (now known as Student.Church), offering grants to churches to fund summer internship positions for 97 students in its inaugural year
- Voluntary Organizations Active in Disaster recognizes CBF as a disaster response organization
- Cooperative Baptists donate more than $1.2 million to Haitian earthquake relief efforts; CBF signs three-year agreement with Convention Baptiste d'Haiti for earthquake recovery, including development strategy, medical ministry and micro-enterprise; CBF helps start Haiti Housing Network, a joint collaboration with partners Conscience International, Fuller Center for Housing and the Baptist General Convention of Texas
- Christy McMillin-Goodwin becomes first person elected as CBF Moderator to have graduated from a CBF-partner seminary (Baptist Theological Seminary at Richmond)
- CBF Moderator Hal Bass appoints 14-member task force (known as 2012 Task Force) to conduct two-year study of the Fellowship's mission and organizational future
- General Assembly workshop titled "A Family Conversation About Same-Sex Orientation" at General Assembly explores what it means to be the presence of Christ among persons of same-sex orientation
- CBF holds inaugural Selah Vie retreat, a yearly end-of-summer gathering for student participants of Student.Go, Collegiate

Congregational Internship Program, as well as other young
Baptists

- Founding CBF Coordinator Cecil Sherman dies April 17
- CBF Executive Coordinator Daniel Vestal and Baugh Foundation President Babs Baugh convene "Fellowship Baptist
Movement" retreat April 27-29 at Callaway Gardens in Pine
Mountain, Ga., for leaders from CBF-related organizations to
reflect on the past and look to the future
- Advisory Council of CBF, on behalf of Coordinating Council,
adopts statement on September 10 condemning a plan by
a Florida church to burn the Quran on September 11 and
encouraging prayers for peace and understanding among all
religions

2011

- Fellowship celebrates 20th anniversary at General Assembly
in Tampa, featuring banquet with keynote address by Molly
Marshall, president of Central Baptist Theological Seminary
- Cooperative Baptist Fellowship of the Bahamas forms October
23 in partnership with CBF of Florida; installation of first
national coordinator, John McIntosh, and first national administrator, Preston Cooper

2012

- Rob Nash resigns as Global Missions Coordinator in June to
return to academia as Associate Dean at Mercer University's
McAfee School of Theology; Jim A. Smith named as Interim
Global Missions Coordinator (Smith and his wife, Becky, were
among the first field personnel appointed by the Fellowship in
1993)
- CBF hosts "CBF Day" during spring at Wake Forest University School of Divinity, Campbell University Divinity School
and the M. Christopher White School of Divinity of Gardner-
Webb University to celebrate their partnership and shared
dedication to theological education ("CBF Day" is an annual
daylong event on campuses of CBF-partner theology schools
started several years prior to celebrate the partnership in training women and men for vocational ministry)
- CBF co-sponsors with Mercer University "A [Baptist] Conference on Sexuality and Covenant," held April 19-21 at First
Baptist Church of Decatur, Georgia, to provide Baptists

with an opportunity for honest, compassionate and prayerful dialogue around matters and questions of sexuality
- General Assembly adopts 2012 Task Force Report; Fellowship staff and leaders begin planning for implementation of recommendations
- CBF announces first two annual "Vestal Scholars," named in honor of Daniel and Earlene Vestal, at General Assembly in Fort Worth, Texas; Daniel Vestal retires June 30 as CBF Executive Coordinator after 15 years of service in the position; Fellowship leader and former CBF Moderator Pat Anderson begins as CBF Interim Executive Coordinator on July 1
- Dawnings, CBF's initiative for congregational renewal, launches with several churches taking part in pilot process focused on visioning, forming and engaging
- CBF Fellows program starts with support of a Lilly Endowment grant to provide encouragement and support for ministers in their first call after seminary graduation; Terry Hamrick directs the first cohort of 25 Fellows

2013

- CBF Coordinating Council selects Suzii Paynter as Executive Coordinator; begins March 1
- 2012 Task Force recommendations implemented, including new CBF governance structure with creation of a Missions Council, Ministries Council, Governing Board and Nominating Committee
- General Assembly approves new CBF constitution and bylaws; organization of state and regional leaders called the Movement Leadership Team further formalized
- CBF launches formal advocacy efforts; Stephen Reeves of Texas Baptist Christian Life Commission hired to coordinate advocacy work

2014

- CBF forms partnership in February with the Baptist World Alliance for international religious liberty and global advocacy efforts at the United Nations
- CBF partners with Wilshire Baptist Church in Dallas, Texas, to create a three-year pilot project focused on congregational advocacy to help congregations discern how they might become effective advocates within their communities

- Steven Porter, a professor at Baylor University's George W. Truett Theological Seminary, named as Global Missions Coordinator
- Kasey Jones begins duties as CBF Moderator, becoming the first African American woman to hold the position
- Longest-serving CBF staff member, Clarissa Strickland, retires June 30 after 23 years of service
- Suzii Paynter meets with President Obama and a small group of faith leaders in the Oval Office at the White House to discuss immigration reform
- CBF and CBF of Florida sponsor in November the first "Academy for Spiritual Formation" for pastors in Cuba, a five-day enrichment event of The Upper Room, the ecumenical division of the United Methodist General Board of Discipleship

2015

- CBF Global Missions begins strategic planning for the 21st century
- First inaugural CBF Seminarian Retreat—students and faculty from all 14 U.S.-based partner seminaries and divinity schools participate
- CBF Advocacy helps start and joins Faith for Just Lending, a coalition of faith organizations aiming to combat predatory lending
- CBF joins BReAD (Baptist Relief and Development Network) to improve collaboration among Baptist groups involved in international relief and development work; CBF takes part in BReAD's response to April earthquakes in Nepal
- CBF launches Sabbatical Initiative in June to invest in the health of ministers and local congregations through making saving funds easier for churches, providing grants and encouraging significant sabbatical experiences; Initiative is a multiple-organization endeavor also including CBF Foundation, CBF Church Benefits and CBF state and regional organizations
- CBF Executive Coordinator Suzii Paynter gives August commencement address at CBF partner Baptist Seminary of Kentucky (formed in 2002) as seminary celebrates receiving accreditation from Association of Theological Schools

- CBF Executive Coordinator Suzii Paynter participates in events surrounding the visit of Pope Francis to the United States
- CBF renews and expands partnership in November with Global Women, an organization addressing women's issues around the world such as clean water, maternal health and sex trafficking awareness and prevention
- CBF receives significant grant from the Lilly Endowment as part of its "National Initiative to Address Economic Challenges Facing Pastoral Leaders;" grant awarded to initiate education and financial initiatives for pastoral leaders of the Fellowship

2016

- CBF announces in January a comprehensive plan for Global Missions, doubling down on its commitment to the long-term presence of field personnel through new sustainable funding model that consolidates field personnel under a single employment category with equitable funding
- CBF Council on Endorsement on March 5 selects Erin Lysse, a chaplain in Winston-Salem, North Carolina as the 1,000th CBF-endorsed chaplain or pastoral counselor
- Cooperative Baptist Fellowship turns 25 years old on May 11
- CBF celebrates 25th Anniversary at General Assembly, June 20-24 in Greensboro, N.C.

Moderators and General Assemblies

Daniel Vestal★
1990-91
"Behold, I Do A New Thing"
  Atlanta, Georgia (1991)

John Hewett
1991-92
"Presence & Promise"
  Fort Worth, Texas (1992)

Patricia Ayres
1992-93
"Faith & Freedom in Christ"
  Birmingham, Alabama (1993)

Hardy Clemons
1993-94
"Pressing Toward the Mark"
  Greensboro, North Carolina
  (1994)

Carolyn Weatherford Crumpler
1994-95
"Come to Joy"
  Fort Worth, Texas (1995)

Pat Anderson
1995-96
"A Time to Behold"
  Richmond, Virginia (1996)

Lavonn Brown
1996-97
"Blessing the Future"
  Louisville, Kentucky (1997)

Martha Smith
1997-98
"Celebrate the Spirit"
  Houston, Texas (1998)

John Tyler
1998-99
"Nurturing Community"
  Birmingham, Alabama (1999)

Sarah Frances Anders
1999-2000
"Come . . . Abide . . . Living
  Missions"
  Orlando, Florida (2000)

Donna Forrester
2000-01
"Following Jesus"
  Atlanta, Georgia (2001)

Jim Baucom
2001-02
"It's Time"
  Fort Worth, Texas (2002)

Phill Martin
2002-03
"It's Time"
  Charlotte, North Carolina
  (2003)

Cynthia Holmes
2003-04
"Being the Presence of Christ
  Today . . . Tomorrow . . .
  Together"
  Birmingham, Alabama (2004)

Robert B. Setzer, Jr.
2004-05
"Being the Presence of Christ in
All of the World"
Grapevine, Texas (2005)

Joy Yee
2005-06
"Being the Presence of Christ for a
World in Need"
Atlanta, Georgia (2006)

Emmanuel McCall
2006-07
"Free to Be the Presence of
Christ"
Washington, D.C. (2007)

Harriet Harral
2007-08
"Embrace the World: Building
Bridges"
Memphis, Tennessee (2008)

Jack Glasgow
2008-09
"Welcome to Your Neighborhood"
Houston, Texas (2009)

Hal Bass
2009-10
"Connect. Discover Your Passion.
Focus on Ministry Essentials"
Charlotte, North Carolina
(2010)

Christy McMillin-Goodwin
2010-11
"God's Mission, Your Passion"
Tampa, Florida (2011)

Colleen Burroughs
2011-12
"Infinitely More"
Fort Worth, Texas (2012)

Keith Herron
2012-13
"With Great Boldness"
Greensboro, North Carolina
(2013)

Bill McConnell
2013-14
"Woven Together"
Atlanta, Georgia (2014)

Kasey Jones
2014-15
"Building Bridges"
Dallas, Texas (2015)

Matt Cook
2015-16
"Christ's Love Compels Us"
Greensboro, North Carolina

*Editor's Note: Daniel Vestal served
as chair of the Interim Steering Committee
of the informal group called "The Baptist
Fellowship" from August 1990 – May 1991.
Vestal and the Interim Steering Committee were selected at the Consultation of
Concerned Baptists at the Inforum Convention Center in Atlanta August 23-25, 1990.
John Hewett was elected the first Moderator
of the Cooperative Baptist Fellowship at the
1991 Convocation of The Baptist Fellowship
in Atlanta May 9-11.*

Editor's Note: The following resolution was presented at the 1992 CBF General Assembly in Fort Worth, Texas, and was referred for comment to CBF Moderator John Hewett, who included it in the call to prayer and repentance in which the Assembly participated during the Friday evening session on May 1. During the Saturday morning business session on May 2, Tim Turnham of Luther Rice Memorial Baptist Church in Silver Spring, Maryland, moved that the statement be brought before the General Assembly for a vote. After three individuals spoke against the resolution (most arguing not against the statement's language but against the Fellowship beginning the practice of adopting resolutions), Mercer University professor Walter Shurden spoke in favor of the motion to adopt the statement. Assembly attendees voted by a narrow margin to adopt the statement of confession and repentance.

During the 1993 CBF General Assembly in Birmingham, Alabama, Assembly attendees adopted a new constitution due to a "sunset clause" requirement per Georgia state law. The new constitution prohibited resolutions and similar motions from being introduced from the floor of an Assembly business session. Resolutions must "pass through and survive a stringent process before being presented to the General Assembly for action," the Fellowship's Constitution Committee stated in its report. "[It] is designed to discourage hastily conceived and highly volatile resolutions being presented for action without the benefit of more deliberate consideration."

A Statement of Confession and Repentance

Keenly aware that the verdicts returned on Wednesday, April 29, in the cases of four Los Angeles police officers accused of the savage beating of Rodney King have called into question the fundamental integrity of the American system of justice and provoked a wave of violence in cities across the nation, we are compelled to address publicly an issue of profound moral and theological import too long neglected by white Baptists in the South.

Holy Scripture records in the book of Numbers 14:18-19 that Moses pled with God for the people of Israel, saying, "The Lord is longsuffering and abundant in mercy, forgiving iniquity and transgression; but God by no means clears the guilty, visiting the iniquity of the fathers (and mothers) on the children of the third and fourth generations. Pardon the iniquity of this people, I pray, according to the greatness of your mercy, just as you have forgiven this people, from Egypt until now."

Following World War II, the people of Germany publicly repented the sins of Adolph Hitler and of their own sins against Jewish people and the whole world. German Baptists similarly have expressed public sorrow and repentance for their compliance with the Nazi regime.

316

Such acts of confession and repentance remind those of us whose own denominational roots are deeply imbedded in the Southern Baptist Convention of the largely unconfessed sin of racism in our own heritage. Indeed, one of the precipitating factors in the formation of the Southern Baptist Convention was the determination to protect the institution of slavery and the position of slave owners in the South. The sins of slavery and the condoning of slavery committed by our Southern Baptist ancestors remain spiritual blights on the relationship between African Americans and Caucasian Americans to the present generation. The time is long overdue for us to repent of these sins.

Accordingly, we who are participants at the Cooperative Baptist Fellowship General Assembly, convened in the city of Fort Worth, Texas, April 30-May 2, 1992, whose roots are in the Southern Baptist Convention, do publicly confess and repent of our historic complicity in condoning and perpetuating the sin of slavery before and during the Civil War and do hereby apologize to all African Americans for that sin. We reject forthrightly the racism which has persisted throughout our history as Southern Baptists, even to this present day.

Furthermore, we pledge our prayers and active efforts to work for the eradication of every vestige of racism in our nation and in our churches. We acknowledge with regret that in the Cooperative Baptist Fellowship we are too white, too middle-class, and too insulated from the seething racial problems confronting our society. We confess that for too long we have remained aloof to what are now full-fledged crises in our cities, many of which are firmly rooted in racism, and pledge to seek ways and means of working with our Christian sisters and brothers in the African-American churches in addressing the critical needs of all people of color.

Particularly in light of the verdicts in the case of Rodney King and the resulting violence in our cities, we offer prayers to God for the healing of our land, even as we offer ourselves as instruments of Christ's reconciling peace.

Editor's Note: During the 2010 General Assembly in Charlotte, N.C., CBF Modera-tor Hal Bass appointed a 14-member task force (known as the 2012 Task Force) to conduct a study of the Fellowship's mission and organizational future. The Task Force's final report was presented and approved by attendees two years later at the 2012 General Assembly in Fort Worth, Texas. Below is the "Identity Statement" from the 2012 Task Force Report.

Identity Statement of the 2012 Task Force Report

What It Means to Be a Cooperative Baptist

For we are laborers together with God (1 Corinthians 3:9).

The Cooperative Baptist Fellowship is a community of Baptist Christians and churches walking together and drawn toward the center of our common life in Jesus Christ. We share this fellowship with God, whom we have come to know through Christ. We serve as co-laborers with the Holy Spirit in God's mission. Within these relationships we freely offer this expression of our identity, not to bind the conscience of any believer or the freedom of any congregation but as an expression of the nature of our fellowship.

Our vision is to be a national and global community bearing witness to the Gospel in partnership with Christians across the nation and around the world. Our understanding of Baptist faith and practice is expressed by our emphasis on freedom in biblical interpretation and congregational governance, the participation of women and men in all aspects of church leadership and Christian ministry, and religious liberty for all people.

Our life together is also shaped by a common ministry focus. Because of our passion to obey the Great Commandment (Matthew 22:34-40) and the Great Commission (Matthew 28:19-20) of our Lord, we are committed to global missions with the least evangelized and most neglected persons of the world through sending vocational and volunteer missionaries. Because of our passion for called, gifted and qualified ministry leaders, we are committed to effective leadership development in partnership with theological education institutions. Because of our passion for local churches as the locus of Christian formation and discipleship development, we are committed to a collab-orative model of resourcing congregations through the development of a robust resource network. Because of our passion for participation in God's mission beyond the capacity of most congregations, we are committed to supporting ministry partners who share our identity, values and goals.

Our community consists of congregations, individuals, regional fellowships, and ministry partners. While we respect the freedom and individuality of each member of our community, we are committed to practices of cooperation, collaboration, and leadership that will enable us to be faithful and wise stewards of our common life and mission.

In summary, Cooperative Baptist Fellowship is a community of Baptist Christians who cooperate together to engage people in missions and equip people for ministry.

ACKNOWLEDGMENTS

Aaron D. Weaver

We talk much in the Cooperative Baptist Fellowship about "forming together"—and this edited volume is an example of that tagline put into practice. No book is written or edited in isolation, and this project certainly was not. The fingerprints of countless are present throughout, and many individuals are owed much appreciation and thankfulness for making this book possible.

First, a special thank you to the contributors. Thank you for sharing your memories and reflections. Thank you for remembering the past aloud as we journey forward as a Fellowship.

Thank you to my CBF colleagues who assisted with this project. Thank you to Carrie McGuffin for proofreading, researching, tracking down information and correcting errors. Thank you for your suggestions from beginning to end. A thank you to Jeff Langford for his excellent graphic design work, from book proposal to book covers. Thank you to my colleague, Candice Young, for her encouragement and input throughout the process. I am greatly indebted to this trio.

I am also indebted to Clarissa Strickland for coming out of retirement to be my professional proofreader and fact-checker. I learn a new Baptist history factoid each and every time I chat with Clarissa. She is a first-class teacher with a passion for preserving and sharing the stories of our history and heritage as free and faithful Baptists. I hope for more opportunities to keep learning from Clarissa.

Pat Anderson is my all-time favorite fellow editor, and I'm thankful for the support he has offered for this project alongside the 25th Anniversary team of Matt Cook, Kasey Jones and Suzii Paynter. I'm especially grateful for the many conversations with Suzii about this project as we brainstormed together about topic after topic.

Along with Suzii, Jeff Huett is owed my appreciation for making this project possible. I pitched the idea to him on a whim, and he immediately said, "Go for it." I ran with it, and he provided support and encouragement throughout the process, as well as the needed resources.

Others who gave great advice and suggestions to make this project a success include Bo Prosser, Pam Durso, Judy Strawn, Grace Powell Freeman, Jim "Global Missions" Smith and Judy Battles. I also appreciate extra editing assistance from Caitlyn Furr and Hannah Minks. Thank you.

Thank you to John Pierce of Nurturing Faith Publishing. Nurturing Faith has my vote of recommendation—what a great publisher!

I must also mention my dad, Doug Weaver, who shared some helpful do's and don'ts from his many years as a Baptist scholar writing and editing books and journals. I hope to one day be the historian that he is.

Last but certainly not least, a thank you to my family: my wife, Alexis, and two children, James Oliver and Miriam Grace. They put up with me working on weekends, editing, fact-checking and flipping through dusty old Baptist periodicals. I love you all.

Pictured above are the three CBF logos from the past 25 years. The top logo is the first, which was introduced in the inaugural issue of *Fellowship News* (now known as *fellowship!* magazine) in December 1991. The second logo, which changed from the original crimson color scheme to that of a global blue and green was introduced in 1997.

The third and current logo is a grayscale representation of the new branding implemented in February 2015. This monogram of CBF is a visual representation of "Forming Together," made up of foundational squares, circles and curvature of community and a cross within the "f" to emphasize the Christian nature of the organization.

Attendees participate in and worship at the 1994 CBF General Assembly in Greensboro, North Carolina.

(Above) CBF's founding Coordinator Cecil Sherman on the campus of Baptist Theological Seminary in Rüschlikon, Switzerland.

(Above) CBF staff smile for group photo in October 1994 at the retirement party for Betty Law (seated center). Back row from left to right: Linda Moore, Nancy Duncan, Gary Skeen, David Wilkinson, Pam Yarborough, Cecil Sherman, Ginny Ireland, Becky Buice Hall, Frank Ivey, Clarissa Strickland, Wanda Hyde (Front row from left to right) Judy Gooch Strawn, Harlan Spurgeon, Betty Law, Keith Parks, Grace Powell Freeman. (Left) Global Missions Coordinator Keith Parks and Moderator Patricia Ayres respond to questions during a session at the 1993 CBF General Assembly in Birmingham, Alabama.

(Below) CBF General Assembly co-chair Suzii Paynter coordinates with an exhibitor at the 1992 General Assembly in Fort Worth, Texas.

(Above) Catherine Allen speaks to 1990 Consultation of Concerned Baptists in Atlanta, using an umbrella "big enough for lots of people to get under" to symbolize inclusion.

(Right) The third graduating class of the Baptist Theological Seminary at Richmond—Class of 1995—poses on graduation day.

(Below) Board members at the first meeting of the CBF Foundation in 1996. From left to right: William Turnage, Patricia Ayres, Pat Anderson, Ophelia Humphrey.

Teen baptized in 2006 at CBF church start Cowboy Church of Erath County in Stephenville, Texas.

(Right) Loyd Allen, left, and Melissa Rogers, center, present Walter Shurden, right, with the William H. Whitsitt Courage Award at the 2009 CBF General Assembly in Houston.

CBF field personnel Lonnie Turner (second from left) visits a village outside of Cabinda, Angola in 2003, one year after the conclusion of the 27-year Angolan Civil War.

Cooperative Baptists and American Baptists gather at U.S. Capitol for "Baptist Unity Rally" sponsored by Baptist Joint Committee for Religious Liberty on June 29, 2007.

(Above) Baptist Women in Ministry supporters proudly sport their "This is What a Preacher Looks Like" t-shirts to celebrate BWIM's 25th anniversary at the 2008 CBF General Assembly in Memphis, Tennessee. **(Top Right)** Students show off their costumes during a western themed dance in 2012 at Selah Vie, CBF's annual end-of-summer retreat for young Baptists. **(Bottom Right)** At 2004 CBF General Assembly in Birmingham, Alabama, Emmanuel McCall (left) introduces 10-year-old Erin Strnad, who brought a wagon loaded with change totaling $915 she had saved to support world hunger efforts of the Baptist World Alliance.

CBF field personnel
Chaouki Boulos prays
with a woman in 2014
at a weekly Bible study
in Lebanon, where he
and his wife, Maha,
minister to Syrian
refugees.

Members of
the Millennium
Development Goal team
of Student.Go
assist local leaders in
digging a water well near
Lake Langano, Ethiopia,
in 2008.

New Global Missions personnel are
commissioned at the 2001 CBF General
Assembly in Atlanta.

(Above) Volunteers in Pearlington, Mississippi, construct a home in 2006 as part of CBF's Hurricane Katrina relief efforts.

(Right) CBF Moderator Donna Forrester welcomes President Jimmy Carter at the 2001 CBF General Assembly in Atlanta.

(Below) CBF Executive Coordinator Daniel Vestal preaches on "being the presence of Christ" (John 20:19-23) at the 2005 CBF General Assembly in Grapevine, Texas.

(Above) Participants pose for group photo at CBF's 2015 Advocacy in Action conference in Washington, D.C.

(Right) CBF field personnel Steve James, left, offers medical care to an injured man in the aftermath of the Haiti earthquake of 2010.

Baptist leaders celebrate Covenants of Action at the New Baptist Covenant Summit in 2013. From left to right: Jeffrey Haggray, Hannah McMahan, Tyrone Pitts, Suzii Paynter, Jimmy Allen, David Key.

(Above) Student.Go intern Abby Pratt spends time with refugee children in Kampala, Uganda in 2013. (Right) CBF Executive Coordinator Suzii Paynter gives address on "ampersand Christianity" at 2015 CBF General Assembly in Dallas. (Below) CBF field personnel Jon and Tanya Parks teach Roma children English skills through song in Košice, Slovakia, in 2015.